The March of Ewyas

An idyllic view of Longtown and the castle in 1794, from James Baker's *A Picturesque Guide through Wales and the Marches*

The March of Ewyas
The Story *of* Longtown Castle *and the* de Lacy Dynasty

MARTIN COOK & NEIL KIDD

LOGASTON PRESS

FRONT COVER, CLOCKWISE FROM TOP LEFT: A reconstruction of an early motte and bailey castle; The small motte at Tre-fedw with the Skirrid beyond; An aerial view of the keep at Longtown (*Adam Stanford, Aerial-Cam*); The gateway to the inner bailey at Longtown; A contemporary depiction of Hugh de Lacy (*from Gerald of Wales's manuscript,* Topographia Hibernica, *courtesy of the National Library of Ireland*); A view of Longtown Castle in 1840 by Charles Walter Radclyffe, published in *Picturesque Antiquities &c. of the County of Hereford*. BACK COVER, FROM TOP: A reconstruction of the keep at Longtown; the development of the fortifications at Longtown, from the Roman fort to the present day

First published in 2020 by Logaston Press
The Holme, Church Road, Eardisley HR3 6NJ
www.logastonpress.co.uk
An imprint of Fircone Books Ltd.

ISBN 978-1-910839-47-8

Text copyright © Martin Cook and Neil Kidd, 2020.
Images copyright © the authors unless otherwise stated beneath each image.

All rights reserved.
The moral rights of the authors have been asserted.

Without limiting the rights under copyright reserved above, no part of this publication may be reproduced, stored in or introduced into a retrieval system, or transmitted, in any form or by any means (electronic, mechanical, photocopying, recording or otherwise), without prior written permission of the copyright owner and the above publisher of this book.

Designed and typeset by Richard Wheeler.
Cover design by Richard Wheeler.

Printed and bound in Poland.

Logaston Press is committed to a sustainable future for our business, our readers and our planet. The book in your hands is made from paper certified by the Forest Stewardship Council.

British Library Catalogue in Publishing Data.
A CIP catalogue record for this book is available from the British Library.

CONTENTS

ACKNOWLEDGEMENTS	vii
INTRODUCTION	ix

PART ONE: The Longtown Castles Project — 1

1	Ponthendre motte and bailey castle today	3
2	Longtown Castle today	9
3	Why build a round keep?	21
4	The excavations	27
5	Post-excavation analysis and interpretation	45

PART TWO: A New History of Ewyas and the de Lacy Dynasty — 57

6	Ewyas in prehistoric times	59
7	The Roman occupation of the southern Marches	75
8	Ewyas in the Dark Ages	87
9	Anglo-Saxons and Vikings in the Welsh borderlands	95
10	William FitzOsbern and the Norman Conquest	107
11	Walter de Lacy I and the castles of Ewyas	115
12	Roger de Lacy – rebel	127
13	Hugh de Lacy I – a nobleman of noble behaviour	133
14	Pain, Anarchy and Gilbert de Lacy	139
15	Hugh de Lacy II – governor of Ireland	153
16	Walter de Lacy II – last of the dynasty	161
17	After the de Lacys	181
18	The borough of Longtown	191
19	The denouement – who built Longtown Castle?	199
20	Summing-up	209

APPENDICES — 215

1	A timeline for Ewyas and the de Lacys	216
2	Were the de Lacy brothers at Hastings?	218
3	Roger de Lacy's holdings in Herefordshire	220
4	The de Lacys in the north of England	228

BIBLIOGRAPHY	231
NOTES AND REFERENCES	237

ACKNOWLEDGEMENTS

We have to thank so many people whose generous assistance helped to make the Longtown Castles Project such a success. **Keith Ray**, former Herefordshire County Archaeologist, suggested the project to the Longtown and District Historical Society and Longtown Village Pride in the first place and gave us the benefit of his experience and advice. The project would not have been possible without the financial support of **The Heritage Lottery Fund**. **Alan and Barbara Williams** who farm at Ponthendre, and **The Nevill Estate** who own Castle Green, graciously gave us permission to dig up their land. **Tim Hoverd of Herefordshire Archaeology** put together a fantastic team of professional archaeologists in **Nigel Baker, Peter Dorling, Simon Mayes, Dale Rouse, Dan Lewis and Jade Beresford**. **Alison McDonald of Historic England** offered wise advice and helped us to obtain Scheduled Monument Consent on not one but two Scheduled sites, and then gave up her leave to do an awful lot of digging. **Adam Stanford of Aerial-Cam** carried out drone flights, to the bemusement of one of the local red kites, and produced excellent computer modelling and otherwise unobtainable views of the two castles. **Chas Breton** gave his expertise in photographing the finds from the excavations. **Peter Reavill of the Portable Antiquities Scheme** and **Judy Stevenson of Hereford Museum** kindly supplied photographs of historical artefacts that have been found in the vicinity of Longtown. **Max Lieberman** investigated the early documentation on Ewyas. Most importantly, we have to thank **all the many volunteers from within the community and further afield**. Without their hard work and enthusiasm the project wouldn't have got off the ground. Lastly but certainly not least, we owe a huge debt of gratitude to our wives for their patience and support during the long incubation of this book.

All illustrations are the work of the authors, unless attributed to others. Watercolours are by **Neil Kidd**. Line drawings by **Martin Cook**.

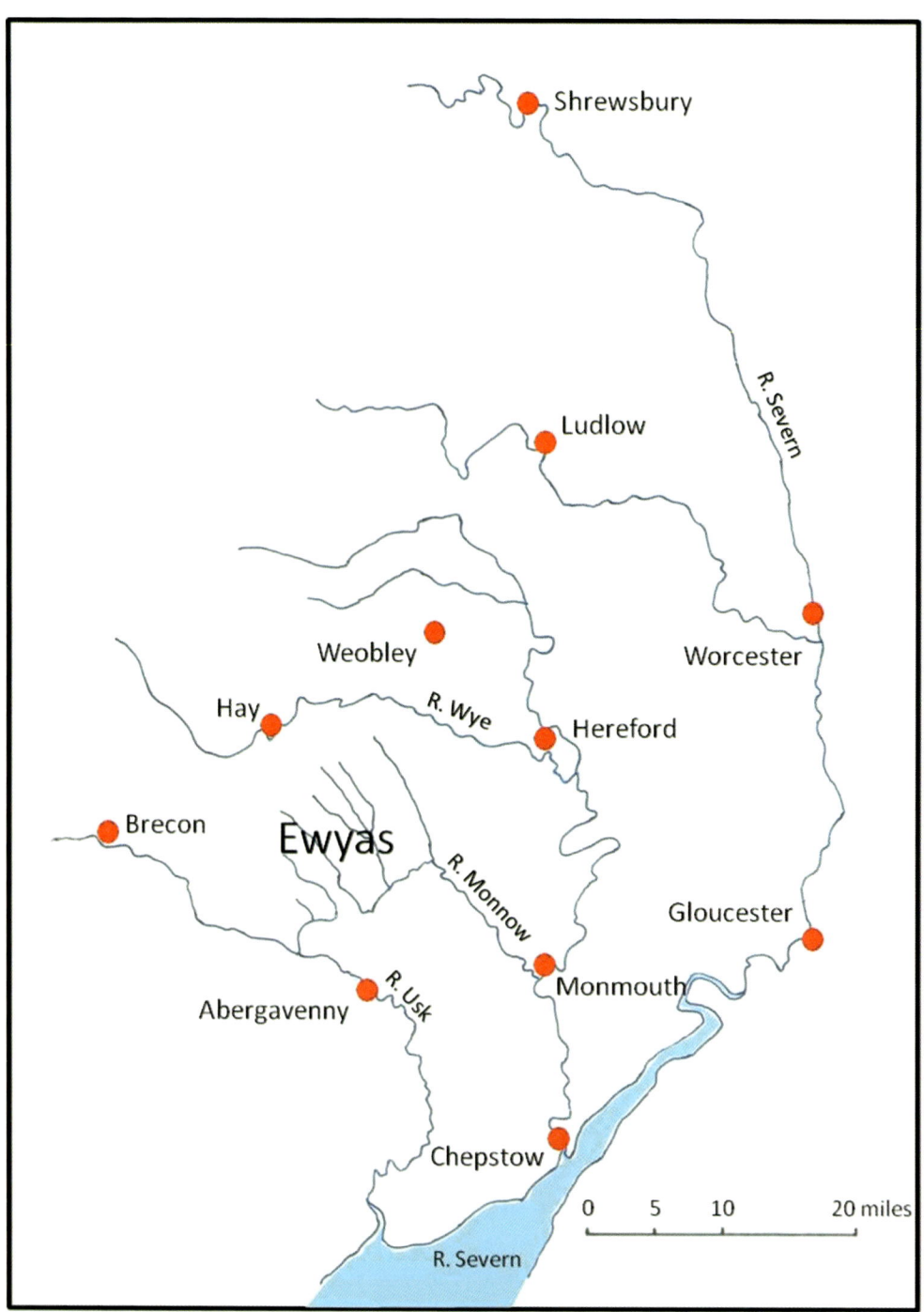

The southern Marches

INTRODUCTION

Never will we find truth if we content ourselves with what is already known …
Those things that have been written before us are not laws but guides.
The truth is open to all, for it is not yet totally possessed.
          Gilbert de Tournai, thirteenth-century master of the University of Paris

This is a detective story – a historical whodunnit. The narrative takes place in the area known as Ewyas, a name that has now almost disappeared from modern maps. Ewyas straddles the present border between south-west Herefordshire and Monmouthshire but it was once a Welsh kingdom, and Welsh continued to be commonly spoken here well into the nineteenth century. In historical times, it was bounded by the Golden Valley to the east and the Black Mountains to the west, extending from the River Monnow in the south, nearly to Hay-on-Wye in the north. In the distant past, Ewyas may have been far more extensive and the Welsh annals claim that it was first governed by the son of Caratacus and then by the ancestors of King Arthur.

In the past, writers have suggested that the name Ewyas meant 'a place of battles', which it was, or 'a land of streams', which it is. If the name were Welsh, it would translate as 'a place of yew trees' of which there are many. It was a local tradition to plant a yew tree next to an outside privy (or perhaps plant a privy next to a yew tree). *The Concise Oxford Dictionary of English Place-names* provides the fanciful idea that Ewyas means 'the sheep district'. The English word 'ewe' has a Germanic root so the compiler had to invent a hypothetical Welsh word for sheep in order to explain his unlikely notion. The Reverend Bannister, vicar of Ewyas Harold in 1902, was more realistic when he wrote,

> The really competent scholars to whom I have applied confess that they have no idea of the derivation of the name, though they all think it is Celtic, or possibly pre-Celtic … In any case no serious student will even hazard a conjecture as to the derivation and meaning of the name.

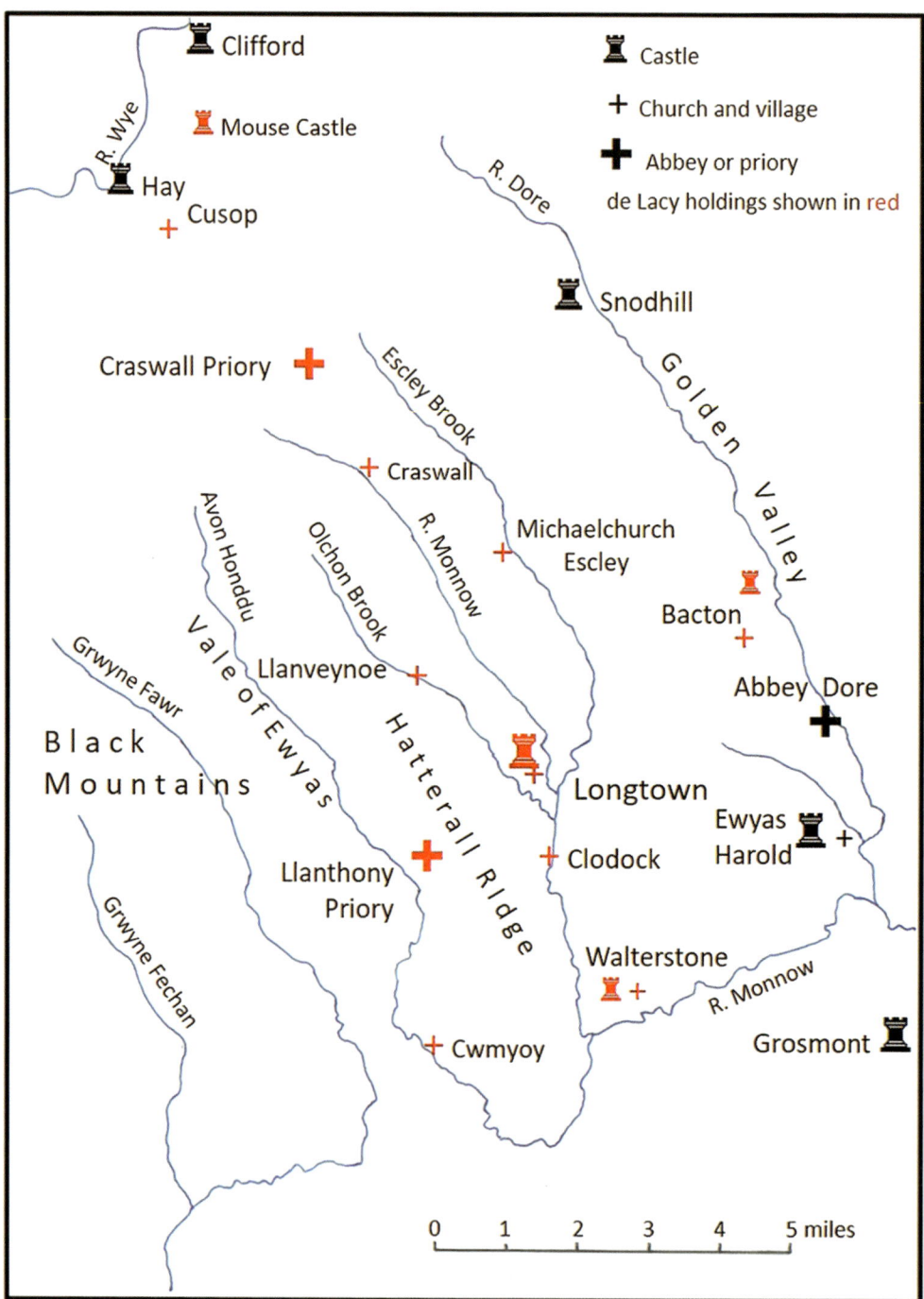

The March of Ewyas

Our story begins in the neighbouring villages of Clodock and Longtown that together form a single rural community stretching for around nine miles in the lee of the Black Mountains. It is an administrative peculiarity that while Longtown is a part of the ancient ecclesiastical parish of Clodock, the village of Clodock is in the township or civil parish of Longtown.

Strangely, this rural parish contains the remains of two castles. The stone castle at Longtown is fairly well known and has many visitors throughout the year, but even some of the local residents are unaware that, just over half a mile away, there are the earthworks of another fortification. This forgotten castle overlooks a group of farmsteads called Ponthendre, clustering around the river bridge that links – or separates – Clodock and Longtown. It was a mystery why, in this small community of fewer than 1,000 inhabitants, there were apparently two castles. Longtown Castle was known to be one of the strongholds of the de Lacy family, but history tells us nothing at all about the castle of Ponthendre. It was not known with any certainty when either of these castles was built, who it was who ordered their construction or for how long they were in use.

Longtown Castle had its own particular mystery. The medieval keep stands on the corner of a massive square embankment. In the eighteenth century, antiquarians recognised its shape as typical of a Roman encampment and believed that they had discovered the site of the Roman town of Blestium. This claim was soon disputed and it is now accepted that in fact Blestium was at or near Monmouth. The Longtown Roman encampment theory lived on, however, and it was reported that when Longtown's first school was being built within the rampart in 1869, 'ancient Roman remains' were unearthed. Unfortunately, all record of the nature of these relics is now lost.

To our knowledge, no Roman pottery or coins have ever turned up in any garden or during any building works around Longtown. In the twentieth century several small-scale excavations were conducted in the castle grounds and the surrounding area, but they found no evidence whatsoever for a Roman occupation. This has led modern historians to cast doubt on Longtown's Roman credentials. Although the rampart has the right shape and area for a small Roman fort, rising to an elevation of up to seven metres it is far too high. Various experts have hazarded that rather than being Roman, it might be Iron Age, Saxon or Norman in origin, but there are problems with each of these theories. The shape is just too regular to be an Iron Age fort. Iron Age forts usually take advantage of the terrain and often have multiple ramparts that follow the contours. Although the Longtown embankment resembles that of an Anglo-Saxon *burh* or fortified town, the persistence of Welsh place-names, surnames and, until recently, the Welsh language clearly indicates that the region around Longtown was never colonised by the Anglo-Saxons. With an area of around four acres, the embankment would be exceptionally large and unusually regular for a Norman castle bailey. In the absence of convincing evidence to back any of the opinions offered, the identity of the rampart builders would have remained an enigma.

LONGTOWN CASTLE,

HEREFORDSHIRE.

LONGTOWN stands in a most secluded and romantic situation, on the banks of the river Munnow, near its junction with the Escle and Olchon, which have their sources not far from each other, and give beauty to the country through which they flow, in a direction from north to south.

In Taylor's Map of Herefordshire, Longtown is marked as the Roman Blestium, most probably from mistaking the place meant by Camden, who fixes that station, (though erroneously), at Castle Hen, or Old Castle, on an eminence, between two and three miles to the south, and which is actually in Monmouthshire, though almost insulated by the lands of this county.

The village of Longtown is in the hundred of Ewyas Lacy, in the parish of Cloudock, and has a chapel dedicated to St. Peter, of the value of 16*l.* *per annum*, in the patronage of W. Wilkins, esq. The resident population in this village in 1801 was 768. It is situated seventeen miles in a south-westerly direction from Hereford, in the neighbourhood of the Hatterell hill, or black mountain, on the borders of the county, near Brecknockshire.

Of the Castle, but a portion of what appears to be the keep remains: it stands on a rising ground, surrounded by a ditch, which is encompassed by a rampart. Its situation is commanding, and the prospects generally delightful. History is silent as to the founder of this Castle, and the date of its erection is unknown. Though not extensive, it has the appearance of having been very strong, and probably was used as a place of defence against the incursions of the Welsh.

Longtown Castle in 1809, from *The Antiquarian and Topographical Cabinet*

Much of our story concerns the de Lacy family, a dynasty of Norman barons originating from the village of Lassy in Calvados. Soon after the Norman Conquest, Walter de Lacy took control of the larger part of Ewyas, which was later known as Ewyas Lacy. Ewyas Lacy was one of the lordships in the Marches of Wales, the more or less autonomous buffer zone established by the Normans along the border between England and Wales. The de Lacy family became extraordinarily wealthy, holding lands in Normandy, England, Wales and Ireland. With their wealth came great power, enough to challenge the authority of the English Crown on more than one occasion. They became innovative and unconventional castle builders. It is generally assumed that one of the de Lacys was responsible for building the stone castle that can be seen today at Longtown, but there is no documentary record as to which one. Historians have offered differing opinions, but none has provided robust evidence for who built either of Longtown's two castles.

In this age of the Internet and 24-hour news, it is difficult to appreciate just how little detailed information we have about the past. Historical records from the early medieval period are extremely sparse. There are far more castles along the border between England and Wales than in any other part of the country, and yet, with a few exceptions, we have no certain knowledge of precisely when they were built or who built them. Baronial and manorial records are effectively non-existent. Often we only learn about a particular landholding when the holder died and his heir was too young to inherit. The Crown then took control of the lordship and farmed the rents until the rightful heir reached maturity. This applied to Ewyas Lacy after Hugh de Lacy was murdered in Ireland. The accounts of the Exchequer, known as Pipe Rolls, for the years 1187 to 1189 were thought to be the only documents that refer to both of our castles. They recorded that the sum of £37 *per annum* was spent on the custody of *Castelli de Ewias* and *Novi Castelli*, the Castle of Ewyas and the New Castle. It was generally accepted by modern historians that these were the castles at Ponthendre and Longtown.

Towards the end of 2013, members of the Longtown & District Historical Society, with guidance from the former Herefordshire County Archaeologist Keith Ray, put together a plan to investigate the history of the two castles, using modern surveying techniques, geophysics, archaeological excavation and historical research. Local volunteers could do much of the work, but we would need the backing and expertise of professional archaeologists and historians. This meant raising a considerable sum of money. As both sites are Scheduled Monuments, it was also a legal requirement to have the support and consent of English Heritage (now Historic England).

We were fortunate that English Heritage welcomed the opportunity to research the two sites, as long as the excavations were limited in size and were conducted and recorded in a professional manner. They even funded a programme of geophysical survey as a preliminary to the main project. For the bulk of the required funding we needed the help of the Heritage Lottery Fund. It was disappointing when they turned down our first application, but we tightened it up, trimmed the budgets and tried again. The second submission was also declined but this time we were informed that it was because applications had outstripped the available funds. They advised us to re-submit it without any further changes. The third application was successful and we were awarded a grant of £78,300. The Longtown Castles Project had become a reality.

As this was to be a community project, the first task was to put out a call for volunteers. There was no telling what sort of response we might get, but it was excellent, far beyond our expectations. We now had a willing workforce to work alongside the team of professional archaeologists who would be digging at both sites simultaneously.

The excavations produced surprising results at both sites. There was no buried treasure but a lot of information, some of which was entirely at odds with what had previously been written about Ponthendre and Longtown. The spadework certainly answered a lot of questions, but it had also thrown up a lot of others. The two of us, who had been managing the project, decided that we would have to dig deeper and over a much wider area. It had become clear that we could never reach a true understanding of our two local castles without taking a more holistic approach and broadening our enquiries to look at the wider context of the whole lordship of Ewyas Lacy. And to understand Ewyas Lacy we needed to be aware of what was happening in the southern Marches in general. Gathering information from modern authors and from earlier sources, we realised before long that there was probably enough material for a book.

Quite a lot has been written about Ewyas Lacy over the years, but we soon learned to treat secondary sources with caution and even an element of scepticism. Different authors using the same historical records have sometimes come to entirely different conclusions. Others have built on their source material, making unsubstantiated assumptions and sometimes producing complete fallacies. These have then been repeated by other writers and so become historical 'facts'.

For this book, whenever we could, we have gone back to the original records, albeit usually in translation as neither of us has the mastery of medieval Latin. The various versions of the Anglo-Saxon Chronicles were extremely useful in providing a brief year-by-year, contemporary account of significant events from the time of King Alfred up to the twelfth century. The Domesday Book, commissioned by King William 19 years after the Norman Conquest, was exceptionally valuable in detailing the de Lacy landholdings, but provided little information about the Welsh Marches, which were exempt from taxation by the English Crown. Several useful histories have been preserved, written by clerics in various parts of the country, such as Henry of Huntingdon, Florence and John of Worcester, William of Malmesbury, Roger of Wendover, Gerald of Wales and the great Orderic Vitalis. They are not always entirely reliable and sometimes their accounts are conflicting. Often they were writing decades after the events they described and at times they are clearly biased by the need to please their patrons. Several of these chronicles were translated in the nineteenth century and brought to the public by the publisher, Henry G. Bohn, and we are fortunate that they have now been digitised and are available to browse on the Internet.

If while researching we found that the historical records failed to provide answers to questions of 'who' and 'when', it was sometimes possible to infer likely answers by considering 'where' and 'why'. Mapping has been an invaluable tool that brought useful insights when we considered different scenarios that might fit what little historical evidence we had. The application of local knowledge, common sense and Occam's razor – the simplest explanation is the likeliest – then helped to eliminate the improbable and point to the more economical and hopefully most credible narrative.

In our attempt to piece together a comprehensive history of Longtown's two castles and the de Lacy family, we have often arrived at conclusions that are different to those of previous writers and, in some instances, even our own historical and archaeological contractors. If this has resulted in errors, they are entirely ours, but we hope that this book will find favour with anyone who wishes to learn more about the March of Ewyas. As our long-suffering wives will readily concur, we have given it a great deal of thought.

CONVENTIONS

Spelling variations are a common stumbling block when searching the internet or printed texts. Standardised spelling is a relatively modern concept and the spelling in historical documents can vary enormously. Medieval scribes were not particularly fastidious about how they spelt the names of people and places, and they were untroubled by inconsistency. For example, we can see in the Bayeux Tapestry that Duke William is variously rendered as VVILLELM: DVX, VVILLELMO DVCI, VVILET DVX and DVX WILGELM.

The fact that personal and place-names have come down to us in many forms is hardly surprising. Usually, the scribes and chroniclers were writing in Latin. This led them to concoct artificial Latinised forms of English, Welsh and Norman-French names. Over the years these may have been transcribed (and mistranscribed) a number of times before eventually being translated into English by modern historians.

In documentary sources, we found the land of **Ewyas** is also spelt Eugias, Euias, Euuias, Euwias, Euyas and Ewias. For the benefit of those readers 'from off', it is pronounced 'you-us', with the stress on the first syllable. In Welsh the letters *w* and *y* are vowel sounds, so in earlier times all of the letters may have been pronounced, giving the name three or even four syllables.

Until recently, the village of **Clodock** could be seen spelt in variations such as Cloddock, Cludock or Cluddock. The eponymous Saint **Clydawg** appears as Clitauc, Clodock, Clydog and Cleodicus.

Ponthendre is often found hyphenated or as two separate words: Pont Hendre. Local residents frequently call it Pont Henry and it can be found spelt that way in several nineteenth-century documents.

The **de Lacy** family name may be spelt as Laci, Lacey or Lasci.

The prefix *fitz*, found in many Norman surnames and meaning 'son of', has multiple variations. Earl William **FitzOsbern** appears as Fitz Osbern, Fitz-Osbern, Fitz Osber and Fitz Osberne, with either an upper or lower case letter F.

Pain FitzJohn comes to us as Payn, Payne or Pagan with all the Fitz permutations. His friend, **Miles** of Gloucester, is sometimes called Milo, while **Joce** de Dinan can be as diverse as Josce, Jocelin, Joceas, Goc', Godso and Gozo.

There are sure to be other variations not listed here – not to speak of the Latin, Welsh and French versions. To avoid confusion we have adopted a standard spelling for all the place-names and personal names that appear in this book, except where found in a direct quotation. These are the ones shown above in **bold type**.

When dealing with Ireland, English versions of Irish names are used, with the Irish in parenthesis at first mention.

And lastly, when referring to the Norman Conquest and its aftermath, we use the word Norman or Normans as shorthand for the coalition of warriors who took part in the invasion of England led by Duke William of Normandy. As well as actual Normans, the invasion force included Flemings, Bretons, Vexinois and contingents from various other parts of France. The English scribes who wrote the Anglo-Saxon Chronicles usually referred to the interlopers as Frenchmen, rather than Normans.

PART ONE
The Longtown Castles Project

☞

The keep of Longtown Castle from above, showing its unique threefold symmetry and the massive thickness of the encircling wall. In comparison, the two remaining of the three turrets are seen to be largely decorative, having very little structural significance

1

Ponthendre motte and bailey castle today

The fortifications that the Normans called castles were scarcely known in the English provinces, and so the English – in spite of their courage and love of fighting – could put up only a weak resistance to their enemies.

Orderic Vitalis, c.1130

WALK SOUTH FROM Longtown in the direction of Clodock. After crossing the stone bridge over the Olchon Brook, and before you pass the splendid stone roof of Ponthendre barn, look over the farm gate to your right. The land rises in an escarpment before levelling off and then rising again to a small, steep-sided hill, its rounded top covered by trees.

Ponthendre

With a height of about ten metres above the surrounding land, this hill is not a natural feature. It was made by man, nearly 1,000 years ago. The base of the hill is surrounded by a circular ditch, visible on one side as just a marshy arc but cut deeply into bedrock on the other side. The ditch separates the hill from a flat area of level land that wraps around the hill, roughly in the shape of a waxing crescent moon. These are the earthworks of an early Norman castle, of the type known as a motte and bailey. (The remains of the castle at Ponthendre are on private land, so please do not attempt to visit them without the permission of the landowner.)

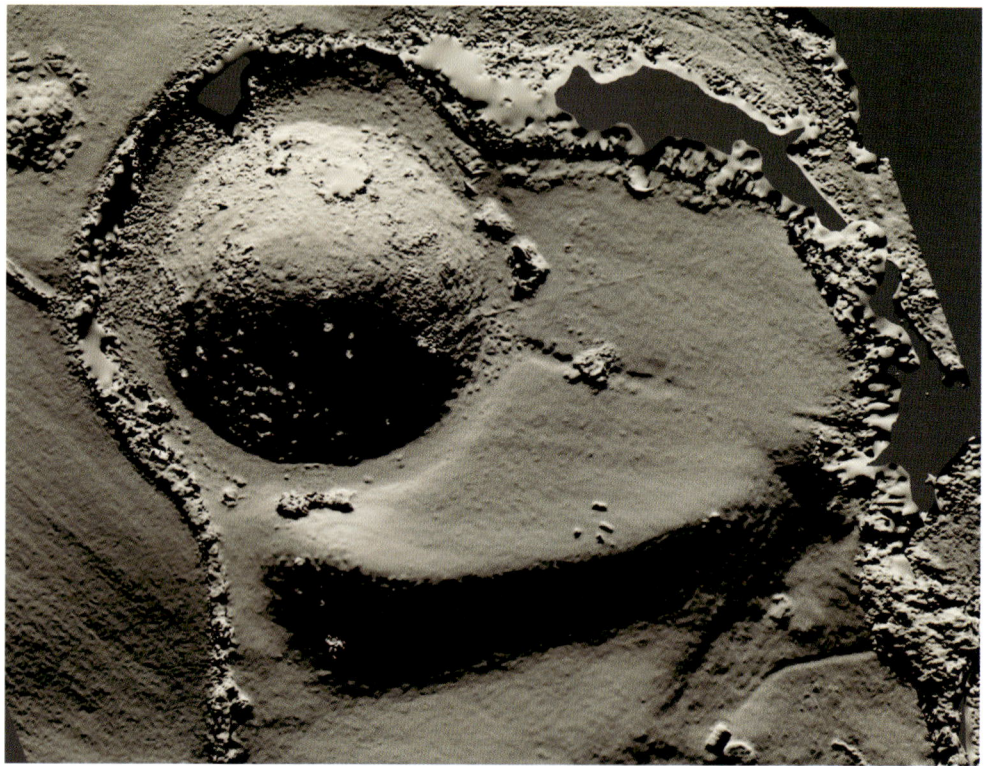

A 3-D terrain model of Ponthendre motte and bailey earthworks (*Adam Stanford, Aerial-Cam*)

The simplest form of early castle was the ringwork. A roughly circular ditch was dug and the spoil thrown up inside to form an enclosing rampart. This would be topped with a timber palisade. It could be built in a short time and provided basic protection for a campaigning force advancing into hostile territory. A more sophisticated version was the motte and bailey castle. Here a circular ditch was dug and the spoil thrown up to form a conical mound of earth and stone, called a motte. A timber tower was then built on top of the motte, often surrounded by a palisade and only accessible by means of a defensible bridge rising up from the bailey. The bailey was a levelled area around the motte, usually crescent-shaped and surrounded by another ditch and a bank. A palisade was erected along the top of the bank and, where possible, the ditches were water-filled by a stream or spring. The bailey could only be entered via a bridge over the ditch, controlled by a gateway.

The wooden tower standing on its motte had four main functions:

i. It housed the personal accommodation of the lord or his constable.
ii. It gave a vantage point to observe what was happening in the surrounding country.
iii. It commanded the bailey by bowshot and could assist in its defence were it to come under attack. This is the reason for the bailey's crescent shape.
iv. It provided a refuge of last resort if the bailey was overwhelmed. The surviving members of the garrison could retreat to the tower and from there negotiate surrender terms.

The bailey contained living quarters for troops and stabling for their horses, as well as storerooms and workshops. It might also have a hall where the lord could entertain and conduct business.

A reconstruction of an early motte and bailey castle

Walter of Therouanne wrote a fairly detailed description of timber motte and bailey castles in 1137:

> It is their custom to build a mound of earth as high as they can, to surround it with a very deep and broad ditch, to fortify the top of the mound on all sides with a solid, wall-like palisade of wooden planks … and to build a house or donjon in the middle of the space within the wall that surveys everything and is disposed in such a way that it can only be entered by means of a bridge that starts at the outer lip of the ditch and is raised little by little and supported by sets of two or even three posts fixed at suitable intervals.

Motte and bailey castles could be quickly built without the need for architects or specialist craftsmen. Famously, the Bayeux Tapestry shows a motte being constructed at Hastings before the battle. The tower was prefabricated in Normandy and shipped over by the invasion fleet. Motte and bailey castles were relatively cheap, normally being built using only local materials. Digging the ditches and levelling the bailey provided all the material for making the motte and the bailey embankment. Rock, clay, gravel and earth could all be used in the construction of mottes, sometimes in alternating bands. If the chosen location was forested (as was Ponthendre) then clearing the site and its surroundings provided all the necessary timber for the tower, palisades and buildings. Construction manpower would be provided by the troops, doubtless supplemented by forced labour from the local populace.[1]

The conical motte and crescent-shaped bailey was a standard pattern that could be varied to take advantage of the local topography. The preferred location was on a natural eminence, but failing this, they were often sited on a convenient promontory or spur coming off a hill. This meant that the ground sloped away from the bailey on three sides, while the motte was positioned on the higher side to defend against a downhill attack. Both Ponthendre and the castle at Ewyas Harold are classic examples of this form of motte and bailey. Where a pre-existing earthwork was available, such as at Longtown, the Normans would make use of it in their defences. Around the country, numerous motte and bailey castles can be found superimposed on earlier Iron Age, Roman or Saxon fortifications.

In recent years academics have been inclined to disparage the essentially military role of castles, often emphasizing their role as symbols of power while expounding on their place in the landscape. The early Norman castle was never merely a symbol of power. While it would have projected power to those under its yoke, it was essentially a practical and efficient instrument of military domination, used to secure captured territory and provide a base for further conquest. Primarily a castle, or better still a chain of castles, was a tried and tested deterrent against local uprisings and external aggression. Small raiding parties would be disinclined to attack an area where there was demonstrably an organised defence force. Larger armies would be confronted with the choice of being delayed trying to take a castle or bypassing it, knowing that they had left a hostile force behind them, capable of harassing their communications and supply lines.

A reason given by the chronicler, Orderic Vitalis, for the success of the Norman Conquest was that the English had no castles. Before the coming of the Normans, both Anglo-Saxons and Danes usually lived in communal halls, the thanes and *jarls* depending on the loyalty of their extended families and followers. The larger Anglo-Saxon settlements, known as *burhs*, were protected by ditches and palisaded banks. For every hide of ploughland they held, landowners were expected to provide an armed man for the defence of the community. In contrast, the early Norman castle was designed to protect only the person of the ruling lord and his troops. Being foreign invaders, the Normans could not command the loyalty of the local populace and their castles served to isolate them from the conquered people. As such, a motte and bailey castle can be regarded as a symbol of insecurity, as much as one of power.[2]

After first appearing in northern France, motte and bailey castles were widely adopted by the Normans during the tenth century and soon proliferated across Europe. There were about 750 in England and Wales. Surprisingly few of them have any accurate recorded history, so it is generally impossible to tell when they were built or for how long they were operational. However, in Britain the highest concentration of motte and bailey castles is along the border between England and Wales. Herefordshire has 66 or more and Shropshire has 70. Their location here strongly suggests that most of them were built in the early years after the Conquest, before the Normans pushed on further into Wales. Once the Marcher lordships were carved out of Welsh territory, many of the simple earth and timber castles built along the old border would have become redundant.[3]

As castles spread and became more sophisticated, there was a parallel development in the techniques of siege warfare. A castle under attack would first be encircled to prevent supplies and reinforcements reaching the defending garrison. The attackers could fill in parts of the bailey ditch and then use scaling ladders to climb the walls or a battering ram to throw down the gates. The height advantage enjoyed by the defenders could be countered by building siege towers and in later years a range of missile throwers came into use. These usually threw stones but sometimes incendiaries were used, as wooden castles were always vulnerable to fire. But a full-on assault of a castle was always a risky enterprise, so sometimes, if time allowed, the most potent weapon against the defenders was starvation.

By the early 1100s, motte and bailey castles were becoming obsolete. In some cases, the timber tower on the motte was replaced with a stone keep or donjon and wooden palisades were replaced with stone walls. The use of the lower storey of donjons for keeping prisoners has given us the English word 'dungeon'. Stone castles were far more secure than timber ones, but they were hugely more costly to build. Because of this, only a small proportion of motte and bailey castles were rebuilt in stone, while the majority of them were simply abandoned.

2

Longtown Castle today

'What does not fade? The tow'r that long has stood
The crush of thunder and the warring winds,
Shook by the slow but sure destroyer, Time,
Now hangs in doubtful ruins o'er its base

John Armstrong, 1744

To access Longtown Castle you must pass through the massive rampart that surrounds both the castle and Castle Green. The rampart rises to a height of between five and seven metres and is roughly in the form of a square with rounded corners. Each side of the square is approximately 120 metres in length. The embankment is surrounded by a ditch, now mostly infilled, but originally about ten metres wide and perhaps as much as five metres deep.

A brown tourist sign on the Green indicates the way to the castle entrance, where there is limited off-road parking. Longtown Castle is in the custody of English Heritage and entry is free of charge.

Longtown Castle originated as a motte and bailey with a timber tower and palisades, but it was important enough to have been rebuilt later in stone. The mass of masonry, seen just to the left of the present entry gate, conceals the sad ruins of the main gateway into the castle (*see overleaf*). Little of it remains and what is left was blocked up and adapted for use by a later building after the castle was decommissioned. The sides of the gateway can still be made out, and it appears to have been a fairly simple opening in the curtain wall, with only a rudimentary gatehouse that lacked any protective projecting bastions. It would have been approached via a bridge over the water-filled moat that surrounded the castle.

The main gateway opened into the outer bailey, which would have held barracks for the men-at-arms and stables for their horses. The buildings in the baileys were probably constructed mainly of timber rather than stone, and now there is nothing left to show how they might have looked.

Opposite: A reconstruction of the keep at Longtown

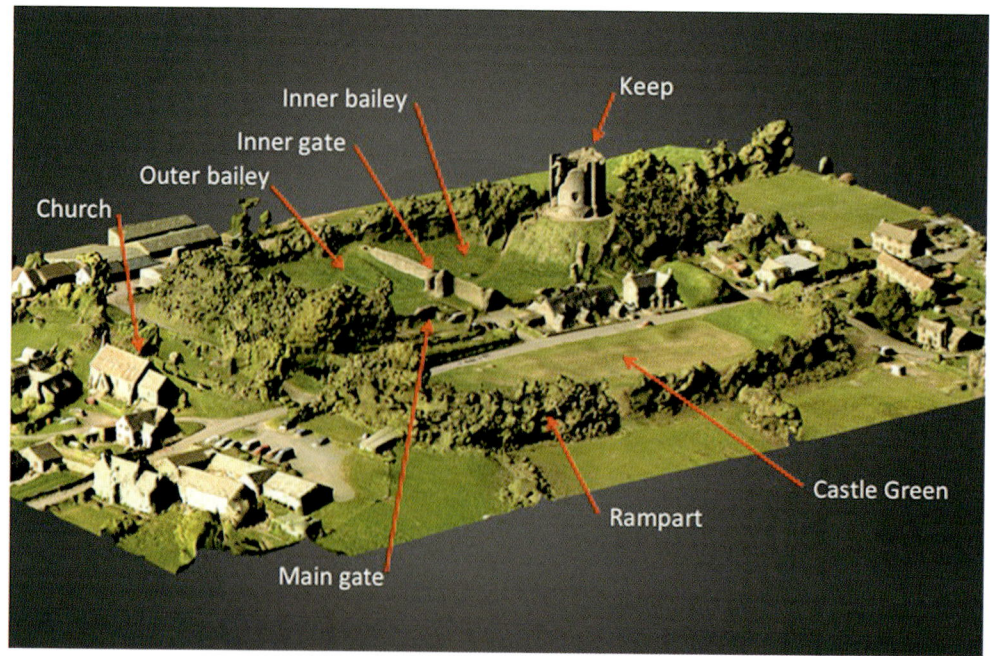

An overview of Longtown Castle (*based on a computer model by Adam Stanford, Aerial-Cam*)

The remains of the main gate

Much of the curtain wall around the baileys has been demolished over the years, its stone taken away and reused for building Longtown's houses and farms. The remaining sections on the east side of the baileys are about two metres thick and rise to a height of over four metres. The western and southern sides of the bailey made use of the great embankment and were far less vulnerable to attack. Here it was felt necessary to build the curtain wall only half a metre thick.

The cross-wall separating the outer and inner baileys was a later modification to improve the defences of the castle. It survives to the height of the soldiers' walkway along the top, but even so it gives only a poor impression of how it would have appeared originally. The ground level has risen considerably since the castle was in use, so when the wall still had its parapet it would have stood nearly twice as high as it does today.

The entrance through the cross-wall to the inner bailey was protected by a remarkably small gatehouse. This too would have stood much higher than it does now. The round-headed arch has the slots for a portcullis that was raised and lowered by a winch housed in a room over the archway.

The two solid bastions projecting in front of the gateway form a narrow passage that would have limited the number of attackers who could attempt to storm the gate. The winch room probably extended over this passage and would have had murder holes in its floor, allowing the defenders to assault unwelcome visitors from above. The gateway is too narrow for carts and packhorses, which suggests that the inner bailey was reserved for important people, such as the knights and their families. When the ground was at its original level, a horseman would have easily been able pass through the gateway without dismounting.

The gateway to the inner bailey

The inner bailey is dominated by the stone keep standing on its motte. The motte was superimposed on the north-west corner of the square rampart and was originally raised to support a timber tower. The motte is currently around 11 metres high but was almost certainly taller when first built and narrower at the top, as the timber tower would have had a much smaller footprint than the stone keep that replaced it.

The drum-shaped keep once stood an impressive 16 metres or so high. Now it is a ruin, lacking floors and roof, with a huge gash on the south side, leaving an opening from top to bottom. Much of the readily accessible dressed stone has been robbed out. And yet, in spite of the ravages of time and the depredation of man, it remains an impressive structure and retains considerable evidence for its original architectural refinement. As well as its military functions, the keep provided secure, comfortable living-quarters for the lord and his family. Apart from the castle guards on lookout duty, it was not designed to accommodate men-at-arms, except when the castle came under siege.

The keep (*photograph by Adam Stanford, Aerial-Cam*)

The keep was built from local Devonian sandstone rubble, with dressed stone for jambs, arches and other features. The circular wall is three metres thick and rises three storeys high before being capped with a wall-walk. A sloping stone plinth (also known as a batter), now mostly robbed out, reinforced the base of the wall. The plinth had a number of important functions. As well as strengthening the lower, most-vulnerable part of the keep, its slope protected the top of the motte from the weather. It also made it difficult for attackers to shelter at the foot of the wall. A plinth provided another less obvious, though perhaps more important benefit when building a heavy stone tower on an earth motte. A plinth spreads the weight of the tower over a greater area, in the case of Longtown more than doubling the size of its footprint, thereby halving the downward pressure on the motte. This is particularly important, as Longtown's keep had no significant foundations.[1]

The keep was buttressed by three projecting turrets, somewhat less than semicylindrical in form, spaced equally around its circumference. The turret on the south side, now largely missing, was slightly larger than the other two and contained a spiral staircase. Projecting turrets are an unusual feature of round keeps in Wales and the Marches. Skenfrith has one turret with a staircase and a small overhanging turret containing a garderobe or toilet. The later keep of Caldicot Castle has just one projecting turret, large enough to contain rooms. No other round keep, anywhere else in the country, has three turrets. It is clear from an aerial view of Longtown Castle that small turrets like these add very little to the structural strength and stability of the keep, and they only marginally enhance the sightlines along the wall. It seems that the primary purpose of the north-western and eastern turrets, which are largely solid, was simply their visual effect – they provide symmetry and give an impression of sturdiness.

An aerial view of the keep (*Adam Stanford, Aerial-Cam*)

The keep now stands in splendid isolation but would have appeared very different when built. Then, the curtain walls ascended the motte in steps before being bonded into the walls of the keep and acting as massive buttresses. From the east side, the wall joined the keep immediately next to the chimney turret. The scar left by its removal can just be detected in an area of new masonry set with a slightly pinkish mortar. The western wall provided essential reinforcement for the stair turret, which had a thinner wall than the rest of the castle.

The keep had three rooms one above the other. The entrance was originally not at ground level but on the next level up. The position of the doorway is revealed by the flat surface of dressed stone on the east side of the gap in the wall. Beam sockets to the right indicate that access was via timber stairs terminating at a landing alongside the doorway. This indirect approach was a simple way of precluding a battering ram from being used against the door.

Nowadays entry to the keep is through the gap in the wall to the lowest room. This undercroft is a little over seven metres in diameter. It has no windows and was presumably used mainly for storage, although it may occasionally have served as a prison. When the castle was in use, it could only be accessed via the spiral staircase from the floor above. A square masonry feature set in the floor appears to be either a well or a cistern for water storage. If it is a well, then it must have gone right down through the motte to the water table beneath.[2]

It was a common feature of Norman castles for the undercroft to be divided in two by a stone wall that supported the joists of the floor above. Longtown Castle had a different arrangement. A large timber, known as a summer beam, spanned the diameter of the keep with its ends resting on a setback in the wall. The word 'summer' is derived from the Old French *sommier*, meaning a packhorse and indicating its capacity to bear a heavy load. Braces rising from two corbels that project from opposite sides of the undercroft provided additional support. The inner ends of floor joists were jointed into the summer beam, while their outer ends also rested on the setback in the wall.[3]

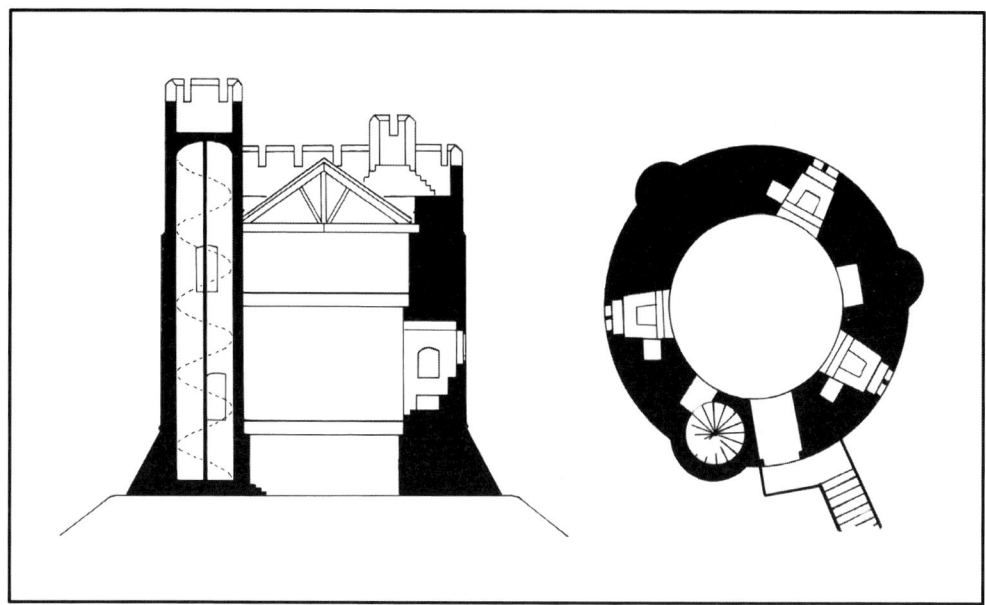

A schematic section through the keep and plan of the principal room

Opposite: A cutaway reconstruction of the keep from the south-west

This middle floor was the principal room of the castle. With its high ceiling, it was certainly impressive but it would also have been a pleasant, comfortable space, lit by three windows and heated by a large fireplace, whose chimney is built into the eastern turret. Internally, the three windows have generous embrasures under segmental arches of pitched stone. These provided useful sitting areas, each lined with stone benches and with a deep cupboard, set into the wall. It is intriguing to imagine what these might have held when the castle was occupied.

Externally, the lintels over the windows were protected from the weight of masonry above by relieving arches of dressed stone, built into the wall during its construction. Two of the arches are plain but the voussoirs of the arch over the north window are carved with ornate medallions. Strangely, this decoration cannot be seen from anywhere within the castle and it is too high up to be visible from outside the castle. Here we have another mystery. Why would anyone go to the trouble of placing such ornamental stonework where it could not possibly be seen?

The north window

Apart from the decoration over the north window, the three windows of the main room of the keep are all the same in form, size and structure. We can see no evidence to support the suggestion that the windows were later alterations or that the external relieving arches were inserted when the windows were widened during some time when defence was not of primary importance. The segmental arches of pitched stone over the wide embrasures and the external relieving arches could not have been inserted without first demolishing all of the stonework above them. And besides, with the increase in the use of crossbows and longbows the tendency was towards narrower rather than wider windows. The three windows must therefore be seen as part of the original build of the keep.[4]

The decoration of the voussoirs over the north window takes the form of medallions made up of beaded rings enclosing flowers and other motifs. Similar beaded medallions can be seen at Llandaff Cathedral, Hereford Cathedral, Leominster Priory and the churches of Kilpeck, Rowlestone and Brinsop. These are all recognised as the work of the Herefordshire School of Romanesque Sculpture that flourished during the second quarter of the twelfth century, producing ornate carvings for ecclesiastical buildings.[5]

The decorated voussoirs

However, although the voussoirs can be reasonably accurately dated, there is a problem. They are decorated on their lower as well as their outer surfaces. The lower surface of a relieving arch is invariably left undecorated, since it is hidden by the masonry infilling the space between the arch and its lintel. Therefore, it is certain that when these stones were being carved, they were not intended for their present position. A close inspection reveals that the central voussoir is incomplete, while the second from the right is unfinished. Its lower surface is plain but flawed. It appears that while these decorated stones were intended for a high status building, most probably a church, they were unsatisfactory or surplus to requirements and stayed in the mason's yard until a less critical use was found for them at Longtown. Their position over the one window, where they cannot be seen from anywhere within the castle, confirms that their use was purely functional rather than decorative.

The spiral staircase led from the principal room to the upper chamber and then on up to the wall-walk. It rose clockwise, giving an advantage to defending swordsmen, as long as they were right-handed. The central column of the stairs would have restricted any attackers to delivering only backhand blows.

The upper chamber provided sleeping quarters for the lord and his family. A small passage, built within the thickness of the wall, separated this room from the staircase, giving additional privacy and isolating the room from the noise of guards using the staircase to reach the wall-walk above. Small rectangular windows within splayed reveals look out to the north-west and south-east. A second passage, again within the thickness of the wall, led to a garderobe, built partially within the north-western turret and containing a privy. The privy projects out from the keep on corbels so that effluent dropped onto the plinth at the base of the keep, where it would remain until rain eventually washed it down to the moat.

Above the upper chamber, between each pair of turrets, there were three holes passing through the wall to the outside. Past reconstructions have mistakenly shown these nine holes as beam slots for a *hourd* or hoarding – a wooden gallery running around the outside of the wall that allowed the defenders to rain stones and other missiles down on anyone attacking the keep. However, with the beams spaced in this

Top: the remains of the spiral staircase
Bottom: The privy

way, the floorboards for the hoarding would have had to be five to six metres long, and with no intermediate supports. Such a long span, pierced by trapdoors, could not possibly bear the weight of piles of rocks and the armoured defenders throwing them.

In fact, the nine holes held the beams and principal rafters supporting a conical roof, probably covered in stone tiles or wooden shingles. Since the roof was set inside the wall of the keep, there had to be a lead gutter running around the wall to collect rainwater and discharge it out through the wall via spouts set in the nine holes.

The roof was circled by the wall-walk at the top of the keep. Defenders posted here were shielded from incoming missiles by a crenellated parapet. Short flights of stone steps went from the wall-walk up to raised platforms at the tops of the two smaller turrets, each protected by a horseshoe-shaped parapet. The spiral stair turret provided an even higher platform. Lookouts on the three turret platforms had clear views along the valleys of both the Monnow and the Olchon. Unlike today, the surrounding area would have been completely clear of trees, leaving no shelter for potential attackers.

Left: the holes in the keep at Longtown (*photograph by Adam Stanford, Aerial-Cam*)

Below: A tower at Caerphilly Castle with holes for both a hoarding and drain spouts

The remains of the walk-way and parapets (*photograph by Adam Stanford, Aerial-Cam*)

From their elevated position, men on the keep could play an active role in defending the castle. We know that on at least one occasion Longtown came under siege. The attack probably began with an assault on the main gate. This was usually the most vulnerable part of a castle, which led to the development of massive, sophisticated gatehouses such as those seen at Chepstow and White Castle. The curtain wall could only be attacked by infilling parts of the moat, so that scaling ladders could be positioned or a shelter brought forward to allow sappers to mine the lower part of the wall. At Longtown, undermining the wall would have been impossible because of the height of the water table that kept the moat filled. If attackers managed to take control of the bailey, those defenders who were able to would retire to the safety of the keep. Because of their inherent strength, keeps were only rarely subject to direct assaults. The defenders were usually left with the choice of negotiating terms of surrender or holding out in the hope of the arrival of a relieving force before their supplies failed.

It is remarkable how many times the number three appears in the description of the keep. As far as we know, Longtown Castle is unique in having the only round keep in all Britain, France and Ireland with a design based on a three-fold symmetry. And yet, Longtown is a very simple castle. Unlike most stone castles, it did not see several phases of redevelopment. The keep was not provided with arrow slits for crossbowmen. The gateways remained undeveloped. No corner towers were added around the baileys to provide enfilading fire along the curtain walls. There were no substantial stone buildings within the baileys. This is in complete contrast to the de Lacys' main strongholds at Ludlow in Shropshire and Trim in Ireland.

3

Why build a round keep?

The world only goes round by misunderstanding
Charles Baudelaire

THE KEEPS OF medieval castles were built to a wide variety of plans. The earliest stone keeps were generally square like Goodrich, or rectangular like Chepstow. During the twelfth and thirteenth centuries, the use of round keeps spread from France into England, then to Wales and Ireland. The greatest concentration of round keeps in Britain is found in South Wales and the southern Marches, extending from Monmouthshire and Herefordshire across to Pembrokeshire. They are largely absent from northern England and are completely unknown in Scotland, which is perhaps surprising as round defensive stone towers called *brochs* were being built in Scotland back in the Iron Age. Almost all modern buildings are built to rectangular plans, so why did cylindrical keeps, and more frequently round towers in walls and gateways, gain popularity in the medieval period?

In our researches we came across some extraordinary claims for the superiority of round keeps over square or rectangular ones. The received wisdom is that the corners of keeps were structurally weak, being particularly vulnerable to battering rams and undermining, and that they somehow restricted the vision of defenders by creating zones of 'dead ground' where attackers couldn't be seen.[1]

Although these notions have not been tested experimentally and are easily challenged, they are frequently repeated in books and academic reports. Sadly, they have even found their way into teaching materials for children. However, any engineer will tell you that the weakest parts of a square or rectangular structure are the midpoints of the longest walls. The corners are in fact the strongest parts because the adjoining walls buttress each other. You can easily demonstrate this for yourself with a cardboard box. Apply pressure to a corner and then to a side, and see which gives the most.

While rams could be useful for breaking down gates or relatively thin curtain walls, they were unlikely ever to be effective against the solid stonework of a keep, some three metres thick and often reinforced at the base with a sloping plinth, whatever its shape might be. Furthermore, rams could not be used against a keep standing on a motte or surrounded by a moat.

The most commonly cited failure of a square keep is that of Rochester Castle. When rebels occupied it in 1215, King John laid siege and brought up stone-throwers to harass the forces within the castle. We don't know what sort of stone-throwers were used – they were described as *petraria* and slings – but by the thirteenth century the trebuchet could hurl stones weighing around 90kg and sometimes as much as twice that. These would certainly have caused serious damage to roofs and parapets but they are unlikely to have brought down the walls of a keep. For comparison, the modern steel wrecking balls used by demolition contractors weigh between 450 and 5,000kg and are capable of delivering repeated blows to the same place.

Roger of Wendover reported that, 'The king, seeing that all his warlike engines took but little effect, at length employed miners who soon threw down a great part of the walls', whereupon the defenders retreated into the keep. King John's sappers then went on to mine the walls of the keep, using the fat of forty pigs to fire the mine props. Even though an opening was made, the defenders continued their resistance, only surrendering when their supplies gave out.[2]

The damage to the keep during the siege resulted in the complete rebuilding of its south-east corner tower. This is often cited as an example of the vulnerability of the corners of square keeps to undermining. However, a detailed survey of the keep, carried out in 2009, showed that the internal face of the original corner tower still survives in the basement, proving that it had not been undermined. The surveyors noted that half of the south side of the keep also had to be rebuilt, and concluded that it was this, rather than the corner, that had been the sappers' target. It was breached not by undermining but with a surface mine. Working under a shelter to protect them from attack from above, the sappers, who had been issued with pickaxes, would have tunnelled into the wall, inserting timber props as they went. These were then packed around with combustible material and set alight. When the props burned through, the unsupported wall would have fallen. The blaze may have spread to other parts of the keep, which show signs of fire damage. The collapse of the adjoining wall and the fire were together enough to destabilise the corner tower and necessitate its rebuilding.[3]

So, Rochester's square keep was able to withstand bombardment from King John's artillery and did not eventually fall because of the undermining of a vulnerable corner. During the medieval period, the design of castles demonstrates that corners were not seen as being susceptible to undermining. Rather, the opposite is the case. At castles such as Goodrich, Chepstow and Caerphilly, later round towers were often built on square plinths to add strength to them.

Top: A square plinth at Caerphilly Castle
Middle: A square, medieval fortified tower
Bottom: A reconstruction of a hoarding at Caerphilly Castle

The perceived problem of dead ground at the corners of square and rectangular towers is also a fallacy. Early castles were defended from the wall-walks around the curtain walls and the top of the keep. From these, the defenders had all-round vision. Anyone approaching the corner of the square tower shown below could clearly be seen – and shot at if necessary – from any of the crenels on two sides of the tower.

Regardless of whether a keep was square, round or polygonal, a problem only arose if attackers could get close enough to the foot of the wall so that they could not be seen from the wall-walk above. Castle designers responded with different measures to counter this problem. Timber hoardings and the later development of stone machicolations allowed defenders to drop missiles onto attackers who were sheltering at the foot of a wall. Later and more sophisticated castles were built with projecting towers with loopholes that allowed crossbowmen to shoot along the length of the walls.

It is often suggested that hoardings were temporary structures stored away in peacetime and only erected when a castle came under attack. This seems to be highly unlikely because getting even prefabricated units out of storage and assembling them would have required considerable time and a large body of skilled labour that was unlikely to be available when a castle was about to come under siege.

Both square and rectangular keeps continued to be built into the fourteenth century, long after round keeps were introduced. Their builders seem to have been oblivious to the supposed problems of corners. Round keeps remained relatively few in number and are completely absent in some parts of the country.

The de Lacys were innovative castle builders who showed no particular preference for the shape of their keeps. In Ewyas Lacy, not far from the round keep of Longtown, there was a polygonal keep at Llancillo. There is no remaining masonry visible at the de Lacy castle of Weobley (just a badly damaged motte), but a seventeenth-century plan shows a rectangular keep with round corner towers. In contrast, at nearby Lyonshall the de Lacys or their tenants, the Devereux family, built a round keep on a motte. At their main powerbase of Ludlow, the de Lacys experimented with the Great Tower that combines a rectangular keep with a gatehouse. This concept of merging keep and gatehouse together was later adopted and developed for the most sophisticated castles in Britain, such as Aberystwyth, Caernarfon, Harlech and Beaumaris, built by Edward I to secure his conquest of North Wales. In Ireland, Hugh and Walter de Lacy built many towers to defend their extensive territories. Their centre of operations was the magnificent and formidably strong, twelve-cornered keep of Trim Castle.

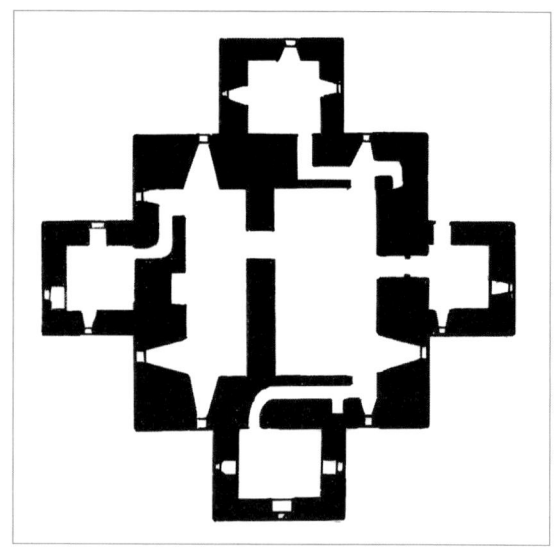

A plan of the keep at Trim

Since there is such a wide variation in the form of surviving keeps – square, rectangular, polygonal and round, with or without projecting turrets or buttresses – it has to be concluded that, as long as the walls were thick enough, the general shape of a keep was largely irrelevant. Only in some limited circumstances were cylindrical keeps perhaps preferable to rectangular.

When building a heavy stone keep on a motte that was originally raised only to support a lightweight wooden tower, the weight distribution was a key factor. A circular structure both spreads the load evenly and fully utilises the limited space available on the top of the motte. On the other hand, the corners of a square keep are its heaviest parts and would be nearer to the edge of the motte, potentially leading to instability. Therefore, when upgrading a wooden tower on a motte to a stone keep, a round tower was the obvious practical choice, although there are exceptions.

Another important factor is that round towers were more economical to build than square or rectangular towers. A circular plan requires less stone to enclose the same area as a square or a rectangular one, and there is no need of expensive ashlar masonry for the corners. The earliest reasonably well-dated round keep in England is at New Buckenham in Norfolk, an area not known for fine building stone. Its curved wall was constructed mainly with mortared flint.

As castles developed, round and D-shaped towers did become common in curtain walls and on gatehouses, either for their economy or perhaps because their curved walls could deflect missiles and absorb their impact better than the straight walls of square towers. But corners are even more effective for this. In later centuries, the increasing power of cannon fire led to the design of star forts, which deliberately incorporated multiple angles because of their inherent strength and effectiveness in deflecting missiles.

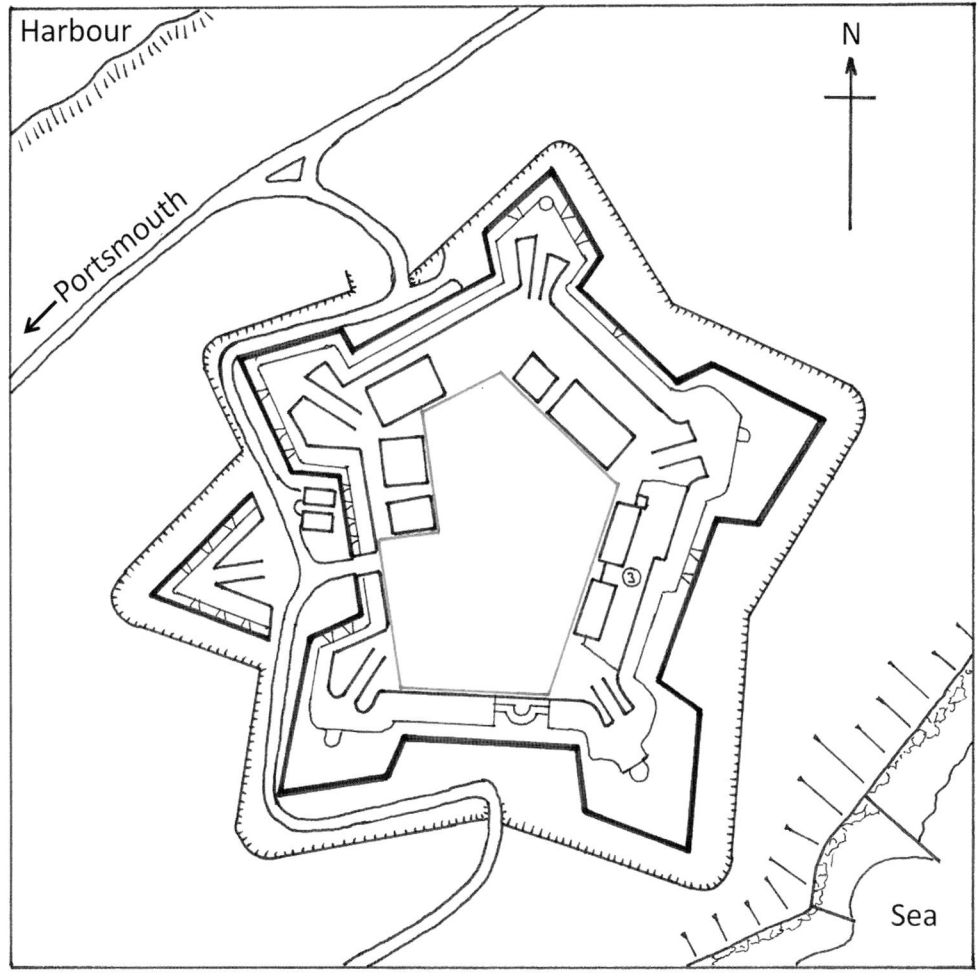

Fort Cumberland, Hampshire

Clockwise from top left: Bronllys, c.1220; Caldicot, c.1221; Skenfrith, 1219–32; Tretower, 1235–50

It is not obvious why there was a concentration of round keeps in South Wales and the southern Marches. Good quality building stone is readily available throughout the area, so the preference for round keeps didn't arise from any lack of it. While some round keeps, such as those at Longtown, Bronllys and Caldicot, were built on pre-existing mottes, others like Skenfrith and Pembroke were built on relatively flat ground where any shape could have been chosen. At Tretower, the inner buildings of an earlier shell keep sited on a low motte were demolished in order to build an imposing round tower.

We can only conclude that the predilection for building round keeps in South Wales and the southern Marches was simply a fashion of the time, a result of Marcher lords and Welsh magnates copying their neighbours.

4

The excavations

There comes a time in every rightly constructed boy's life when he has a raging desire to go somewhere and dig for hidden treasure

Mark Twain

ARCHAEOLOGICAL EXCAVATION IS a destructive process. Although it can produce useful and instructive insights into the past, it invariably results in partial and often complete destruction of the evidence. It is therefore essential to consider why you need to excavate and what you might reasonably hope to achieve by doing so. This is particularly the case when working on Scheduled Monuments, which are by definition of national importance and have statutory protection. A necessary part of the project plan was to think carefully about a set of archaeological objectives for both of our sites.

After much discussion we agreed that the objectives for our archaeological excavations were to provide answers to some or all of the following questions.

At Ponthendre:

a. Over what period or periods was the motte and bailey occupied?
b. Was it completed and was it a single or multiple phase construction?
c. What form did any keep structures take and what materials were used?
d. What were the form and materials of the bailey defences?
e. What activities took place within the bailey?
f. Are there any structural remains still in place?
g. Were any of the structures subsequently robbed out or slighted?
h. Is there any evidence for earlier occupation of the site?

At Longtown Castle Green:

a. When was the square embankment constructed?
b. Was the embankment a single phase or multiple phase construction?
c. What materials were used to build it?
d. Is there an internal structure to the embankment?
e. Was it faced with either timber or stone?
f. Was it topped by a wall or palisade?
g. Was there an internal ditch as suggested by the geophysics?
h. Is there evidence for buildings within the embanked enclosure?
i. What activities took place within the embanked enclosure?
j. Over what period(s) was the enclosure occupied?
k. Is there evidence for earlier occupation of the site?

These questions would be used to target where and how we would dig. The success of this part of the project could be judged on how well these questions were answered.

Before deciding where to excavate, we commissioned a comprehensive geophysical survey of Ponthendre, Castle Green, and part of Longtown Castle's outer bailey. Although three different techniques were used – resistivity, gradiometry and ground-penetrating radar – the results were largely uninformative and frankly disappointing. There were no obvious indications of buried buildings and those anomalies that were detected were amorphous and could not be resolved into anything recognisable. It was clear from the visible earthworks that we were on important archaeological sites, so it was extraordinary that the geophysics failed to provide any useful information. Only excavation was going to explain why this was so.[1]

We arranged for both Ponthendre and Longtown to be overflown by a camera-carrying drone that took several thousand high-definition photographs. These were processed to provide accurate 3-dimensional models of the two castles and their surrounding areas. Later this technique was also applied to the motte and bailey at Walterstone.

The 3-D models are used in the two previous chapters and again in this chapter to show the positions of the excavation trenches. We planned the location of trenches for where they were most likely to provide answers to the research questions we had posed. Site visits were arranged with our archaeologists and Historic England to discuss and agree our plans. It is illegal to carry out any work on Scheduled Monuments without the formal consent of the Secretary of State for Culture, Media and Sport. It is Historic England who advises the minister and either commends or opposes the application for consent.

We were to excavate at both sites simultaneously, over two 3-week seasons during July of 2016 and 2017. Tim Hoverd, Herefordshire Council's Archaeological Projects Manager, provided an excellent team of five professional archaeologists who set up camp in the orchard of Clodock Mill. Work at Ponthendre was supervised by Peter Dorling, while Nigel Baker headed up the work on Castle Green. Each day the professionals had the help of an average of 11 volunteers. Many of these were complete beginners with no previous experience of excavation. They received training and were closely supervised. Others came with a wealth of specialist knowledge and experience from previous digs. Most were from the local community or the surrounding area but others had travelled some distance to take part. Two of them, Kevin and his daughter Shannon, came over from Alaska and spent some of their holiday digging. Over the 30 days of excavation, 79 volunteers gave up their time to join the project.

Volunteers working at Ponthendre (*photograph by Simon Mayes*)

SEASON 1 AT PONTHENDRE

During the first season at Ponthendre, Trench 1 exposed the north-east quarter of the summit of the motte, to determine the nature of the keep. Trench 2 extended 20 metres over the southern edge of the bailey and down its scarp, to see how the perimeter was fortified. Trench 3 was located within the bailey, to look for buildings and investigate any activities that had taken place there.

Being raised features, motte and bailey castles are unlikely to have accumulated a thick overburden of soil, so we expected that as soon as we had removed the turf we would be straight on to archaeology. Although they are very common, comparatively few motte and bailey castles have been excavated. It was with great anticipation that we cut and stacked the turf from our three trenches.

Trench 1 on the top of the motte was expected to tell us whether there had been a wooden tower or a stone keep. This might be either square or round. Even if there

The trench locations shown on a 3-D model of Ponthendre (*model by Adam Stanford, Aerial-Cam*)

were no actual remains, we should at least still find massive post-holes or foundation trenches. Below the topsoil the motte was shown to be made up of purplish clay containing small pieces of sandstone rubble, but after we had trowelled off an entire quadrant, there was nothing else visible whatsoever. We went deeper, and deeper again, but there was still no sign of any structure. If there ever had been a tower it must have been built on sill beams that left no archaeological trace in the ground.

Trench 2 was more productive. Before excavation, it appeared that only the scarp of the hill had protected the southern edge of the bailey. Now it was clear that there was a low rampart of turf, earth and broken stone. As the trench extended down the scarp, a ditch was revealed. Material from the ditch had been used to form the rampart. Picks had then been used to enhance the slope of the natural scarp above the moat, and the resulting rubble was added to the rampart. In spite of the dry summer weather, the ditch began to fill with water. We now knew that the bailey had been protected by a wet moat. Even though the resulting rampart was only 0.7m higher than the bailey, the advantage of the natural slope meant that the height from the bottom of the ditch to the top of the rampart was around 6m, providing a formidable defence. We looked carefully for the expected post-holes of a stockade on the rampart but strangely only found one.

A small section of the rampart was removed. The soil type under the rampart indicated that the site had been forested before the earthworks were constructed. In just a small sample of this soil, two pieces of worked flint were found, demonstrating that Ponthendre was occupied in prehistoric times and that people had been making stone tools here.

Trench 3, opened up inside the bailey, was expected to reveal the remains of buildings for housing men and horses, along with cooking hearths or other signs of occupation. However, like Trench 1, this trench was completely sterile, with no signs of any activity whatsoever. It now seemed fairly certain that our castle at Ponthendre had progressed no further than the earthworks of the motte and bailey. Of course, it was just possible that we had been unlucky in where we had placed our trenches, but there was no doubt that the first season of excavation had raised more questions than it had answered.

SEASON 1 AT CASTLE GREEN

We decided that we would open up two trenches on Castle Green during the first season of excavation. Trench 1 was to be a section through the square rampart which extends around the Green and the castle. Trench 2 would investigate what had taken place on the Green itself.

The rampart stands around five metres high on the east side of the Green but at some time in the past it

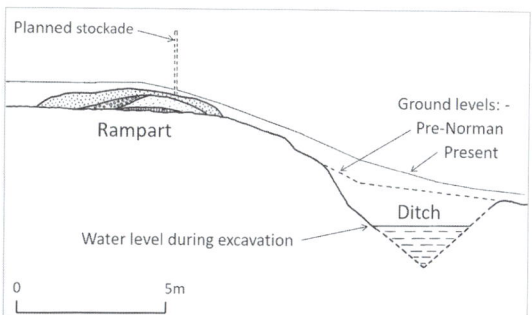

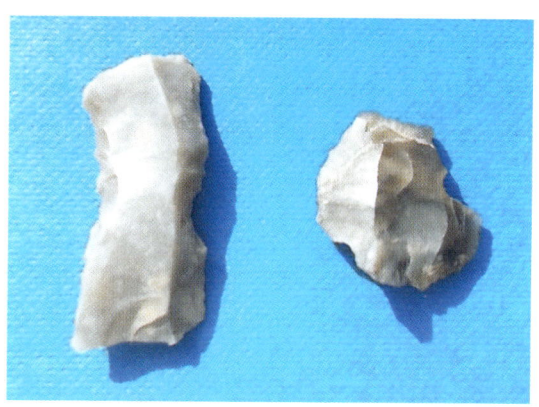

Top: A simplified section of Trench 2 at Ponthendre
Middle: Trench 2 (*photograph by Simon Mayes*)
Bottom: Worked flint from Ponthendre

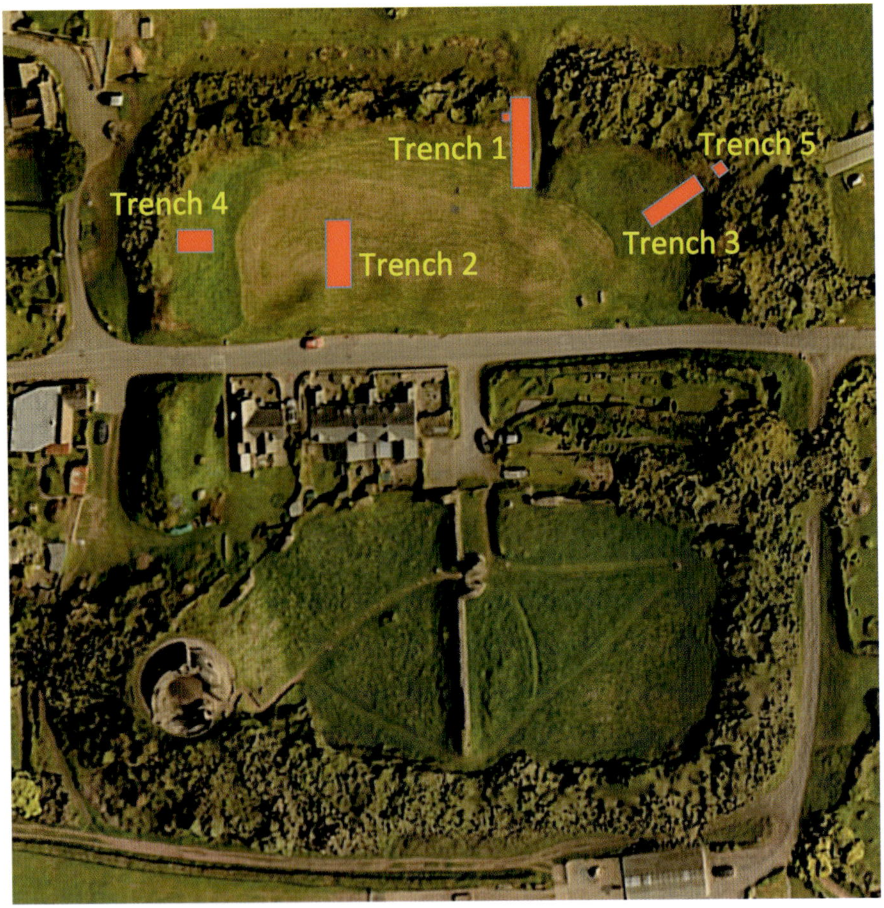

Above: Trench locations shown on a 3-D model of Longtown Castle (*model by Adam Stanford, Aerial-Cam*)

Left: The 1718 plan of Longtown Castle (*photograph © The British Library Board, Add. 60746 f11*)

NB *for a larger version of this plan, see p. 256*

32   THE MARCH OF EWYAS

had been breached to allow access to the fields beyond. This was presumably done before 1718, because the earliest image we have of Longtown Castle is a plan of that date, drawn for the Right Honourable George Lord Bergavenny, and showing a field gate there.

We had permission from English Heritage and the present Marquis of Abergavenny to make use of this breach to cut a complete section through the rampart. Because of the height of the rampart, for safety considerations the section was cut in 1-metre steps. One of our volunteers, Tim, made life easier for the others by bringing his JCB to lift the turf and begin cutting the steps.

Trench 1 at Castle Green (*photograph © Herefordshire Archaeology*)

Turf blocks at the base of the rampart around Castle Green

As work on the section progressed with mattocks and trowels we began to see that the rampart was made up of loose layers of material without the use of a timber or stone revetment. Soon more details began to emerge. Blocks of turf had been stacked up to form the core of the rampart. These stood to a height of 0.55 metres but would have been higher when they were first laid.

The bulk of the rampart was then built up with layers of earth, then clay and degraded mudstone, piled up to a height of over four metres. Presumably this material was derived mostly, if not entirely, from excavating the surrounding ditch. The rampart remained at this height long enough for a layer of turf to grow, before its height was raised by a further 0.3 metres or so. A small area of the top of the rampart was sampled to see if there was evidence for a wall or a timber stockade, but surprisingly we found no sign of any additional defences.

We were desperately looking for dating evidence that could tell us when the rampart was built but all we found were a few pieces of abraded thirteenth- to fifteenth-century pottery in the upper layer. Unfortunately, these could not be used to give a reliable date because of the amount of disturbance from tree roots and animal burrows on the top of the rampart. At the very lowest level there were a few small fragments of charcoal embedded amongst the turf and we collected some of these in the hope that they might provide a radiocarbon date for when the rampart was started.

One intriguing feature was a 3-metre-deep drain that cut through the inner slope of the rampart and then curved out through the breach towards the outer ditch. This contained some sherds of blue and white glazed pottery from the nineteenth century. Its depth suggests that it was probably the drain for a sawpit, known to have been located on the Green in the 1890s and presenting something of a hazard to the local children. The Longtown School logbook for 1892 reported,

> 'Clara Edwards whilst playing on the Green fell into the sawpit and cut her head rather badly. I had to send her home after it was attended to and her sister went along.' The sawpit was still there in 1899 when the teacher's log says, 'I am to enquire what steps are taken to ensure the safety of children when playing about the sawpit adjoining the school which HM Inspector reports is dangerous.'[2]

Trench 2 was opened in an uneven area near to the centre of the Green, to investigate some lumps and bumps, and to see what lay beneath them. Below the turf the upper layer of soil contained some small change, slate pencils from the school, pieces of clay tobacco pipe stems and odd sherds of pottery dating from the fifteenth to the nineteenth and

The whetstone (*photograph by Chas Breton*)

twentieth centuries. One very promising find, perhaps brought up from medieval strata by a burrowing mole, was a small whetstone for sharpening knives, pierced at one end to be worn around the neck on a thong.

There were also two very corroded arrowheads, one leaf shaped, the other with a diamond section. These seemed to be too lightweight for military use and may have been post-medieval sporting arrows. Below this layer was a dump of broken stone containing some pieces of stone roofing tile and various pottery fragments, some medieval, others seventeenth-century. This deposit probably derived from demolition work connected with building the school on the opposite side of the road in the nineteenth century. Below was another dumped layer of broken stone and marl. A bowl-shaped pit dug into this layer contained a few pieces of medieval pottery.

Beneath these dumps of material was a layer of redeposited marl spread across the entire area of the trench and presumably placed there to level the site. It contained pieces of black cooking pots, animal bone, iron nails and a piece of a horseshoe. Two features cut into this layer suggested the remains of a simple building. One was a stone-filled gulley that may have held a sill beam supporting a timber-framed wall. The other was a post-hole, still containing vertically-placed packing stones. We were beginning to reveal medieval Longtown.

One mysterious find generated a lot of discussion. It was a flat piece of hard sandstone, about 30cm by 25cm. One side was scored with several U-shaped grooves, as if it had been used repeatedly for sharpening something. The other side had a number of similar but smaller grooves and much of it was covered with peculiar brown blotches. When examined under a microscope, these were found to be the result of the stone having been splashed with tiny spheres of molten iron. Presumably it had been used in some manufacturing process that involved working with extremely hot metal.

Towards the end of the first season of excavation we uncovered a surface of small compacted stones. This surface was scattered with fragments of medieval black cooking pots and crushed animal bone. Alongside it lay a row of flat stones, perhaps the remains of a wall or the foundations for a sill beam. It appeared that we had reached the

The 'mystery stone' (*photographs by Chas Breton*)

floor or yard of a domestic building. Unfortunately we could not investigate further, as time had run out, but we would return to this trench during the next season. The exposed archaeology was covered with a plastic sheet and then backfilled by machine. Our first season of excavation had been largely exploratory, carefully working our way through layers of redeposited material. The next season we would be starting off in the thirteenth century.

Trench 2 at Castle Green (*photograph by Dale Rouse*)

Excavation entails a lot of hard physical labour and some of us are no longer in our prime. During that first season, we baked in sweltering temperatures. Nearly every day, while most of us took a well-earned lunch break in the shade, Dan, one of the professional team, ran to the top of Hatterall Ridge and back – a circuit of about six miles with a climb of 1,000 feet – and then joined us for another afternoon's excavating.

After three weeks of digging we had not found anything that might suggest a Roman presence in Longtown. Since all previous excavations had also failed to find evidence for the Romans, we were now utterly convinced that Longtown had never been the site of a Roman fort.

SEASON 2 AT PONTHENDRE

A year later, our volunteers were all keen to start the second season of excavation and discover more about the two castles. At Ponthendre, new trenches were opened up to check the findings of the first season and investigate particular features of the earthworks.

At the point where the southern horn of the bailey meets the moat around the motte there is a substantial mound looking like a miniature version of the motte. This mound might be either the base for a defensive tower or possibly the abutment for a bridge from the bailey up to the motte. Trench 4 was positioned on top of the mound, to look for any evidence of a built structure. A wooden tower or bridge up to the motte should have left obvious foundations or at least substantial post-holes but we found no indication that anything had been built on the mound. A number of burrows suggested that the mound might have seen later use as a rabbit warren, although the holes may just have been the work of wild rabbits.

Trench 5 was opened up in the bailey in a further attempt to look for signs of any buildings or activities. Again we found no indications that the bailey had ever been occupied. There were no foundations or post-holes, no residue from fires and only two pieces of late medieval or post-medieval pottery were found. These had probably arrived during later agricultural use when the bailey was lightly ploughed and cultivated.

Trench 6 was an extension to Trench 2 along the top of the rampart. It was intended to locate additional evidence for a stockade but, since no more post-holes were found, we had to conclude that a stockade had never been built.

Trench 7, the entrance to the bailey at Ponthendre (*photograph by Simon Mayes*)

Trench 7 was cut across a depression at the east end of the bailey scarp, which looked as if it may have been the entrance to the bailey. Excavation confirmed that this was indeed an entranceway. The end of the rampart was similar in construction to the section uncovered in Trench 2, with the addition of some larger stones. If there was a proper masonry gateway, it had subsequently been completely robbed out. A few large, irregular stones had been randomly placed across the entrance to provide rough metalling, either for the construction phase or during later agricultural use, but it was apparent that no proper access road had been laid through the gateway.

Trench 8 was a deeper, 1-metre-wide transect across the top of the motte, from the centre to the edge and taking in an anomaly that had shown up on the ground penetrating radar survey. The anomaly turned out to be only some larger buried stones disturbed by tree roots. It was clear that no tower or palisade had ever been built on the motte.

SEASON 2 AT CASTLE GREEN

At Castle Green, Tim the digger-driver came on the first day and reopened Trench 2, extending it further towards the east, away from the dumped material we had to go through the previous year. He also removed the turf for two other trenches, Trench 3 in the south-east corner of the Green and Trench 4 on the northern edge of the Green, against the rampart.

In Trench 2 we uncovered more of the compacted stone surface that we had found the previous year. It now became clear that it was a medieval road, running east-west across the Green. The surface was cambered and metalled with small stones and gravel.

The thirteenth-century road

We were amused to find a deep thirteenth-century pothole (it was a particularly bad year for potholes in Herefordshire in 2017). The road was bounded on its south side by a line of stones that may have supported the sill beam of a timber building, and on the north side by a deep ditch. The ditch fill included pieces of medieval cooking pot, a complete horseshoe and a considerable quantity of charcoal, suggesting the nearby presence of a blacksmith's forge.

With only limited time available, it was decided that we should cut two sondages or trial pits to determine what lay beneath the road. Immediately below the road surface, a layer of gravel and clay contained pieces of cooking pot, burnt bone and daub from a demolished building. Then the sondage to the north of the trench, cutting into the roadside ditch, came up with a thick chunk of pottery, about the size of a hand. The professional archaeologists immediately recognised it as a piece of amphora, the large vessel used by the Romans for shipping wine, oil and fish sauce around the empire. That one piece of distinctive pottery was unavoidable proof that the Romans had been in Longtown after all. We had been digging for five weeks before we found it, but soon there were other finds of what appeared to be Roman pottery and a rather fine Roman glass bead. It seemed that the ditch alongside the medieval road had followed the line of an earlier Roman ditch. Beneath this ditch was a broken stone base covered with charcoal, probably the remains of a kiln or oven. A horizontal flue or duct from this extended the full width of the trench.

A second sondage was cut through the road across the western end of Trench 2. This uncovered an orange mass of fired clay, presumably the remains of another oven, although of a very different type to the one in the other sondage. The fired clay was found to be covering seven or more short wooden planks. These had been laid down on a metalled surface and appeared to be either a base for the oven or perhaps duckboards along a walkway. Their remarkable preservation was due to their being sealed by the clay oven and then subjected to its heat. Although completely carbonized, they were still recognisable as oak.

It was an extraordinary experience and a privilege to be excavating timbers that were at least 700 years old and

Excavating the carbonized planks

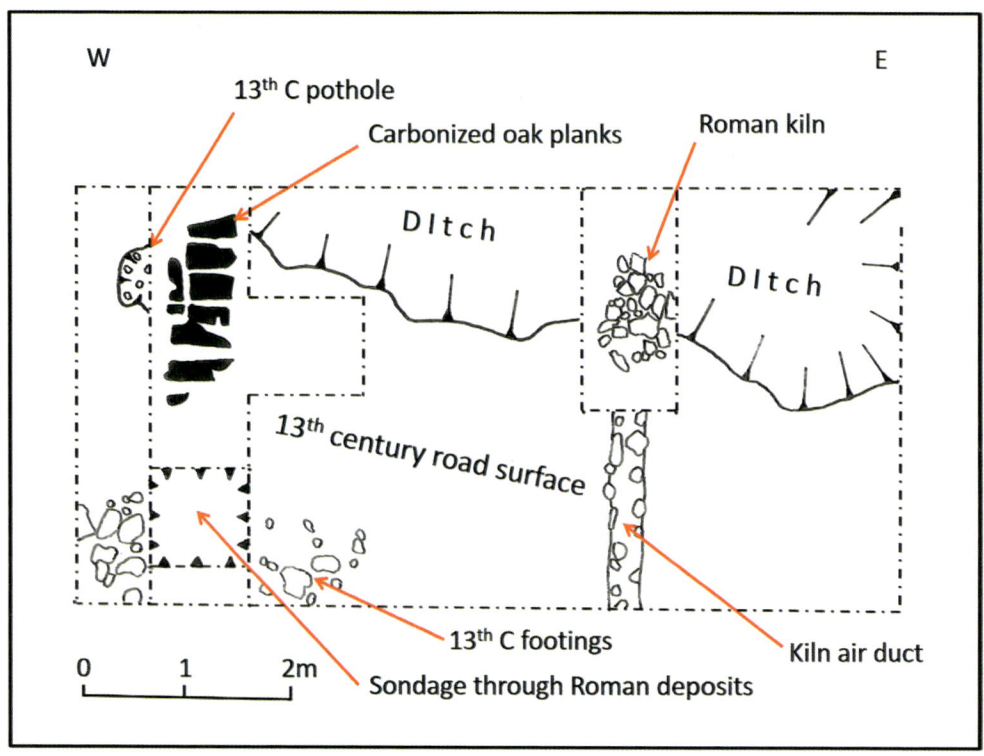

A plan of Trench 2 on Castle Green

possibly considerably older. The sondage was deepened another metre beside the planks, cutting through a thick deposit of silt and gravel, down to the natural surface. The fragments of pottery that were recovered from this deposit all appeared to be Roman, rather than medieval.

It is clear from all the lumps and bumps across the Green that over the centuries it has been a place used to dispose of unwanted debris. This was nowhere more obvious than in the south-east corner where Trench 3 was located. The excavators there soon found themselves digging into a massive quantity of builders' rubble. But it had not been left here in the nineteenth or twentieth centuries. It had been dumped here in medieval times. The trench began as a large rectangle, 8m by 3m, but excavating through the rubble was so difficult and time-consuming that after digging down a metre, it was decided for convenience and safety to progress with just a 1.5m square sondage.

At the highest, and therefore latest levels, a stone wall had been built on top of the demolished remains of an earlier clay-walled and clay-floored building. Pottery sherds suggested that these structures were in use during the medieval period. Below them were thick layers of tipped clay and rubble containing a considerable amount of daub, some still with the impression of wattle. Wattle and daub is a building technique used for the walls of timber-framed buildings. A lightweight panelling, woven from hazel or willow, was fixed to the building frame and then daubed with a sticky mixture, such as clay, mud and animal dung. Scattered amongst the clay and rubble were horseshoe nails, smithing slag, a chunk of Wye Valley millstone with a pecked working face, and medieval pottery. These layers, which were a metre deep, appeared to be the remains of demolished buildings that had been cleared from elsewhere.

Below the layer of demolition debris there were various thin strata, rich in charcoal and containing pieces of cooking pot. These lay over a metre-deep mass of sandstone rubble in large blocks, interleaved with clay. This was distinguishable from the layers above by its different tip lines and a complete absence of any occupational debris. It was suggested that this 'clean' material was derived from digging a defensive ditch.

Trench 4 was positioned at the northernmost part of the Green butting against the rampart. As in the other trenches the topsoil contained a few small-value coins, slate pencils and a number of broken stone roof tiles, recognisable by their peg holes. More interesting were a musket ball and a pistol ball, possibly from the time of the Civil War.

Further excavation exposed three working surfaces, laid consecutively, one above the other, across the entire area of the trench. The upper two surfaces showed the telltale burnt patches left by hearths, along with fragments of medieval cooking pot and burnt bones. A single post-hole suggested the presence of some sort of rudimentary shelter. A later pit that cut through both surfaces contained medieval pottery, burnt bone and what appears to be a stout iron knife blade.

The lowest surface was of red clay, laid directly on the natural bedrock. A depression in this surface had then been lined with a distinctive pale-green clay. This appeared to be the waterproof lining of a cistern, which had been truncated when the area was levelled to lay the next working surface (*see overleaf*). It extended beyond the excavated area, making it impossible to determine its size or shape. The cistern held a deposit of loose silty clay containing a high concentration of charcoal, a solitary white glass gaming piece and two fragments from a Roman pottery jar.

An interesting find from this trench was a turned-stone spindle whorl (*see overleaf*). In the Middle Ages spinning was a common occupation for most women. A clump of wool to be spun was held on a rod called a distaff. Strands of wool were pulled out and attached to a spindle weighted with a spindle whorl to act as a flywheel. The spindle was then spun to twist the wool into yarn. Spinning has given us the word 'spinster' for an unmarried woman and the expression 'distaff side' for the female members of a family. A long spun-out story, whose thread is difficult to follow, is called a 'yarn'.

Trench 5 was opened at the top of the rampart in the south-east corner, in a further attempt to determine if there had been any supplementary defences. Again, there were no indications of either a wall or a timber palisade, which should have been obvious in the corner. Either it was deemed that the rampart and its moat was an adequate defence, or the rampart may have been fortified with a barrier that left no archaeological trace, such as thorn hedge or an entanglement of cut thorn.

The cistern in Trench 4

Above: The spindle whorl from Trench 4
(*photograph by Chas Breton*)

A spindle whorl in use

42   THE MARCH OF EWYAS

Various small finds from Castle Green (*photographs by Chas Breton*): **a.** A piece of Wye Valley millstone; **b.** A flint blade; **c.** Pieces of cooking pots; **d.** Metal mounts for a wooden casket; **e.** A Roman glass bead; **f.** A glass gaming piece; **g.** A thirteenth-century horseshoe; **h.** A fragment of a Roman amphora

As our second three-week season of digging came to an end, it was essential to ensure that the excavations were all fully recorded. The finds and samples were bagged up and packed away for future analysis. Throughout the excavations, plans had been made of any features as they were exposed. Now sections had to be drawn for each of the trenches. We had been remarkably lucky with the weather but, in accordance with Sod's Law, our last day was one torrential downpour. Fortunately, archaeological drawings are done on waterproof matt plastic drafting film, so in spite of the persistent rain, the work was completed.

It is a sign of camaraderie and a good atmosphere on an excavation when a decent number of volunteers turn up to help with the arduous but unglamorous chore of back-filling the trenches and relaying the turf over them. Over the two seasons we shifted an estimated 400 tonnes of soil and stone, and it all had to be put back where it came from. Fortunately our digger driver came back to help on Castle Green but at Ponthendre all of the reinstatement had to be done by hand. Biodegradable netting was then pegged over the steeper slopes to hold the soil and turf in place until it could stabilise. On both sites, clover and wild flower seeds were sown.

Once the excavations were over it was time to involve the specialists. Finds of pottery and metalwork were sent off for analysis. Samples of charcoal were subjected to radiocarbon dating and species identification.

5

Post-excavation analysis and interpretation

'I yield to him who knows more of these things than I do
Nennius, *c*.830

So what had we learned from the excavations? We would have to wait for the specialists' reports before we could carry out a full analysis of the Castle Green findings, but in the meantime we could think about what we had discovered at Ponthendre.

PONTHENDRE

Eight trenches were dug at Ponthendre, sampling the top of the motte, the bailey, a length of the rampart and the bailey entrance. It was very clear that no structures had been built at any of these locations. In fact, there was no evidence that the site had ever been occupied. The usual indicators of occupation were all missing. Only a minimal amount of pottery was found, an insignificant amount of charcoal and no bone. We could now say with absolute certainty that the motte and bailey castle at Ponthendre was not completed and it had never performed its intended purpose as a fortress. And it was quite obvious now why the geophysics results had been so uninformative.

Of course, it had been disappointing not to find the remains of an operational castle and discover clues as to how it functioned. We had learnt a little about the construction and details of the earthworks but, with virtually no finds, we had no accurate dating evidence for them. On the other hand, we had proved that almost everything written about the castle at Ponthendre was incorrect. Knowing that it had not been the precurser to Longtown Castle, we had to come up with a new history. We'd set out to discover why Longtown had two castles, not much more than half a mile apart. Now we had to explain why one of them had never been finished.

We looked at past theories and mulled over new ones. Each was carefully considered:

1. Nearly a century ago, Alfred Watkins, the Herefordshire photographer and originator of the theory of ley lines, gave a lecture to the Woolhope Naturalists' Field Club, claiming that rather than being castles, the mottes at Ponthendre and Tref-fedw were early British surveyors' platforms. Whether or not you believe in ley lines, no other civilisation has ever felt the necessity to pile up thousands of tonnes of earth and stone for a surveyor to stand on.[1]

Ley line enthusiasts of the Long Straight Track Club scaling Ponthendre motte in 1933 (*photograph courtesy of Herefordshire Libraries: herefordshirehistory.org.uk*)

2. A farmer neighbouring Ponthendre told us, 'It were a lookout for the castle at Longtown, but they was asleep on the job, 'cos look at the state of her now.' However, a simple observation post doesn't require the same investment in earthworks as a motte and bailey. And besides, Ponthendre is only a ten-minute walk from Longtown, so it couldn't have given much warning of when an attacking force was approaching.

3. A PhD thesis advocated that Ponthendre was abandoned because the bailey was boggy, making it unusable. In fact the only boggy area is the moat around the motte, which is fed by a spring. The ditch crossing the bailey was cut in relatively recent times to take water away from the moat and not to drain the bailey. Since the land falls away sharply on three sides, the bailey has always

been perfectly well drained. Excavation showed that before the earthworks were started the area was forested. Later, the bailey became ploughland and then pasture. It was never a bog.[2]

4. It has also been proposed that one of the de Lacys had the Ponthendre earthworks raised in readiness for a 'spare' castle, just in case it might be needed. This makes little sense, as felling timber and erecting the tower, palisades and other buildings could not happen overnight. It would be too late to start building the timber structures on the earthworks once an enemy had been sighted.

5. A more serious proposition was that Ponthendre was built as a siege castle for an assault on Longtown during the twelfth-century civil war known as the Anarchy. However, siege castles were usually ringworks without a high motte. These were serious investments undertaken by large armies, usually only built when it was absolutely necessary to take possession of a crucial military or commercial asset. Also, Ponthendre is the wrong place to build a siege castle. If an attacker held Walterstone and Ewyas Harold there would be little need for a siege castle south of Longtown, though it might be useful to place one on the higher ground to the north. Conversely, if the attacker didn't hold Walterstone and Ewyas Harold, it would be military suicide to attempt to build a siege castle within a triangle of three hostile castles.

6. A respected castles researcher suggested that one of the de Lacys' tenant knights began building a castle of his own at Ponthendre, within view of Longtown Castle, but without his lord's permission. Under Norman law and with the de Lacys in control of justice, such a foolishly defiant knight was likely to have lost his eyes and his testicles before he had collected his workforce together and started clearing the site.[3]

7. Another rather silly theory was that the earthworks were a job creation scheme to keep soldiers or the conquered peasantry occupied. It is very clear from historical accounts that the Norman military had its work cut out just keeping order, and there was certainly no shortage of useful work for the peasantry, since 20 years after the Conquest much of the farmland along the border was still described as waste, following the earlier depredations by Welsh raiders.

It is clear that none of these theories holds water. There is, of course, a host of other reasons that might explain why building at Ponthendre was suspended, such as royal disapproval, the death or banishment of the lord, cashflow problems, local opposition, diversion of resources to trouble spots elsewhere, plague or persistent bad weather. Perhaps it was just no longer needed. But there had to be a rational explanation for why, after so much work had been done at Ponthendre, it was left unfinished, while a castle was built at Longtown, such a very short distance away.

In order to understand why Ponthendre was never completed, it is perhaps necessary to ask why the decision was made to build a castle here in the first place. We will return to this matter in chapter 11. Meanwhile, our pottery specialist informed us that a single sherd of black cooking pot, found below the rampart, *could* be from the late eleventh century. Similar pottery was found below the ramparts of Wigmore Castle and Stafford Castle, both built around 1070. A single fragment of pottery was not enough to give a reliable date for the Ponthendre earthworks but it did raise the possibility that they could have been erected very soon after the Conquest.

The fact that Ponthendre was never finished raised another question, of course. If the two castles mentioned in the Pipe Rolls of 1187–89 were not Ponthendre and Longtown, then where were the Castle of Ewyas and the New Castle?

LONGTOWN CASTLE GREEN

When the specialist reports on Longtown Castle Green came in, they gave us plenty to consider. Together, the pottery analysis and radiocarbon dating provided a much more detailed timeframe for the activities that had taken place on the Green. This allowed us to expand on some of the theories we had been developing about the history of the castle.

The pottery experts informed us that we had found 29 sherds of Roman pottery. It was not much to go on, but these came mainly from just the two small sondages in Trench 2. Most was of an oxidised orange-coloured fabric, some being coarse wares, while others were typical of Severn Valley tableware and included part of a distinctive ring-necked flagon.

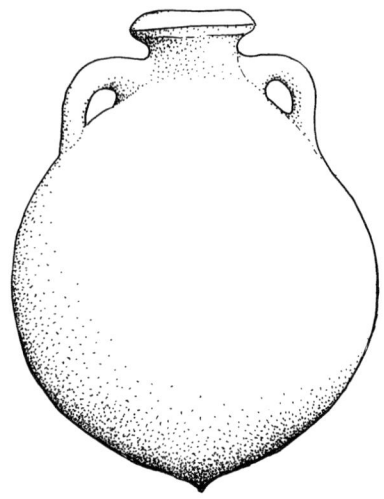

A Severn Valley Ware ring-necked flagon   A Dressel Type 20 amphora

There were two items of imported pottery. One was a tiny piece of the characteristic red glossy fabric known as Samian Ware made at La Graufesenque in France. The other was the chunk of amphora. This was identified as part of a Dressel Type 20 amphora, manufactured in southern Spain from the first to the third century AD and used for exporting olive oil.

This small assemblage of pottery dated mainly from the first century, probably extending to the second century and was typical of what might be found at an early Roman fort. This confirmation that there had been a Roman presence at Longtown set us thinking about the square rampart around the castle and the Green. Its height and composition certainly wasn't typical of Roman work. But there was that core of turf at the bottom. In first-century Britain, the Romans had used turf to build the ramparts of their forts. Could it be that the bulk of the Longtown rampart was a later development that had taken advantage of the remains of a Roman fort?

We were excited to learn that the radiocarbon laboratory confirmed that they could give us a date for the small amount of charcoal collected from the lowest layer of turf. This should either prove or disprove our theory that the turf embankment was Roman. When it came through, the result was not what we expected. The charcoal dated from between 355 BC and 117 BC. Did this mean that the lowest part of the rampart was Iron Age, rather than Roman? Well, probably not. The radiocarbon date was for the charcoal found in the turf and not for the turf itself. It might have been there a long time before the turf was cut. Also, radiocarbon dating of wood only gives the date when the tree was growing, not when it was cut down. So, charcoal from the heart of a 300-year-old oak tree gives a date 300 years earlier than when it was burnt. The radiocarbon date was therefore not incompatible with a Roman construction of the turf embankment.[4]

The pottery gave us secure evidence for a Roman occupation of Longtown during the first century AD, and the regular shape of the rampart, a square with rounded corners, was far more suggestive of a Roman fort than an Iron Age camp. Unfortunately, we had nothing to show when the rampart had been built up to its present height. All we could say was that this was done after the Romans and before the Normans raised the motte over it. A rough calculation found that widening the ditch and using the spoil to build up the rampart had involved the movement of an estimated 40,000 tonnes of soil and stone. This had to be the work of a sizeable army.[5]

The carbonized planks uncovered in Trench 2 were confirmed as being oak and were shown to be Roman rather than medieval, because the strata immediately above and below contained Roman pottery. Radiocarbon dating of the wood gave a similar result to the one from the base of the rampart – a range of 352 BC to 56 BC with a most likely date in the second century BC. This suggests that the planks were sawn from a mature tree. The charcoal-bearing deposit lying below the planks, which contained 11 sherds of Roman pottery and continued all the way to bedrock, returned a radiocarbon date range of 24–125 AD. The stratum immediately below the piece of amphora and the glass bead, had a similar date. We can infer from this that the fort probably first came into use in the second half of the first century AD.

In Trench 2, the medieval road had truncated the Roman deposits. The medieval activity in Trench 4 had been more disruptive. Although some Roman pottery was found, radiocarbon dating and pottery from the red clay below the cistern indicated that it was a twelfth-century feature. It appears that in preparation for its construction, the area had been cut right back to bedrock, disturbing and clearing away all the Roman deposits.

This has left a gap in the archaeological record of nearly 1,000 years, from before the abandonment of the Roman fort until the arrival of the Normans. It does not mean that Longtown was deserted for all that time, only that in the small sample revealed by our trenches there was nothing visible from this period. This was not surprising. Outside of urban areas and cemeteries, archaeological evidence for the Anglo-Saxons and the contemporary Welsh is notoriously elusive. Their pottery is rarely found, usually being of poor quality and very poorly preserved.

The bulk of the pottery from the excavations on the Green was identified as having been made in the twelfth and thirteenth centuries. Mostly it was pieces of coarse, black cooking pots, manufactured around Malvern and Worcester. There were also a few pieces of distinctively decorated green-glazed tableware.

Left: Medieval black cooking pot. *Right*: Medieval green-glazed tableware

It was the pottery that provided us with dates for the two massive dumps of material found in Trench 3. The upper layers, made up of the debris of demolished buildings, contained pottery from the first half of the thirteenth century. This suggested that a major redevelopment of the castle had taken place between 1200 and 1250. The most likely interpretation is that this dump resulted from buildings being cleared from the bailey prior to inserting the stone dividing wall and inner gateway.

Pottery analysis told us that the earlier dump of sandstone and clay, containing no occupational debris, lay below strata containing only twelfth-century pottery. It had been suggested that this material came from digging a defensive ditch; however, if that were the case, why would anyone go to the trouble of carting it onto the Green to dump it, rather than throwing it up alongside the ditch to form a rampart? There had to be a better explanation.

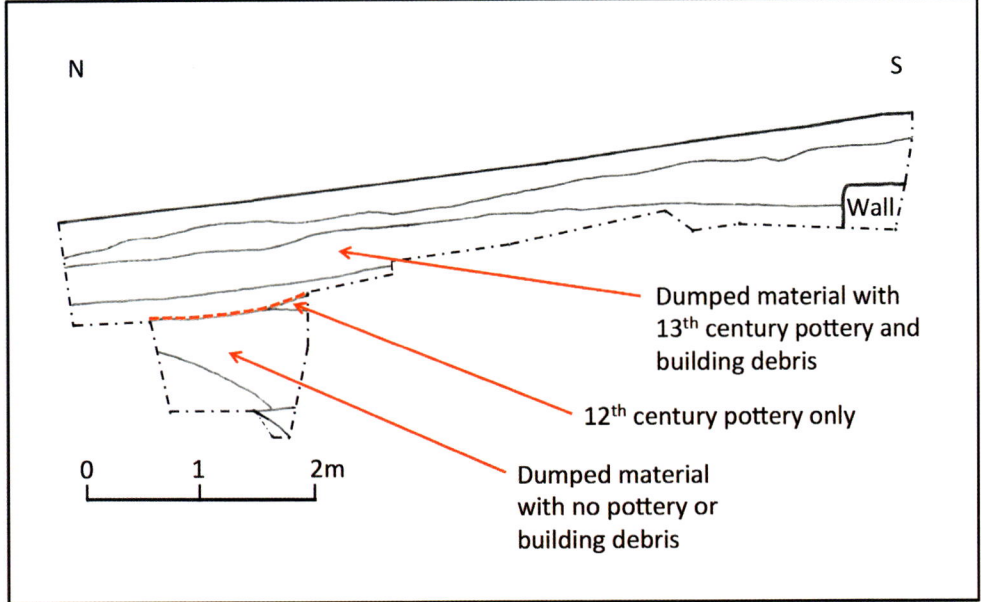

A simplified section of Trench 3

Early Norman mottes, built for timber towers, are generally conical with a fairly small flat surface at the top. Those at Ponthendre and Walterstone are both about 12 metres across, but Longtown's motte is around 20 metres across at the top. When the original wooden tower was replaced with the stone keep, if the motte had been reduced in height sufficiently to increase the diameter of the top from 12 metres to 20 metres, it would be necessary to remove around 575 cubic metres of material. The simplest way of disposing of this would be to take it out through the main gate and drop it in a corner of the Green.[6]

The deepest and oldest features uncovered in Trench 3, found below the two episodes of dumping, were a small section of pebbled surface, likely to be a floor or a yard, through which a cesspit had been cut. A radiocarbon date for these indicated that they were medieval, so even though this trench plumbed over two metres below the present ground level, it still did not reach the underlying Roman occupation deposits. Excavating down through massive dumps of builder's waste had not been a particularly pleasant experience. But at least now we had rational explanations for the two episodes of dumping, and we had gained an important insight. If our interpretation was correct, then the stone keep was probably built before the end of the twelfth century.

We now also understood why the geophysics results for Castle Green were so disappointing. The Roman deposits had been destroyed by medieval activity at the north end of the Green, and elsewhere they were too deep to show up, having been overlain with multiple layers of medieval and nineteenth-century dumping. Below all this dumped material, there is a good chance that earlier archaeological remains are well-preserved.

A reconstruction of life on the Green

The Green was a busy place during the twelfth and thirteenth centuries, where a variety of insubstantial buildings or shelters housed artisans working on behalf of the castle. Their occupations would probably have included blacksmithing, butchery, food preparation, clothmaking and possibly corn milling.

Given the amount of activity on the Green during the medieval period, it is remarkable that there was no evidence for any sustained activity later. There were no signs of any permanent buildings and it seems that the Green was reserved as an open space, presumably used, when required, for mustering and drilling troops before it eventually reverted to pasture.

Returning to the research questions we had formulated when planning the project, we could now see the extent to which they had been answered.

At Ponthendre:

a. Over what period or periods was the motte and bailey occupied?
The motte and bailey was never occupied, apart from during its construction, which probably took place in the late eleventh or early twelfth century.

b. Was it completed and was it a single or multiple phase construction?
It only had a single phase of construction, which was not completed.

c. What form did any keep structures take and what materials were used.
No keep was ever built.

d. What were the form and materials of the bailey defences?
On its south side the bailey was defended with a low embankment and a wet moat. A single posthole suggests that a timber palisade was intended.

e. What activities took place within the bailey?
We found no evidence for any activities.

f. Are there any structural remains still in place?
No.

g. Were any of the structures subsequently robbed out or slighted?
No.

h. Is there any evidence for earlier occupation of the site?
The site was forested but worked flint and waste flakes indicated that there had been human activity there.

At Longtown Castle Green:

a. When was the square embankment constructed?
Initially it was constructed by the Romans in the first century.

b. Was the embankment a single phase or multiple phase construction?
The original Roman embankment was later greatly enhanced. A third and final phase was added later still.

c. What materials were used to build it?
First turf and then earth and stone.

d. Is there an internal structure to the embankment?
The three phases were clearly visible on excavation. The earth and stone had simply been built up in layers.

e. Was it faced with either timber or stone?
There were no signs of any revetment in timber or stone.

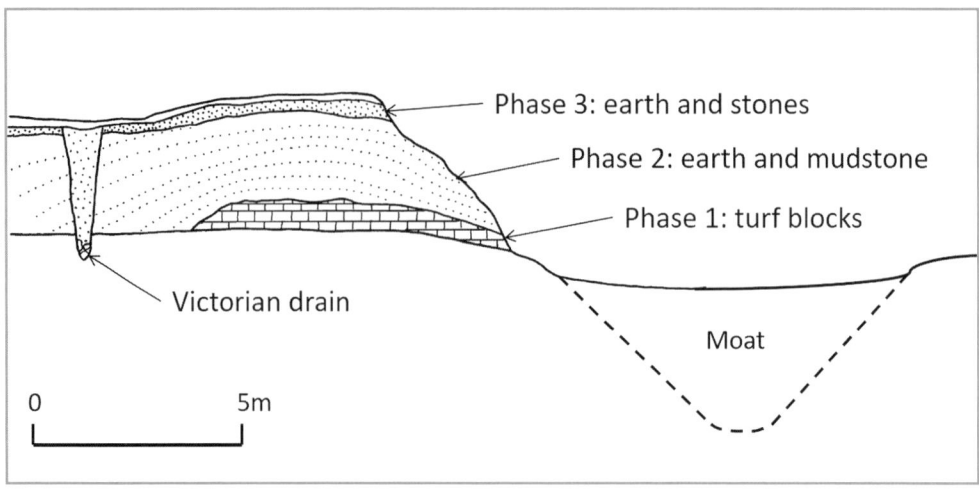

A simplified section through the rampart

f. Was it topped by a wall or palisade?
    There was no wall or palisade on the excavated sections, which included a corner.

g. Was there an internal ditch as suggested by the geophysics?
    No. This signal probably came from the medieval clay-lined cistern.

h. Is there evidence for buildings within the embanked enclosure?
    Floors, post-holes, hearths and ovens all indicate that there were Roman and later medieval buildings. These would have been timber-framed not masonry.

i. What activities took place within the embanked enclosure?
    The enclosure was a fort during the Roman period. During the medieval period there was light industrial activity, presumably connected with the castle.

j. Over what period(s) was the enclosure occupied?
    The clearest periods of occupation were in the first century AD then the twelfth and thirteenth centuries. Later the enclosure reverted to agricultural use.

k. Is there evidence for earlier occupation of the site?
    A small amount of worked flint probably indicated pre-Roman activity.

It is extremely unusual for a community excavation to answer so many of its research questions. On this basis alone the project has been highly successful, thanks to the combined efforts of the professional archaeologists and the community volunteers. We also now had a much better idea of how the earthworks at Longtown had been adapted to meet the needs of the different fortifications. But we still hadn't answered the fundamental questions of why we had two castles and exactly when they were built. Although we had learned a lot from the excavations, it was clear that we would not reach a proper understanding of our two castles without exploring their wider context.

The development of the earthworks at Longtown:

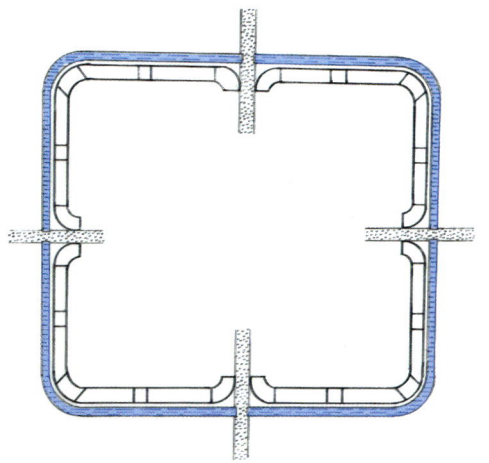

The turf banks of the Roman fort, with gates and corner towers

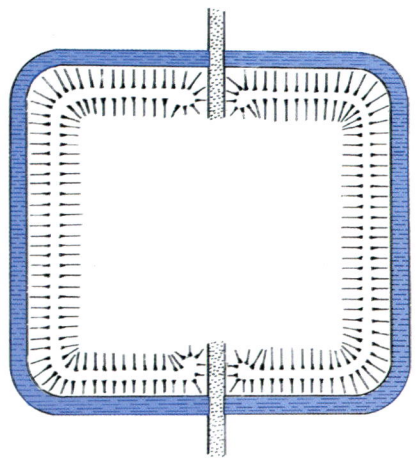

The later earth embankment with a larger ditch

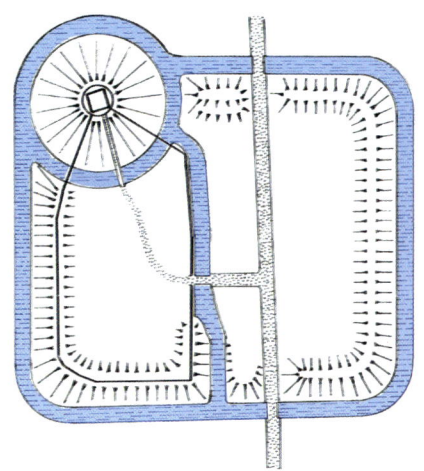

The early Norman timber castle superimposed on the embankment

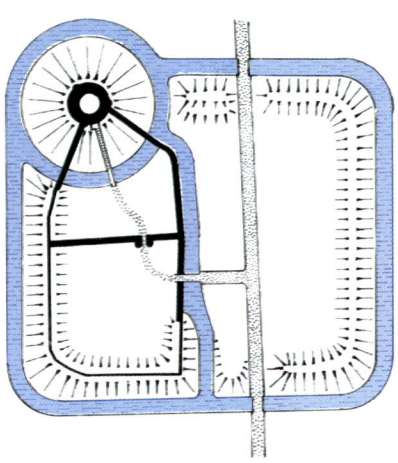

The medieval stone castle and later cross wall

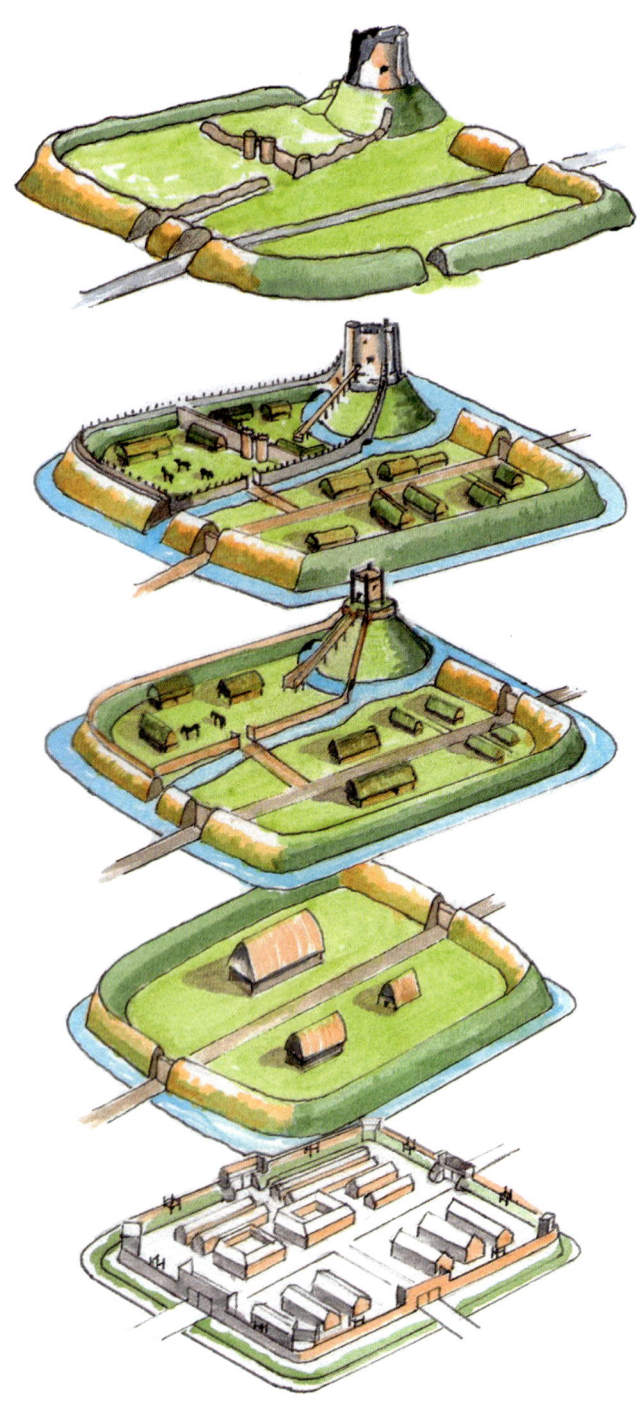

The development of the fortifications at Longtown from the Roman fort to the present day

PART TWO

A New History of Ewyas and the de Lacy Dynasty

A contemporary depiction of Hugh de Lacy (d.1186), the Marcher baron who held Ewyas, Weobley and Ludlow along the Welsh border, and later became the first lord of Meath and governor-general of Ireland. He is the only member of the de Lacy dynasty for whom we have a portrait.
(Taken from Gerald of Wales's manuscript, Topographia Hibernica, courtesy of the National Library of Ireland)

6

Ewyas in prehistoric times

*Then by slow degrees the iron sword came to the fore, the bronze sickle fell into disrepute,
the ploughman began to cleave the earth with iron*

Lucretius, *c*.60 BC

THE STONE AGE

For a hundred millennia the uplands of Britain were covered with a sheet of ice, and glaciers carved out today's river valleys. Humans were absent, unable to survive such harsh conditions, until climate change eventually brought higher temperatures. Around 35,000 years ago retreating glaciers allowed Ice Age hunter-gatherers to return to western Britain, following their prey. It is possible that for a time mammoths and woolly rhinoceros grazed in the Monnow Valley. Their teeth and bones were found, along with early stone tools, only 15 miles away from Longtown at the classic Palaeolithic site, known as King Arthur's Cave at Great Doward Hill, overlooking the Wye Valley near Symonds Yat.[1]

Mesolithic flints from Herefordshire (*Photo © The Portable Antiquities Scheme: UID. HESH-45F7FI*)

Around 10,000 years ago temperatures began to rise rapidly, the river valleys became forested and Mesolithic hunters came in search of wild boar, aurochs and deer that browsed the clearings. Britain was then still attached to Europe, but as the ice-sheets and glaciers continued to melt, sea levels rose and Britain eventually became an island. Where food was plentiful, the hunters built themselves insubstantial shelters, probably temporary or only seasonally occupied. Archaeological evidence for these rarely survives, but their presence can sometimes be inferred from scatterings of flint that show where the hunters made and used their often distinctively small tools, known as microliths.

The Mesolithic way of life lasted for about four millennia but was to be swept away around 4,000 BC, when new migrants arrived by boat from Europe. This was the start of the Neolithic revolution in Britain. The incomers were farmers, who used fire and polished stone axes to clear sections of forest where they raised crops and kept domesticated cattle and sheep. They also introduced the use of pottery. From the little evidence available, it appears that they lived in settlements of rectangular houses, each large enough to contain an extended family. How permanent these settlements were, is open to doubt, as the land would most likely have been quickly exhausted, forcing the people to move on and allowing the forest to re-establish. Over time, these pale-skinned people with dark hair and brown eyes, originating from the Iberian Peninsula, largely replaced the blue-eyed, dark-skinned, indigenous population of hunter-gatherers.

We know little about the complex social organisation and religious practices of these Neolithic farmers, but they could clearly plan and co-operate on a grand scale. They produced some of our most iconic ancient monuments – megalithic tombs, alignments and stone circles, including the early phases of Stonehenge. Another archetypal feature in the landscape left by these early farmers was the hilltop causewayed enclosure, most often found in southern Britain. The purpose of these enigmatic structures is still not well understood. They are roughly circular in area and surrounded by a bank thrown up from an internal ditch. The ditch is not continuous, instead being dug in segments separated by 'causeways' allowing access to the central area. From the animal bones, broken pottery and, in some cases, disarticulated human bones deposited in the ditches the feature has usually been interpreted as a meeting place where isolated farming communities could get together for celebrations, feasts, funeral ceremonies and to exchange goods.[2]

On the hill to the east of Dorstone village in the Golden Valley, a causewayed enclosure has been shown recently to contain tools made from rock crystal originating from North Wales, and polished stone axes from the Lake District. Adjacent to this enclosure the archaeologists also uncovered the remains of a remarkable Neolithic structure. Three huge timber-framed halls, arranged end to end in an east-west alignment and dating to around 3,800 BC, were deliberately burned and levelled and eventually replaced by three chambered cairns enclosed in earth and turf to create a massive extended mortuary.

Arthur's Stone, near Dorstone

So far, this type of extended long-mound appears to be unique in Britain, but may be related in some way to the other funerary structures common around 3,600 BC. One of these, the burial chamber called Arthur's Stone, lies only a short distance away.[3]

The polished stone axes used by Neolithic farmers have been found around Longtown. These were not made from the local sandstone but were brought considerable distances by trade or as gifts. A greenstone axe found at St Margaret's came from near Penzance, while a hornfels axe found at Craswall came from the Mynydd Rhiw axe factory in Gwynedd. Recently, a broken Neolithic axe, made of polished dolerite, possibly from the north of England, was found in a field by a river near Longtown. The damage at both ends suggests that it may have been deliberately broken before being deposited as a votive offering.

A Neolithic axe from Longtown (*photograph* © The Portable Antiquities Scheme: UID. HESH-216050)

EWYAS IN PREHISTORIC TIMES

The excavations at Ponthendre and Longtown provided evidence for prehistoric activity at both sites. We recovered a small number of flint tools and waste flakes, which indicated that they were made locally. Flint isn't found in Longtown's sandstone geology, so the material for making these tools was brought in from elsewhere. Although there is some flint in the glacial moraines found in the uplands, it is frost damaged and unsuitable for tool-making. Analysis of the flint of tools found in Gwent showed that it was brought both from the English chalklands and from as far away as County Antrim in Ireland.[4]

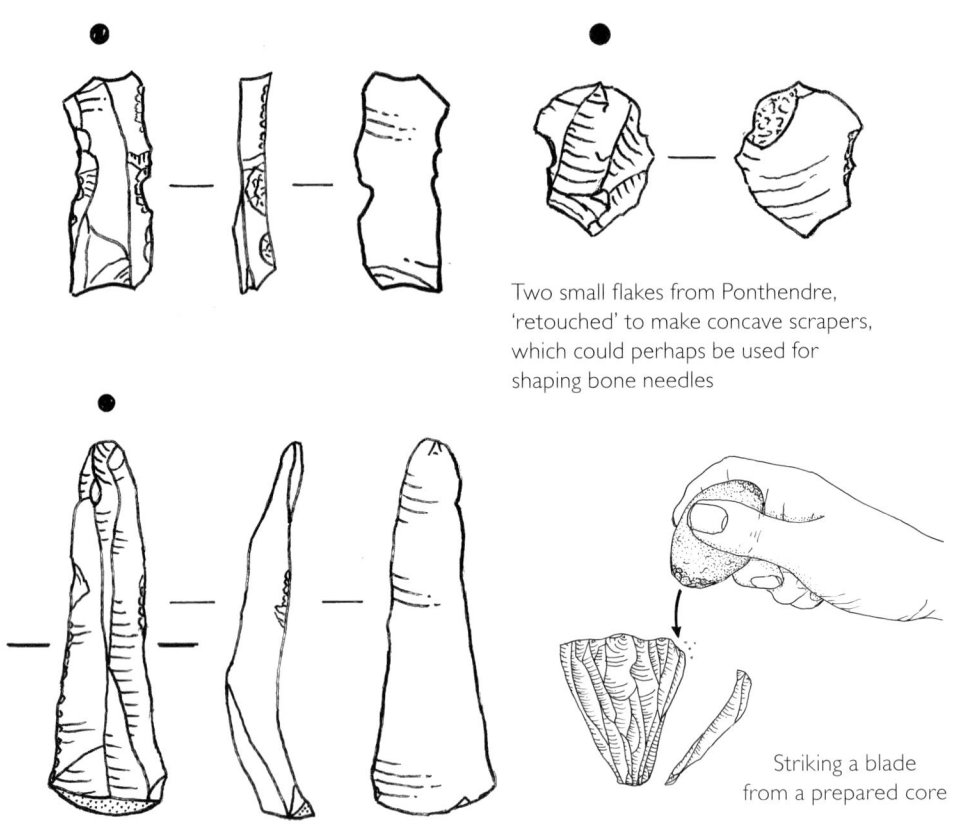

Two small flakes from Ponthendre, 'retouched' to make concave scrapers, which could perhaps be used for shaping bone needles

Striking a blade from a prepared core

A pointed flint blade from Longtown Castle Green, possibly used for making holes in wood or skins

Thin flints like these are referred to as blades and can have razor-sharp edges. Using a hammer stone, a large number of blades can be struck from a prepared flint core. The black dots on the illustrations show the points of percussion. It is impossible to tell when exactly these tools were made, as the same technique was used throughout the Stone Age and the Bronze Age, and sometimes even into the Iron Age in areas where flint was readily available.

THE BRONZE AGE

The Bronze Age in Britain began around 2,500 BC, with the introduction of metal tools and weapons, first of copper and later of bronze. This coincided with the arrival of the 'Beaker' people, who are named after their distinctive pottery drinking vessels and may have brought the skill of copper smelting with them. Our knowledge of the Beaker culture comes largely from their burials, the most famous being that of the 'Amesbury Archer', interred near Stonehenge around 2,300 BC. His spectacular collection of grave goods included five beakers that may have contained beer or mead, three copper knives, 18 flint arrowheads, two stone archer's wrist-guards, an assortment of 122 flint tools and a pair of finely-wrought gold hair ornaments.

The Amesbury Archer's grave goods (*photograph © Wessex Archaeology*)

In 1932, two rather more modest Beaker burials were discovered in the Olchon Valley, not far from Longtown. They were contained in cists – essentially stone-lined boxes, each with four sides and a capstone made of local sandstone. The larger cist contained the bones of an adult male, lying on his side with knees drawn up to the chest. A complete bell-shaped beaker and a flint arrowhead had been placed in the cist beside the body. The other cist contained the fragmentary remains of an adolescent male, a broken beaker and a flint flake. After the internments, the cists may have been covered over with earth barrows or stone cairns. Early Bronze Age round barrows and cairns and cist

A beaker from the Olchon Valley cist grave (*photograph © Hereford Museum: accession number 1345*)

burials are widespread across the border landscape, mostly to be found on the higher ground. Those located in the valleys are mainly lost, having been covered or erased by millennia of farming.[5]

Until very recently, it was thought that the Beaker culture was introduced to Britain through trade or other contacts, rather than mass migration, but recent genetic studies have completely overthrown this idea. The extraction of DNA from the bones of ancient skeletons has shown that there was roughly a 90% replacement of both men and women in Britain during the Beaker culture expansion. This may have been the result of warfare and genocide, but there is an alternative possibility.

The Beaker culture appears to have originated in Portugal around 2,800 BC and then spread into central Europe by cultural transmission. The people of central Europe had by that stage a high component of genetic ancestry from migrants from the Steppes to the east, a signature that was absent from Britain until the arrival of the Beaker culture. This genetic signature then became predominant, showing that there had been significant migration of people from central Europe, who largely replaced the local population. There is good evidence now that the steppe migrants also brought plague with them from the east. DNA of the plague bacterium, *Yersinia pestis*, is first found in European bones from the Early Bronze Age, this being the air-borne pneumonic form, rather than the medieval rat-and-flea-borne bubonic variety. The indigenous British population, never before exposed to this disease, would have had no immunity, resulting in widespread loss of life across the whole country.[6]

The Early Bronze Age (2,500–1,500 BC) was a period when farmers began clearing upland forests to provide cultivable soil and summer pasture for sheep and cattle. This

Above: Early Bronze Age flat axe from Ewyas Harold (*photograph © Hereford Museum: acc. no. 2012-200*)

Right: Middle Bronze Age palstave axe from Herefordshire (*photograph © The Portable Antiquities Scheme: UID. PUBLIC-491928*)

EWYAS IN PREHISTORIC TIMES 65

would have been mainly accomplished using fire. The bronze flat axe, while a more effective tool than the old polished stone axe, was not suitable for the wholesale felling of large trees. The attachment to the shaft was a weakness likely to result in its splitting. This led during the Middle Bronze Age (1,500–1,000 BC) to the development of the flanged axe or palstave, which was more securely fastened to its handle.

During the Bronze Age, burial rituals changed and cremation became prevalent, with the remains often being buried in urns. In 2009, Longtown volunteers were involved in the initial excavation of a large round cairn in the Olchon valley, not far from the two Beaker burials. On full excavation the following year, this was found to be an Early Bronze Age burial mound. The primary burial was a collared urn and a smaller cup containing the burnt remains of a man, a pregnant female and two children. The accompanying grave goods were two worked flints and a copper alloy pin. The urn appeared to have been initially covered with a small earth barrow and then by a revetted stone cairn. This was later mounded over with turf held in place with a ring of stones. Subsequently, nine pits and cists were dug into the mound to deposit the cremated remains of at least 16 other individuals.[7]

Excavation of the burial cairn at Olchon Court
(*photograph* © *Adam Stanford, Aerial-Cam*)

Around 1,200 BC a major change in climate brought colder and wetter conditions to the uplands, gradually changing many of the once lush pastures to the waterlogged peat bogs that we see today. The resulting competition for fertile land may have resulted in conflict between communities. Bronze socketed spears and rapier-like swords came into use. Territorial boundary dykes became a feature of the uplands and some settlements were enclosed by ramparts and possibly wooden palisades.

Increased militarisation during the Late Bronze Age (1,000–700 BC) saw further developments in weaponry, with less of an emphasis on archery and a greater use of daggers, spears and swords, which became larger and heavier. Other pieces of armoury such as shields also started to appear. At the same time, a new style of axe came into use. The axe head had a socket for the wooden shaft to fit inside, making it much stronger than the earlier flat axes and palstaves.

The Olchon Court urn
(*photograph © Adam Stanford, Aerial-Cam*)

Late Bronze Age socketed axes from Herefordshire
(*photograph © The Portable Antiquities Scheme: UID. NMGW-C9E537*)

Many examples of bronze weaponry have been recovered from lakes and rivers, often deliberately damaged, suggesting that they may have been deposited as offerings to a deity.

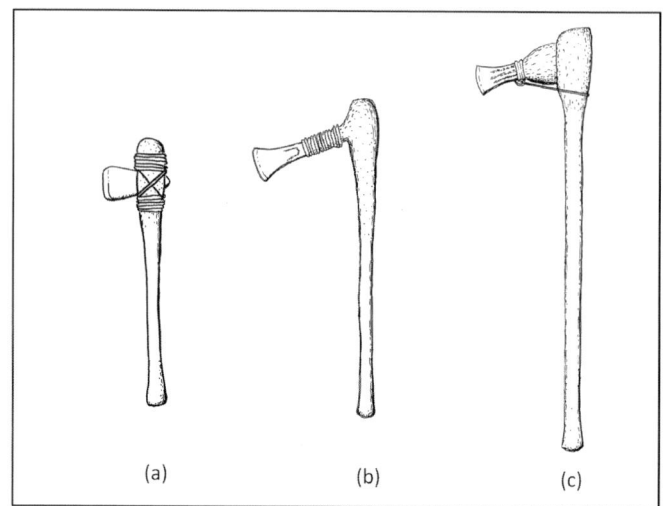

The development of Bronze Age axes and their hafting:

a) An Early Bronze Age flat axe, bound into a split shaft

b) A Middle Bronze Age palstave, set on a branched shaft

c) A Late Bronze Age socketed and looped axe, mounted on a weighted shaft (from a recent find at Must Farm, near Peterborough)

THE IRON AGE

In Britain, the Iron Age is usually taken to begin around 700 BC, when iron implements started to spread across the country. The technology of iron smelting appears to have been first developed in the second millennium BC by the Hittites in what is now central Turkey. The advantages of iron over copper and bronze were soon realised. While the copper and tin ores required for making bronze are relatively rare, iron ores are commonly found across the world. Iron, especially when processed into steel, is harder, tougher and keeps a sharp cutting edge for longer. However, it was only after the collapse of the Hittite empire around 1,200 BC that iron working started to spread across Europe, with the first iron weapons and tools being made in Britain around 750 BC.

Despite its advantages, iron implements remained relatively uncommon in the Early Iron Age and bronze continued to be the most commonly used metal. Life for most people was probably much as it had been in the Late Bronze Age, being mainly centred on small farmsteads with their associated fields. The trend towards enclosure of settlements by simple ramparts continued and in places developed on a larger scale into the construction of hillforts. These may have been defensive in function, as the evidence from archaeology shows that trade with the Continent was declining at this time and communities were probably becoming more insular and protective.

By the Middle Iron Age (500–150 BC), hillforts were starting to dominate the landscape in central and southern England and the Welsh Marches. As iron implements became more widely used, agricultural production increased and population density followed. This led to major changes in social organisation, with small rural communities coalescing into larger groupings centred on individual hillforts and their associated farms and fields. Some researchers have taken these changes to be indicative of an emerging hierarchical social system, with the elites, possibly local warrior chieftains and their entourages, occupying the forts, with the rest of the population working the farms. On excavation, many hillforts have revealed evidence for their occupation. Circles of post-holes show the location of roundhouses. Groups of four post-holes arranged in a rectangle are usually interpreted as granaries and store huts for animal feed. The high density of post-holes at some hillforts has been interpreted as the beginning of communal, semi-urban living. Other hillforts show little or no evidence of occupation. Whether they were only used intermittently, as meeting places or refuges, or whether they were never completed, remains a mystery.

Reconstructed Iron Age roundhouses at Llynon Mill, Anglesey

There are thought to be over 4,000 Iron Age hillforts in Britain and Ireland. They are extremely variable, ranging from small univallate enclosures with a single rampart, to the stunning complex of multivallate ramparts and ditches that encloses a settlement of 19 hectares at Maiden Castle in Dorset. Two main types of fort predominate. One is the contour fort, located on a hilltop, often between the confluence of two rivers. The ramparts roughly follow the contours of the hill, resulting in the fort having an irregular shape. The ramparts were sometimes revetted with stone to make vertical faces, and they were topped with wooden palisades. The other common type of hillfort is the promontory fort. Coastal promontory forts jutted out into the sea and were protected from landward attack by one or more ditches and banks across the neck of the promontory. An inland promontory fort was similar but, instead of the sea, used the steep-sided slopes of a suitable spur projecting from a hill for its defence.[8]

In Herefordshire between 30 and 40 hillforts have been recorded, as well as hundreds of smaller enclosures that appear to be defended farmsteads. Not all of these were occupied throughout the period, and some of the enclosures may not even be Iron Age. Even so, the fertile soils of Herefordshire appear to have been supporting a relatively high population at the time.

One rectangular enclosure on Garway Hill has been the subject of small-scale excavation. Surrounded by an earthen bank faced on the outside with large stones, there was a single entrance leading into the enclosure. Inside, there was a beaten earth floor, with the stone and earth footings of a circular or oval hut, placed centrally. Pottery dated the enclosure to the Middle to Late Iron Age.[9]

As the Middle Iron Age progressed, some of the earlier hillforts were abandoned while others were expanded and given more elaborate multivallate ramparts with more complex entrances. In Herefordshire at Little Doward, situated close to the River Wye, dating evidence puts this transformation after about 370 BC. The period seems to have coincided with an expansion in trade and exchange of goods, together with an increase in metalworking.

The platforms of roundhouses have been found at British Camp, Midsummer Hill, Little Doward and Eaton Camp, but at other hillforts the evidence for roundhouses has been elusive. At Credenhill and Croft Ambrey, excavations revealed arrangements of four post-holes that have been variously interpreted as domestic dwellings and storage huts. At Credenhill it is clear that these were raised off the ground, presumably to keep the contents dry and to deter vermin. A typical feature of hillforts in southern England that so far appears to be absent from Herefordshire is the grain storage pit. It may seem strange to store corn in a pit, but experimental archaeology has shown how effective it can be. After a pit was filled, the top was sealed with an airtight cap of clay. Grain in contact with the pit walls would then begin to germinate, which used up oxygen and raised the concentration of carbon dioxide to levels that prevented further germination, while killing off bacteria that might have caused rotting. The bulk of the grain remained wholesome to eat, free from vermin and still viable as seed corn.[10]

Extensive excavations at Croft Ambrey found evidence for a thriving community using iron agricultural implements, pottery, worked bone and antler, spindle whorls, loom weights, nails and grinding stones. Some of the inhabitants wore rings and brooches, and used iron weaponry including swords, knives, spears and iron helmets.[11]

Credenhill, to the west of modern Hereford, is the largest hillfort in the county. It encloses an area of 20 hectares and was probably a tribal centre for the area. On the basis of some questionable assumptions it has been estimated that as many as

4,000 people may have occupied the site by the time of the Roman invasion. If true, Credenhill might be regarded as an example of an early British town.[12]

Ewyas is surrounded by Iron Age forts, with three impressive contour forts along its southern border. Twyn-y-Gaer and Pentwyn lie on the ends of the ridges either side of the Vale of Ewyas, while Walterstone Camp is a fine, roughly circular trivallate fort overlooking a bend in the River Monnow. Each of these three forts is in view of a probable fourth on the imposing height of the Skirrid mountain.

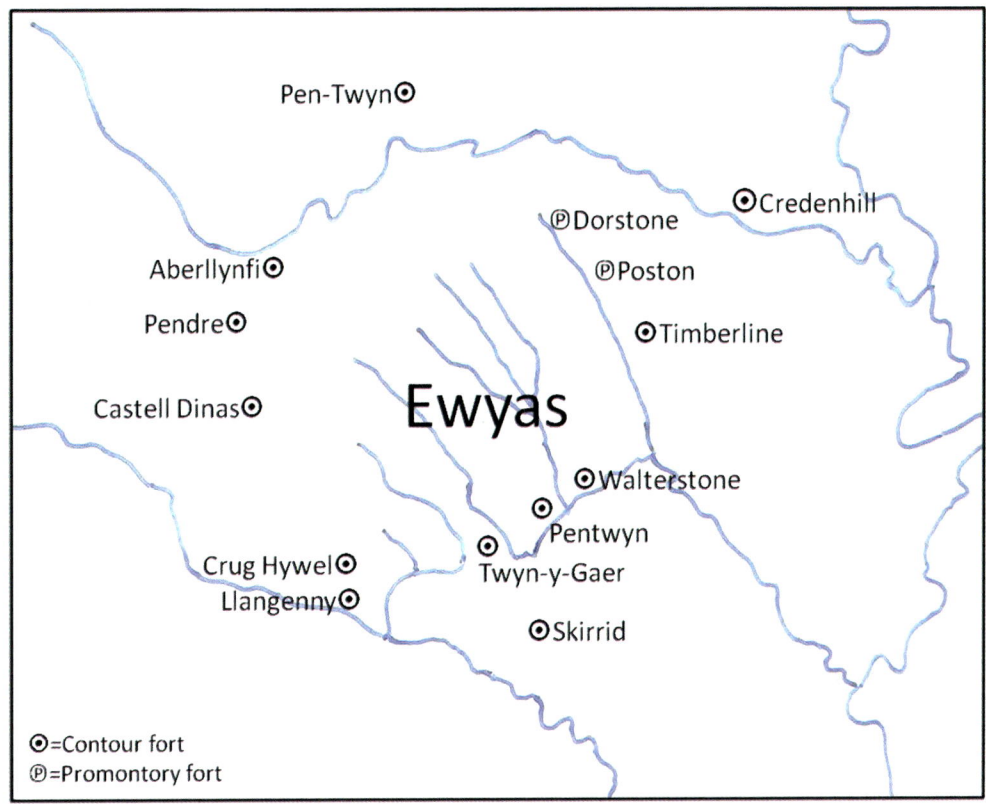

Hillforts around Ewyas

Of those three or four forts, only Twyn-y-Gaer has been investigated archaeologically. Excavations in the 1960s showed that Twyn-y-Gaer began in the Early Iron Age as a fenced enclosure of about 0.7ha. Around 390 BC, this was expanded to an area of 1.5ha surrounded on three sides by a rampart and ditch with an additional counterscarp bank, except on the southern side where the steep slope of the hill provides protection. The ramparts were made more effective by stone revetments, particularly around the single in-turned entrance at the eastern end. In later years the fort contracted to an area of just 0.4ha at the west end of the early enclosure, which appears to have been occupied until the arrival of the Romans.

EWYAS IN PREHISTORIC TIMES   71

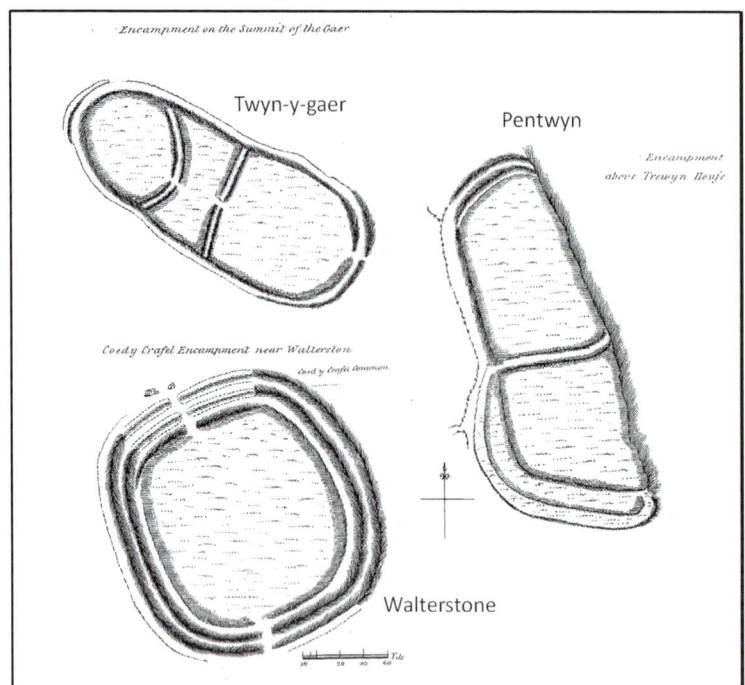

Plans of Twyn-y-Gaer, Pentwyn and Walterstone hillforts

The excavations uncovered objects of iron and copper alloy, brooches, glass beads made in Somerset, querns for grinding corn, iron-working debris and pottery, mostly from the Middle and Late Iron Age periods. This included briquetage, the pieces of coarse ceramic vessels used for making and storing salt. These have been found at other hillforts in Herefordshire and were imported from the salt workings at Droitwich and Cheshire. Salt was probably used not only for seasoning but also for preserving meat and as a fixative for dyeing fabrics. Post-holes within the enclosure may have been part of the entrance to a roundhouse, but there is little now to indicate the number or type of buildings within the fort, as these probably had turf walls, of which nothing remains.[13]

In the immediate Longtown area, Iron Age finds are scarce. In 2016, part of an Iron Age cloak pin was found in a field adjoining Longtown Castle. This worked rather like a modern safety pin. Although known as a 'Colchester-type', pins like this were used across the country during the first century AD.

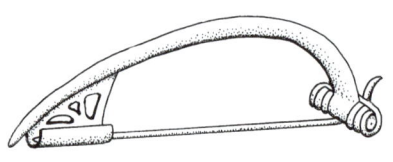

Part of a cloak pin from Longtown and a complete pin

By the Late Iron Age most of the country was divided up into large tribal confederations, governed by an aristocratic ruling class and a priestly order of druids. Ewyas may well have already become border country. From the evidence of their coinage, the Dobunni tribe appear to have occupied most of Herefordshire, as well as Gloucestershire and Somerset, while to the west the Cambrian uplands were held by the Silures in the south and the Ordovices in the north.

A gold quarter stater found near Vowchurch

Fighting between neighbouring tribes may have been endemic, but the imposing presence of the larger hillforts must have acted as a powerful deterrent. There is no question that they were primarily defensive structures rather than mere status symbols. The entrances were often complex and overlooked by additional ramparts to forestall any unwelcome approach to the gates. Hostile forces could be held at a distance by defenders using slings from the ramparts. Sling stones – carefully selected smooth ovoid pebbles – have been found cached in their thousands at several hillforts, and their lethal effect should not be underestimated. Even children with slings were capable of bringing down elite armed warriors. The famous encounter between David and Goliath occurred during the Palestinian Iron Age. If any attackers did reach the gates or manage to scale the embankments, they would then be vulnerable to the spears of the defenders behind the palisades.

Following his expeditions to Britain in 54 and 55 BC, Julius Caesar wrote a striking description of British warriors using two-wheeled chariots in battle:

> First they drive [their chariots] in all directions hurling spears. Generally they succeed in throwing the ranks of their opponents into confusion just with the terror caused by their galloping horses and the din of their wheels ... They then jump down from their chariots and fight on foot. Meanwhile, the chariot drivers withdraw a little way from the fighting and position their chariots in such a way that if their masters are hard pressed ... they have an easy means of retreat ... Even on steep slopes they can control their horses at full gallop, check and turn them in a moment, run along the pole, stand on the yoke and get back into the chariot with incredible speed.[14]

However, when attacking a hillfort, chariots would have been useless – in fact a liability, as they would have to be left some distance away and guarded in case of counter-attack. The extent to which chariots were used across the whole of Britain is questionable. They had long fallen out of use in Gaul, and Julius Caesar's excursions only took him to the south-east of England. The best archaeological evidence for chariots comes from chariot burials, where a high status individual was buried complete with chariot and horses. These are found almost exclusively in Yorkshire. Linch pins for securing wheels and terret rings for guiding the reins are occasionally found across the country, but the great majority have been recovered in the eastern counties from Yorkshire to East Anglia and Kent, areas where there are few hillforts. Conversely, where hillforts are common, linch pins and terret rings are rare finds. At the time of writing, in the counties along what is now the Welsh border, Cheshire and Shropshire have only produced two linch pins each and not one has been found in Herefordshire. It would appear that those tribes who built hillforts had little use for chariots. The hillfort effectively rendered them obsolete as a weapon of war.[15]

By the end of the Iron Age, population levels were probably at their highest level, due to a combination of warming climate and more effective agricultural implements. Julius Caesar wrote,

> The number of people is countless, and their homesteads exceedingly numerous, for the most part very like those of the Gauls: the number of cattle is great ... As in Gaul, there is timber of every description ... The climate is more temperate than in Gaul, the cold being less severe.[16]

Caesar was describing the communities of the south-east of Britain, where his short forays had established some diplomatic ties and extracted some tribute. Commercial links increased, with British traders exporting lead, tin, woollen goods, slaves and hunting dogs across the Channel. But Britain had certainly not been absorbed into the empire. Rome considered how it could increase its influence over this populous country and its resources. It would be almost a century before the legions came again and their task was not going to be easy.

7

The Roman occupation of the southern Marches

*'Remember, Roman, it is for you to rule the nations with your power,
for that will be your skill, to crown peace with law,
to spare the conquered, and to subdue the haughty*

Virgil, *c*.20 BC

LEAVING ASIDE JULIUS Caesar's brief forays into Britain in 55 and 54 BC, the real Roman invasion of Britain came about in AD 43 during the time of the Emperor Claudius. Some 40,000 troops were involved, comprising four legions: *legio II Augusta*, *legio IX Hispana*, *legio XIV Gemina* and *legio XX Valeria Victrix* – about 20,000 foot-soldiers with the same number of auxiliaries and cavalry. So successfully was the campaign carried out by Claudius's governor, Aulus Plautius, and his legionary generals, that within three years much of south and eastern Britain was under Roman control. A new road, the Fosse Way between modern Exeter and Lincoln, marked a rough boundary between the new Roman territories and the unconquered barbarian tribes. Plautius retired to Rome to receive great honours for his service and was replaced in AD 47 by a new governor, Publius Ostorius Scapula.[1]

Ostorius's mission was to continue the war to the west and north into what is now Wales. Here, two tribes in particular were proving hostile to Roman interests – the Silures in the south and the Ordovices in the north. Attacks by these and other hostile tribes in the north kept Ostorius busy for the first two years of his governorship. By AD 49, *legio XX* had been brought from Colchester (*Camulodunum*) to a new fort at Kingsholm, near Gloucester (*Glevum*). This fort would become the legionary base for Ostorius's campaign against the Silures. To complicate matters, Caratacus, leader of the Catevellauni, defeated twice in battle earlier in the Roman campaign, had now joined the Silures and was stirring up resistance.

The Roman historian, Tacitus, provides us with a vivid description of Ostorius's campaign against the Silures but, frustratingly, does not give us sufficient geographical detail to follow troop movements on the ground. Webster, writing in 1981, gave his best guess

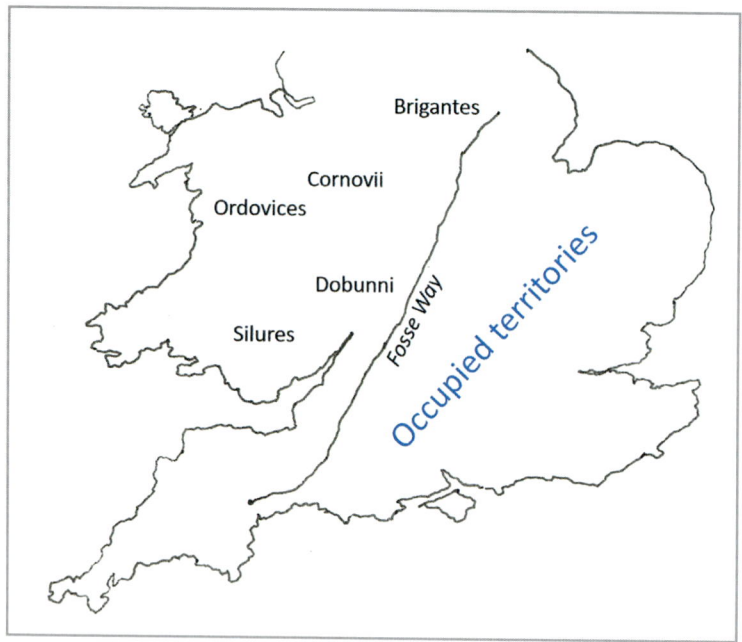

Roman occupation and unconquered Britain in AD 47

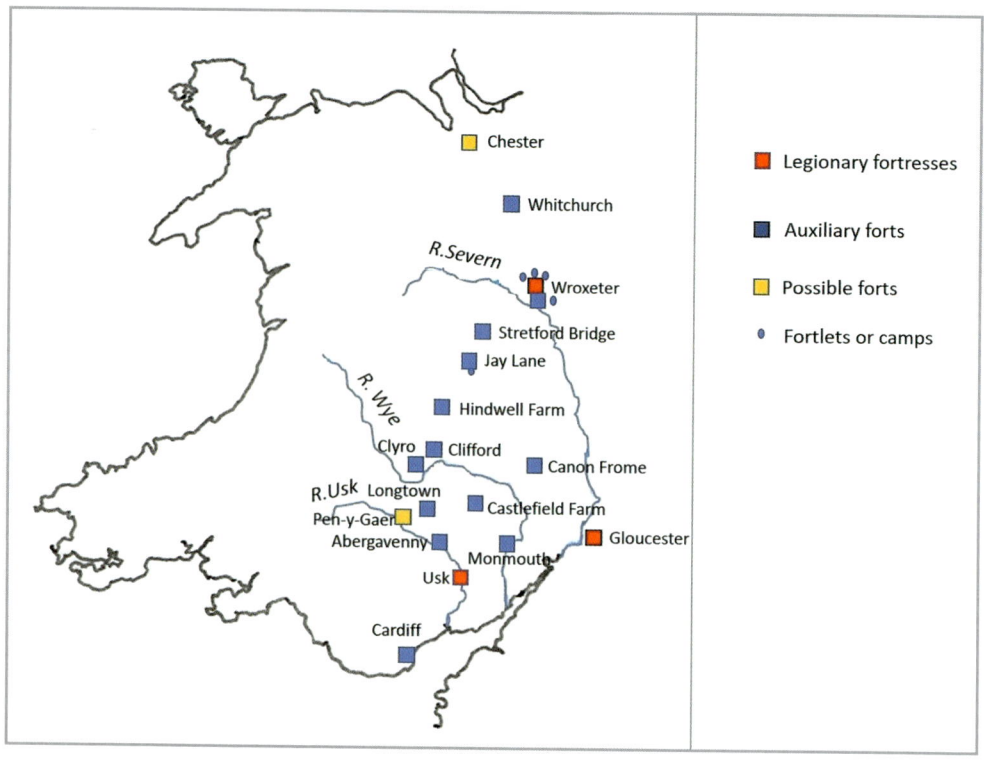

The distribution of Roman military bases before AD 60

at Scapula's campaign routes, but important forts and dates were unknown at that time. Archaeological work in recent decades has provided us with a better understanding of the positions and occupation dates of Roman forts in the area. With a careful examination of the terrain, it is now possible to reconstruct plausible routes for Ostorius's advance into Silurian territory. It may be that Ostorius also began campaigning against the Ordovices to the north at this time, but, if so, Tacitus remains silent. The early forts and marching camps identified in Radnorshire and north to Wroxeter and beyond may be from this period, or they could date to around the time of a later battle with Caratacus in AD 51 (*see below*).[2]

In the absence of roads, the most obvious routes for any army to follow are the river valleys. By the Late Iron Age, most of these low-lying areas would have been under cultivation, unless boggy or marshy. The first obstacle to the legion's western advance would have been the River Wye, which was probably crossed close to modern Ross-on-Wye. Later, the fort and settlement of *Ariconium* would be built not far from this crossing. The main part of the legion probably continued north on the eastern bank of the Wye, bringing it into contact with the people of Credenhill hillfort. Certainly, archaeology has uncovered no evidence for a battle. Nevertheless, the hillfort was taken over by the Romans and is thought to have been used as a campaign supply base. In time, the important town of *Magnis* would be founded close by.

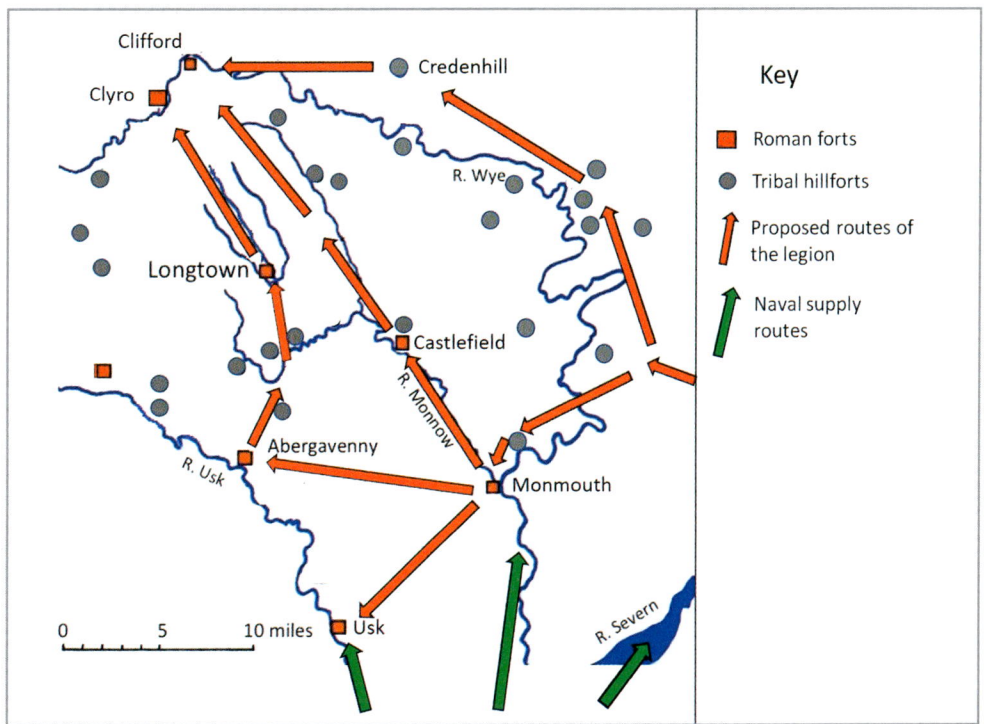

Probable routes taken by the Roman advance

Beyond Credenhill the army would eventually have arrived in the vicinity of modern Clifford, where two large campaign fortresses have been discovered, presumably built as bases for further incursions into mid-Wales. These fortresses would soon be abandoned in favour of the site at Clyro, on the north bank of the Wye, close to the modern town of Hay-on-Wye. Interestingly, there are some sites in Herefordshire which, it has been suggested, bear names which may recall Ostorius Scapula's presence in the area. Caplar Wood, near Fownhope, for example, sits beside the River Wye on the probable route taken by the legion. Oyster Hill near Ledbury is another possibility.[3]

A section of the legion must have continued south-west to the confluence of the Wye and Monnow rivers, as pottery from the period confirms that a fort was established here at what would later become the town of *Blestium* (Monmouth). This was a strategically important site, defended by water on three sides and with easy access to the coast by river. It seems highly likely that the provincial navy (*Classis Britannia*) would have been bringing in supplies for the army via the Severn and Wye estuaries. Whether over one or a number of campaigning seasons, Monmouth would have been the base for further western incursions by *Legio XX* through the Monnow and Usk valleys, establishing forts near modern Kentchurch (Castlefield Farm) and at Abergavenny. Both the Abergavenny and Castlefield forts are approximately a day's march from the base at Monmouth, but Ostorius's plan appears to have been to continue north-west to rendezvous with the main force at Clifford, a two-day march away. This conclusion is based on the presence of the strategically significant Longtown fort lying midway between Abergavenny and Clifford/ Clyro. Its position suggests that Ostorius's plan was to create a network of equally-spaced forts on the eastern side of the Black Mountains, before campaigning further south and west into the Silurian heartland.

Ostorius's territorial gains to this point were only achieved with great difficulty. The Silures under Caratacus harried the legion at every turn, using the hilly terrain to their advantage with ambush and guerrilla tactics. The disposition of Silurian hill-forts in the area perhaps gives some indication of likely trouble spots. At some point, however, Caratacus overreached himself and suffered a defeat sufficient for him to abandon the Silures and join the Ordovices in the north. Here, he was brought to battle by Ostorius in AD 51 at an unknown place, possibly in Radnorshire. The Ordovices were roundly defeated and, although Caratacus escaped, his family was captured. Freedom was short-lived, however, as Caratacus was handed over to the Romans by Cartimandua of the Brigantes, with whom he had sought refuge. Caratacus and his family were transported to Rome where he spent the rest of his life as something of a celebrity, if not a curiosity.[4]

If Ostorius thought that this victory would end Silurian resistance, he was wrong. His ill-judged threats to annihilate the tribe simply hardened their resistance, and the frequency of attacks and ambushes increased. Tacitus gives us a very vivid description of the problems faced by the legion:

some legionary cohorts, left behind to construct garrison-posts in Silurian territory, were attacked from all quarters and, if relief had not quickly reached the invested troops from the neighbouring forts – they had been informed by messenger – they must have perished to the last man. As it was the prefect [fort commander] fell, with 8 centurions and the boldest members of the rank and file. Nor was it long before a Roman foraging party and the squadrons despatched to its aid were totally routed.'[5]

Which of the previously mentioned forts is featured in this dramatic account cannot, of course, be confirmed, but given that it was one of the smaller, later-built forts, there is a good chance that it could have been Longtown. The passage also indicates that rapid troop movements were possible between neighbouring forts, suggesting that a system of connecting roads may already have been in place.

This attack took place in AD 52 and was part of a wider breakdown of order in the region. Worn out by the strain, Ostorius paid the 'debt of nature', as Tacitus puts it, and died in office later the same year. His replacement, Aulus Didius Gallus, quickly restored order in the region, despite having suffered a serious legionary defeat before he took office. Nevertheless, according to Tacitus, he made only small territorial advances, building few forts. His main contribution during his period as governor (AD 52–57) seems to have been the establishment of the legionary fortresses at Usk and Wroxeter, both completed around AD 55. *Legio XX* moved to Usk from Gloucester to focus the campaign against the Silurian heartland of what is now Gwent, Glamorgan and the south Wales valleys, while *XIV Gemina* used Wroxeter as a base for campaigning in mid and north Wales. Several possibly earlier camps or forts have been discovered close to Wroxeter fortress, showing the strategic importance of this site as a supply base next to the River Severn.[6]

It was during the governorship of Didius that the Emperor Claudius was murdered in AD 54, to be replaced by Nero, thus providing archaeology with a dateable change in coinage. Forts of Neronian date, however, are few in number in the region. A notable exception was the large fort at what is now Cardiff, which was in operation by AD 60, no doubt providing another shipping supply base for future campaigning. It may also have been under Didius Gallus that the Usk Valley boundary was extended to the fort at Pen-y-Gaer, near Bwlch. However, despite strong offensives against the Silures and Ordovices by Didius's two successors, Quintus Veranius (AD 57–58) and Seutonius Paullinus (AD 58–61), the frontier failed to move forward significantly during this period. One of the reasons was the number of insurrections and revolts across the province, partly fuelled by Nero's taxation policies. These revolts included the major Icenian uprising led by Boudicca in AD 61, which took both the *XIV* and *XX* legions away from the western frontier.

The decade after AD 61 appears to have been fairly quiet militarily. Nero took this opportunity to withdraw the *XIV Gemina* from Britannia in AD 66/67 and replace them at Wroxeter with the *XX Valeria Victrix*. It is thought that Usk continued to be manned by auxiliary cavalry and possibly a cohort of legionaries, but plans may already have been in place to replace Usk with the large fortress at Caerleon, which came into operation in the 70s. Caerleon was garrisoned throughout its long occupation by the *II Augusta* legion. By the end of the first century the legionaries were supplemented by 8,000 auxiliaries.[7]

It was only after Nero's death and the advent of the Flavian dynasty (Emperors Vespasian, Titus and Domitian: AD 69–96) that territorial expansion and fort-building began again in earnest in the west. Some 18 forts of Flavian date have been identified in south Wales, with a further 16 in mid and north Wales. An important addition to the Usk Valley forts was the one built at Brecon (*Brecon Gaer*), showing the importance of the river valleys for troop movements at this time. The periods of most active and successful campaigning were under governor Sextus Julius Frontinus (AD 74–77), who ended the Silurian war, and governor Gaius Julius Agricola (AD 77–84), who finally defeated and pacified the Ordovices.

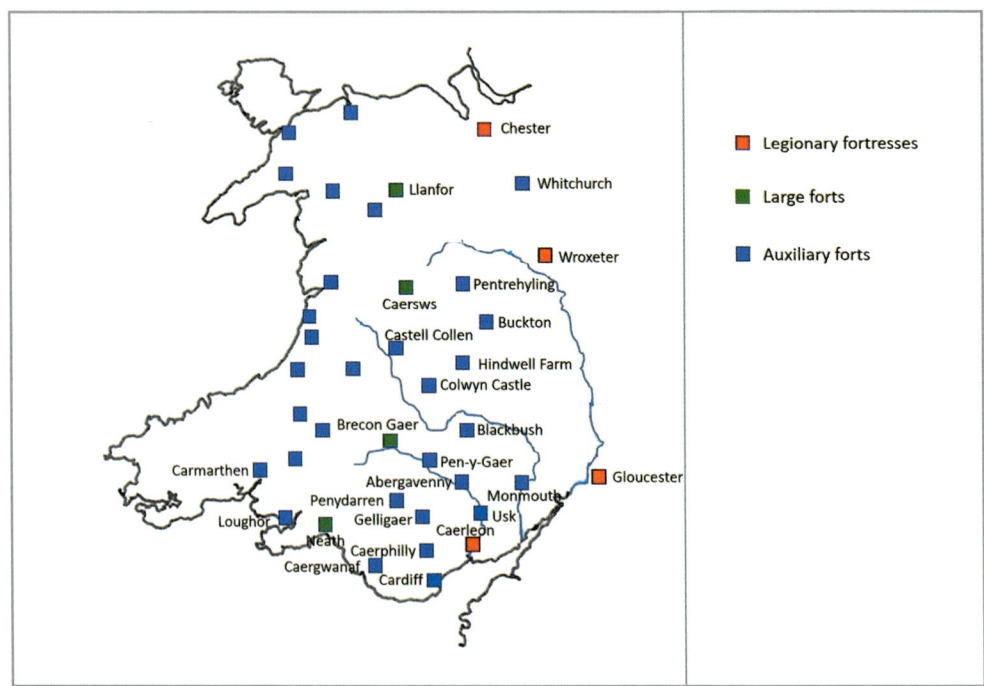

The distribution of Flavian forts in Wales and the Marches

During this Flavian expansion, the early forts like Longtown, now comfortably behind the front line, would have been manned by auxiliary troops, usually recruited from the provinces, and charged with more of a policing and peace-keeping role. Longtown's size (1.5ha) suggests that it was garrisoned with a battalion of 500 foot-soldiers (*cohors quingenaria peditata*).[8]

Once the threat of rebellion had subsided, some of these early forts, possibly those with no civilian settlement, were abandoned. This phase coincided with Agricola's new campaign against the Caledonian tribes in the north, begun in AD 79, which necessitated the redeployment of troops from the Welsh theatre of operations. There is no evidence to show whether or not the Longtown fort was abandoned at this early stage or continued in use into the second century. It seems unlikely, however, that the fort would have survived much beyond the early second century, given that it was never rebuilt in stone. Many of the other early forts in Wales had also been abandoned by this time.

LONGTOWN FORT

Small, square Roman forts, although not of the typical 'playing card' shape, are relatively common in Wales and the Marches. At least 13 have been recorded so far, under 2.5 hectares in area. Typical first-century frontier forts would have had a rampart of stacked turf to a height of at least 2m, possibly with a central core of earth. There were normally four gated entrances, one on each side. The rampart would have been topped with a wooden palisade and walkway, with wooden watchtowers at the entrances and corners. Watchtowers may also have been placed at mid-points along the ramparts, as was typical of larger forts. The arrangement of internal buildings is well known from

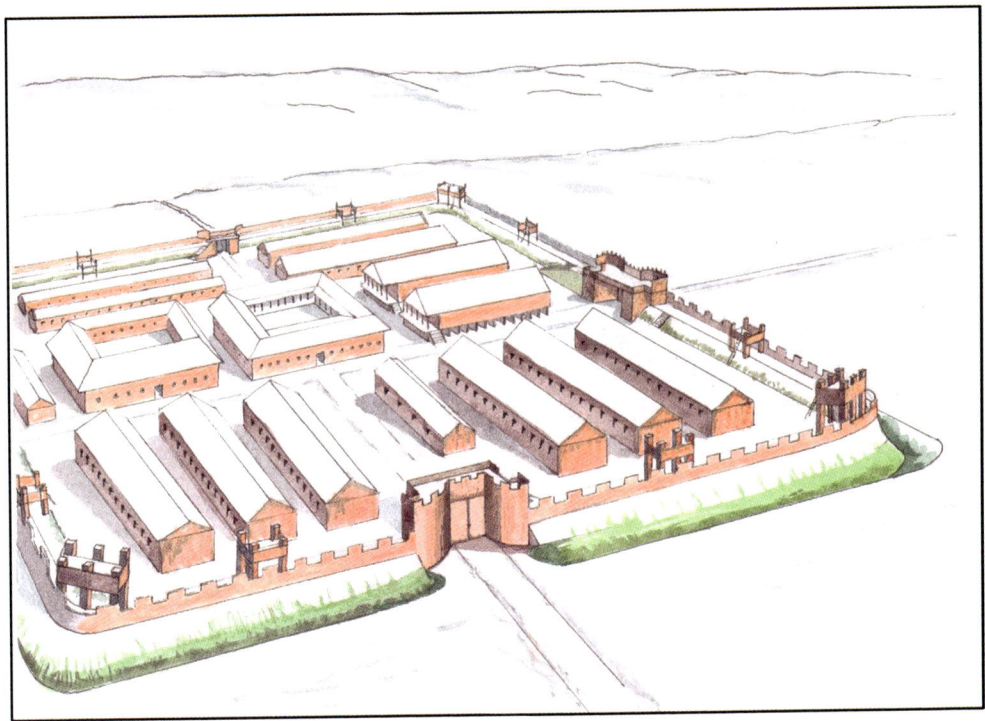

An impression of Longtown fort around AD 75, based on the excavated timber fort of similar size at Elginhaugh in Scotland

later forts rebuilt in stone, but some excavated timber forts have also revealed a similar layout. A headquarters building (*principia*) would have been centrally located on the *via principia* between the north and south gates, with the commanding officer's house (*praetorium*) and a number of granaries situated nearby. Six to eight barrack blocks, together with workshops, would then have been built around these central facilities. Each barrack block is thought to have housed a century of 80 soldiers, with ten rooms of eight men. Each room had a space opposite for equipment and cooking food. These arrangements may have varied from fort to fort, however, depending on size and the presence of additional troops.[9]

At Longtown the south entrance to the fort is still in evidence as a sunken lane cutting through the rampart just to the west of the modern road. The original north entrance has been obliterated by later development.

The south entrance to Longtown fort today

The gateways on the west and east sides of the fort gave access to water supplies. Although these entrances were blocked by the later enhancement of the rampart, the lines of the roads using them are still evident in today's landscape in a farm track running west to the Olchon Brook and a raised field boundary running east towards the River Monnow.

THE ROMAN ROADS AND THEIR WIDER CONNECTIONS

The Roman military strategy of placing each fort at one day's march from the next certainly facilitated rapid troop reinforcement at trouble-spots. It did, however, depend on good communications and at the time that meant good roads. The Roman system of road-building has justly taken its place in the popular imagination, but much of this is based on misconception. Construction methods varied according to terrain and resources available. While some roads, such as the Appian Way in Rome, were surfaced with paving stones and edged with corbels, those in Britannia were usually faced with impacted gravel, with or without edging stones. Roads could be straight for long stretches, but in difficult terrain, bends and twists were not unusual. Roads could also vary considerably in width. Standard features tended to include a raised central 'agger', made from the material dug from drainage ditches on either side of the road. To this raised mound a substrate of larger stones was added before the cambered surface was metalled with impacted gravel. This created a strong, impervious road capable of resisting, at least for a time, the wear and tear of weather, army boots, horses and wheeled vehicles. Whenever necessary, repairs could be made by adding further substrate and gravel.

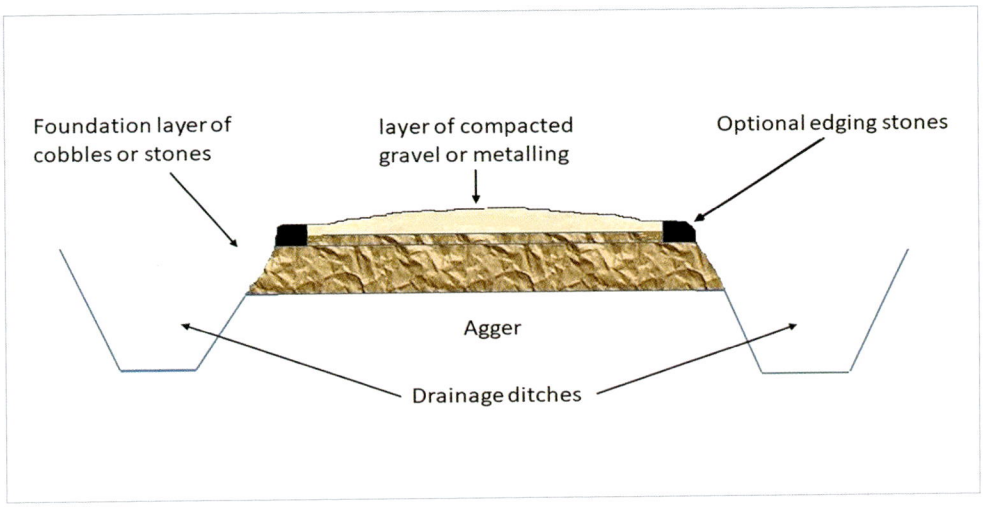

Cross-section showing construction of a typical Roman road

A system of roads would have linked the fort at Longtown to neighbouring forts and towns in the area. The roads would not only have been used for troop movements and communicating orders and despatches, but just as importantly for bringing in supplies. Some food would no doubt have been commandeered locally, but even a small garrison like Longtown's would need restocking with rations and materials from the neighbouring forts, such as Abergavenny or Monmouth.

The Roman road connecting Abergavenny and Longtown is not at present clear. It may have followed the route of the modern Hereford road as far as Pandy, turning left along the Monnow to Clodock and hence Longtown – a day's march distance of 15 miles. North of Longtown there are also old trackways on the hills on either side of the Monnow, which could be contenders for Roman roads between the fort and the legionary fortresses at Clyro and Clifford, again a day's march distance.

An important road to the east would also have connected Longtown fort by way of Stone Street to Credenhill and the town of *Magnis*, a total distance of 12 miles. Some vestiges of the Longtown extension to Stone Street still remain. The long straight road across the common at Lower Maescoed is traditionally thought to have been Roman in origin, while old maps of the early 1800s show that it once continued across the Dulas brook to join the road at Tremorithic. Another stretch of old, raised track is to be found passing to the north of Holling Grange Farm, which bears some of the hallmarks of Roman engineering. These vestiges of road can be joined on a map to form a remarkably straight line which, if continued to the east, joins the end of Stone Street between Bacton and Abbey Dore, close to the site of a later fort at Blackbush Farm.

Left: The raised trackway at Holling Grange Farm

Below: The eastern section of the Roman road between Longtown and Bacton (in red). The position of the Holling Grange Farm section shown left is indicated by the yellow arrow

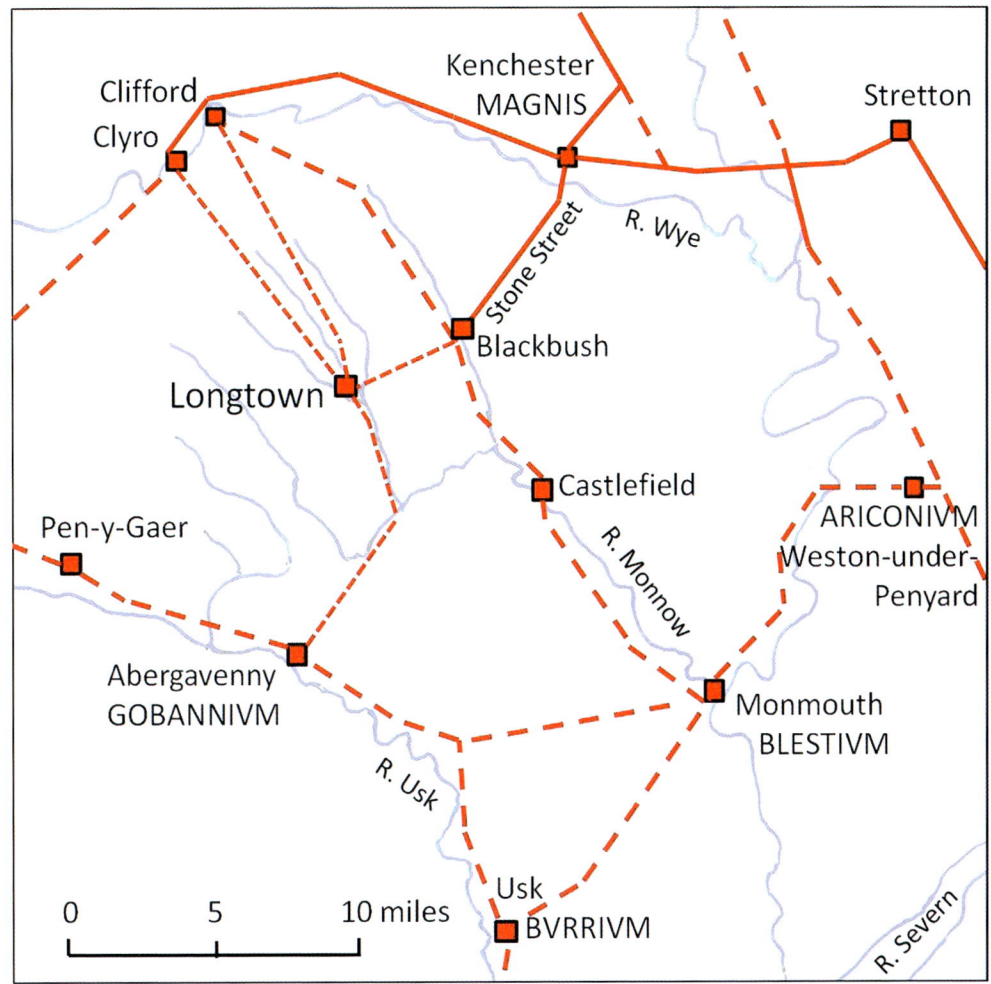

The forts and interconnecting roads of the southern Marches

This junction was also an important crossroads. An ancient track, probably Roman judging by its construction, was initially discovered at Abbey Dore Station in 1908, but has been more recently excavated at a number of other places. The track runs from Abbey Dore to Dorstone along the Golden Valley and, judging by its direction, probably continued on to Clifford and later Clyro. The road probably also ran south from Abbey Dore to Castlefield fort and even on to Monmouth, although no trace has yet been detected.[10]

By the late AD 60s or early 70s, the mosaic of approximately equally-spaced forts was probably interconnected by a complex network of roads. As the early campaign forts, such as Longtown, and possibly Castlefield, fell out of use and were abandoned by the second century, their connecting roads would have continued to be used for a long time afterwards. In all likelihood, the road from Abergavenny through Longtown and on to *Magnis* would have become part of the longer Watling Street west extension from Wroxeter to Carmarthen, listed as Journey 12 in the later Antonine Itinerary. The fort at Blackbush Farm, thought to have been built by AD 85, may have been placed at the southern end of Stone Street precisely to protect the *Magnis* to Abergavenny section of this road.

An impression of the Roman road at Bacton

8

Ewyas in the Dark Ages

Sometimes legends make reality, and become more useful than the facts
Salman Rushdie

THE TERM 'DARK AGES' has become unfashionable with academic historians writing about the first few centuries in Britain after Roman rule. We could call them the 'Early Middle Ages', but the idea that the Middle Ages are anywhere near the middle of man's time on earth completely ignores the millennia of pre-history. The term 'sub-Roman' used by archaeologists is equally unsatisfactory, as it seems to over-emphasise the importance of the Romans – and besides, is meaningless to the general public. The Dark Ages rightfully expresses the lack of written history that we have for this period, when 'now we see things through a glass, darkly.' The 'glass' referred to in St Paul's letter was a mirror of polished bronze, giving only a dark and distorted reflection, a perfect metaphor for our perception of this period in British history.

Archaeology informs us that during this time coinage fell out of circulation, markets collapsed and trade effectively came to a standstill. Pottery and glassware were no longer produced or imported to any extent. Road-making ceased and people stopped building in stone. In terms of their economy, manufacturing and the arts, most parts of Britain effectively seem to have more or less reverted to the culture of the early Iron Age. Literacy was almost unknown. The myths and legends that have come down to us are the memories of history, passed on as tales told around the fire on winter nights.

The withdrawal of the Roman legions led to the arrival of Germanic tribes, first as mercenaries but soon, in greater numbers, as colonists. Angles, Saxons and Jutes overran most of lowland Britain. The invaders referred to the indigenous British people as *Walas* or Welsh, meaning foreigners. The term didn't just apply to the Britons. It was used to describe the Romans and any other inhabitants of the Roman Empire.

In what was later to become England, many of those enclaves still populated by subjugated Britons were given names such as Walbrook, Walden, Walford and Walton. The western upland region, where the Britons successfully fought to keep their independence, became known to the invaders as Wales. Here, the Brythonic language remained in use and the people called themselves *Cymry*, meaning fellow-countrymen. Yet Wales was not a united country. It comprised a number of small independent kingdoms or principalities. Although these might occasionally combine through conquest or marriage, they soon separated again, sometimes as the result of rebellion but often by the division of territory between sons. The borders of the Welsh kingdoms were ill-defined, always fluid and constantly disputed.

One of these small kingdoms was Ewyas. It is not known when Ewyas was founded but it was probably in existence during the Dark Ages. Some have noted the similarity between Ewyas and *Gewisse*, the name used for the early Saxons in Wessex, but, according to Geoffrey of Monmouth writing in the twelfth century, having much older origins. He says that Vortigern, the British ruler responsible for inviting Saxon mercenaries to settle in Kent after the Romans had left, had the title *consul Gewisseorum*, lord of the Gewisse. The *Brut Dingestow*, a thirteenth- or fourteenth-century Welsh translation of Geoffrey's history is more explicit, stating that Vortigern was '*yarll oedhvnnv ar Went ac Ergyng a Yeuas*' – earl of Gwent, Archenfield and Ewyas.[1]

Vortigern was a very unpleasant character who, with the help of the Saxon leaders, Hengist and Horsa, used trickery and murder to usurp the throne of Britain and went on to marry his own daughter. He came under attack from the sons of the king he had deposed, Ambrosius and Uther Pendragon, and was eventually burned to death in his castle of *Genoreu* on the hill of *Cloartius*, overlooking the Wye in Archenfield. This has been identified as the Iron Age fort with Roman/ post-Roman enhancements on Little Doward hill, near to the village of Ganarew in south-west Herefordshire (*Cloartius* being a transcription error for *Doartius*).[2]

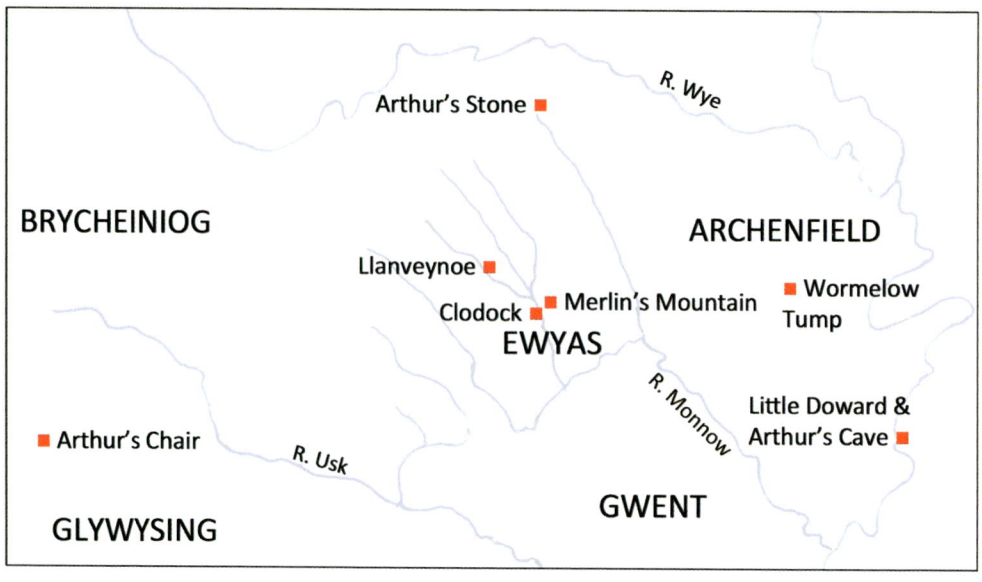

Places with Dark Ages associations around Ewyas

88 THE MARCH OF EWYAS

KING ARTHUR

Like many places, Ewyas has associations with the Arthurian legends. King Arthur, the son of Uther Pendragon, is a symbolic figure, a Briton who won fame holding back the Germanic invaders. The stories of Arthur and the prophet or wizard, Merlin, come from an oral tradition that was only set down and then heavily embroidered in the medieval period. Some academics claim that Arthur is entirely mythical but with so many sources in English, Welsh and French literature, it seems unlikely that there isn't at least a germ of truth behind the legends.

During the eighteenth and nineteenth centuries the hill to the east of Longtown was known as Moneyfarthing Hill. This is a charming corruption of its Welsh name, *Mynydd Ferddin*, which means Merlin's Mountain. Merlin was the wise wizard who advised King Arthur and reputedly was responsible for bringing Stonehenge from Ireland to Britain. It has now been proved that the 'bluestones' of Stonehenge came from the Preseli Hills in Pembrokeshire. The fact that this area was colonised by people from Ireland in the fifth century may go some way to explaining the legendary source of the stones. We don't know what Merlin was doing in Ewyas, and the reason for naming Mynydd Ferddin after him is lost in the mists of time.

This isn't the only landmark near Longtown connected with the myths of King Arthur. Only 14 miles to the north, near Dorstone, is a Neolithic chambered tomb that is known as Arthur's Stone. Although it predates King Arthur by three or four millennia, there have been folk stories to the effect that the tomb marks the place where Arthur slew and buried a giant, or was himself buried. Pits in one of the stones are

Arthur's Stone

supposed to be marks left either by the giant's elbows when he fell or by Arthur's knees when he prayed. Kilvert wrote in his 1878 diary that it was believed that the marks were made by Arthur's fingers and knees when he heaved the stone up on his back and set it upon the pillars.

Fourteen miles east of Longtown there was once another prehistoric tomb, known as Wormelow Tump, sadly lost to road widening in the nineteenth century. According to legend this is where Arthur buried his son, Amr, after killing him – though why he killed his own son is not recorded. The Welsh monk Nennius, writing in the ninth century, said that whenever the tomb was measured it was never the same length, sometimes being six feet long, sometimes nine feet, sometimes twelve or even fifteen feet. Nennius claimed to have put this to the test himself.[3]

Fifteen miles south-east of Longtown, on a curve of the River Wye just a short walk from Vortigern's burnt-out fortress, is King Arthur's Cave. Apparently, when Arthur was on the run from his enemies, he hid his treasure here. Merlin cast a spell over the cave so that Arthur's pursuers could not find it. Merlin himself had his own cave not far away.

The Brecon Beacons rise to the west of Longtown. The medieval historian and commentator, Giraldus Cambrensis or Gerald of Wales, refers to the highest of them as '*Cadair Arthur*, or Arthur's Chair, so called from two peaks which rise up in the form of a throne.'[4]

Arthur's Chair – the peaks of Corn Du and Pen-y-Fan

Ewyas is mentioned in connection with Arthur in *The Mabinogion*, a set of Welsh legends compiled during the medieval period but based on a much older oral tradition. In what is thought to be one of the earliest stories, Arthur's cousin Culhwch sets out to wed Olwen, the daughter of Ysbaddaden, the chief of the giants. To win her hand he invokes the help of Arthur, along with a long and humorously unlikely list of his knights. As well as more familiar figures like Kei and Bedwyr (Kay and Bedivere), there are warriors with droll names like Sufficiency, the son of Surfeit, and Earth, the son of Acre. Some are gifted with improbable superpowers. One can hear an ant stirring 50 miles away. Another can run across the tips of reeds, and a third, while standing in Cornwall, can shoot an arrow across the sea through both legs of a wren in Ireland.

When Arthur's band of heroes confronts the giant Ysbaddaden, he agrees to his daughter's marriage but only if Culhwch can perform 39 seemingly impossible tasks. One of the tasks is to take a comb, a razor and shears from between the ears of Twrch Trwyth, a warrior who has been turned into a ferocious boar. Presumably these seemingly mundane objects had a significance now lost to us.

By the time Arthur and his army find Twrch, he and his seven piglets have destroyed a third of Ireland. When Arthur attacks, Twrch swims across to Wales, where Arthur and his men harry him, killing the piglets one by one but suffering dire casualties in the process. At Ewyas, Twrch is turned back towards the River Severn. Arthur summons the men of Devon and Cornwall, and they drive Twrch into the river by the mouth of the Wye and manage to seize the razor and shears. Twrch escapes again and is hunted to Cornwall where Arthur's men finally capture the comb, before driving Twrch into the sea. Having gained these and various other treasures, Culhwch eventually wins his bride. Her father, the chief of the giants, having been defeated, submits to being beheaded on a dunghill.[5]

It is impossible to know the meaning of this strange, barbaric story, which combines the comedic with a catalogue of bloody mayhem. Although it first appears in fourteenth-century manuscripts, it owes far more to Dark Age mythology than to chivalric virtues, and perhaps contains the memory of a seaborne attack on Britain during the fifth or sixth century.

KING CLYDAWG

A Dark Age figure more closely associated with the Longtown area is King Clydawg, who gave his name to Clodock. Clydawg, the son of Clydwyn, ruled over Ewyas during the sixth century. He wisely administered justice in his kingdom and was renowned for his virtue and chastity. A young woman, the daughter of a wealthy man, was in love with him and told her suitors that she would marry no one but the illustrious Clydawg. One of the companions of the king, who she had refused, was tormented by lust for her and became filled with hatred for Clydawg. One day, when the king was waiting by the River Monnow to meet a party of hunters, the jealous courtier killed him.

The king's companions and nobles found the body and placed it on a carriage drawn by oxen. They attempted to cross the River Monnow by a ford but once in the river the yokes started to break and the oxen refused to move another step, even though they were repeatedly goaded on. It was as if Clydawg's body had miraculously become incredibly heavy, although immediately after his death it had seemed to be wonderfully light. Filled with amazement, the courtiers had no option but to bury Clydawg beside the river. They gave praise to God and that night a column of fire was seen over the grave, which was taken as a sign that God approved of the place of burial. Because King Clydawg had led such an excellent and virtuous life, he was declared to be a saint.

The River Monnow can be forded at several places near to Clodock, but the most likely place for King Clydawg's ford is at the weir belonging to Clodock Mill, which has its sluicegate beside the corner of the churchyard. The earliest records for Clodock Mill refer to it as 'the mill of Seynt Cladok'. If you stand at the weir and look across the river to the bank opposite you can just make out a hollow way across the field, which may well mark the intended route of Clydawg's last journey.

The weir at Clodock

The bishop of Llandaff ordered that an oratory be built over the grave and from that time onwards it was held in veneration as the church of *Merthyr Clydawg*, on account of the blessed martyr who was buried there. Later, three hermits came to live nearby and built an improved church. This early church is thought to have been where the chancel of the present church now stands, with King Clydawg's tomb below the altar.[6]

Writing in 1919 the vicar of Clodock said, 'There is an interesting tradition that the builders tried at first to place Clodock Church where Llanwonog stands today. Day after day with the greatest diligence did the workmen build, but each morning the previous day's work collapsed until they recommenced their efforts where Clodock Church now stands.' Llanwonog is just east of Longtown Castle. Its name could come from a church dedicated to either Saint Gwynnog or Saint Gwenog, and perhaps this legend reflects an early rivalry between the communities of Longtown and Clodock, possibly resulting in acts of sabotage.[7]

In the first half of the eighth century Ithael, the son of Morgan the Generous, ruled over much of south-east Wales, including Glywysing (Glamorgan), Gwent, Ewyas and Archenfield. He gave Clodock Church and the surrounding area to the bishop of Llandaff,

> with all its liberty and commonage given to the present and future inhabitants in field and in woods, in water and in pastures, and without any payment, great or small, to any mortal man besides the Church of Llandaff and its pastors for ever; and as an island placed in the sea, free from every service … and with refuge according to the will of the refugee, without limit; and as long as he should choose to remain, be safe under its protection as if he were in the sanctuary of Llandaff.[8]

This meant that Clodock was effectively a tax-free zone where fugitives from the law were permitted to remain safely and without fear, for as long as they needed – a tradition that in some minds continues to this very day.

A ninth-century grave stone found beneath the nave of Clodock Church.
It reads 'This grave holds the remains of a seemly woman, Guinnda's dear wife who was of this place.'

SAINT BEUNO

Beuno was another early Welsh saint associated with Ewyas in the sixth century. *Buchedd Beuno*, the life of Beuno written in 1346, records that his aging parents despaired of having children until his forthcoming birth was announced to them by an angel. Ynyr, the king of Gwent, noted Beuno's sanctity and gave him a village in Ewyas, with its people, where he could build a monastery. Ynyr, whose name is a Brythonic version of the imperial Roman Honorius, then became his disciple. The community, in the Olchon Valley just north of Longtown, took the name of the church of Beuno – Llanveynoe.

An early crucifixion carving in Llanveynoe Church. Not only does it predate the present church but it also appears to reuse a stone with cup and ring marks from the Neolithic period

Beuno didn't stay long in Ewyas. On hearing that his father was dying, he returned to his family home. There he planted an acorn at his father's grave, which grew into a great oak tree. A branch from this tree touched the ground and then grew up again, forming an arch. It is said that if an Englishman went under the arch he soon died, though a Welshman could pass through unscathed.

Beuno went on to found a number of monasteries. These were nothing like the spectacular edifices erected by the great monastic orders of later centuries. They were small Christian communities centred on a simple church, as likely to be built of timber as of stone. One was in Powys where King Cynon gave Beuno some land. Cynon's grandsons stayed there while hunting, and expected Beuno to provide them with food. Reluctantly, Beuno killed a young ox and put its meat in a cauldron to boil. After several hours on the fire, the water wasn't even warm, although the huntsmen had been feeding the fire continuously. For a saint, Beuno had a very dark side. When one of the party complained that Beuno was using his arts to prevent the water boiling, Beuno cursed him and he was dead before nightfall. Beuno told Cynon's grandsons that Cynon had given him the land freely and he had no obligations to feed them. He then prayed that the young men would never inherit Cynon's kingdom and so it came to pass. When their father died, the crown of Powys passed to his brother, rather than to them.

Beuno went on to perform many other wonders. His most notable miracle was to reunite a beautiful virgin with her head and bring her back to life after she had been decapitated by a thwarted suitor. The beautiful virgin's Welsh name was Gwenffrewi, known in English as Saint Winifred. Beuno's prayers were to raise several people from the dead and at least three of them had been beheaded. This suggests that his legend perhaps preserves elements of earlier Celtic mythology concerning the severed head, a theme that also appears in the Arthurian romance of *Sir Gawain and the Green Knight*.[9]

9

Anglo-Saxons and Vikings in the Welsh borderlands

A certain vigorous king called Offa ...
had a great dyke built between Wales and Mercia from sea to sea

Asser, biographer of Alfred the Great

During the Dark Ages, ragtag armies of Angles, Saxons, Jutes and Britons, both heathen and Christian, had fought for control of the more productive lowlands. When it was expedient, the leading families made alliances and intermarried. Powerful warlords emerged and were able to extend their control over larger territories that eventually coalesced into kingdoms. The Saxon kingdoms in the east, south and west became known as Essex, Sussex and Wessex. The Angles gave their name to East Anglia and ultimately to the whole of England. The area in the Midlands where the Germanic tribes and the Britons still struggled for dominance was known as the *mearc*, meaning the border. This region eventually became the Anglo-Saxon kingdom of Mercia. The word *mearc* has the same linguistic root as 'marches', the name later adopted by the Normans for their border with Wales.

Mercia became a dominant power during the long reign of King Offa (757– 796) and he exerted influence across much of England. But Offa was frequently in conflict with the various Welsh kingdoms. The border was an intractable problem, and Hereford was both a target for Welsh raids into Mercia and a launch site for Mercian raids into Wales. Hereford's name

The early Anglo-Saxon kingdoms

comes from the Old English word *here* meaning an army, specifically a raiding army. So, Hereford was the ford where invading forces crossed the River Wye. The Welsh rendered Hereford into their own language as *Henffordd*, which means 'old road'. This was probably a reference to the Roman road that followed the west-east course of the River Wye and skirted to the north of Hereford. Roman roads continued to have military use well into the medieval period, so both versions of its name, Hereford and *Henffordd*, encapsulate the military importance of the city.

Offa's response to the perpetual warring between the Welsh and the English was to lay down a physical demarcation (another word based on the Old English *mearc*). Offa's Dyke is an earth embankment and ditch that defined the border between the Welsh kingdoms and Mercia. The ditch on the east side was the primary quarry for the banked material. The slope from the bottom of the ditch to the top of the dyke was generally between three and five metres high and formed a formidable obstacle. It extends from near Prestatyn in the north to the mouth of the Wye in the south – from sea to sea. Offa may not actually have built it all. Along parts of the border there are other dykes running more or less parallel to Offa's. Radiocarbon dating suggests that some of the dyke was built long before Offa's time, so it may have incorporated sections of earlier dykes.

Offa's Dyke is nothing like Hadrian's Wall. There are no mile castles or forts along its length, and gates are few and far from obvious. There is no evidence that it was permanently manned although it could have been regularly patrolled. Whereas the dyke could never have been a complete defence against a determined army, an agreed or accepted border would have discouraged incursions in either direction. For much of its length it would have been at the least a highly effective check to small groups of raiders attempting to rustle cattle.[1]

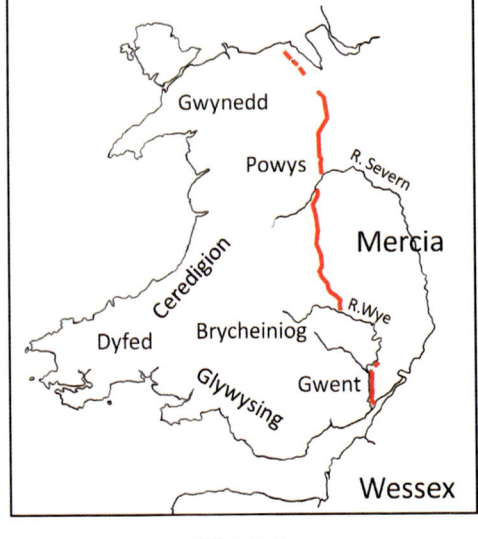

Offa's Dyke

There is a notable gap in the dyke across much of Herefordshire where the border seems to have been defined by the River Wye. However, the area south and west of the Wye, known as Archenfield, was already coming under Mercian influence, which may account for the absence of the dyke here. South of Herefordshire, the dyke resumes along the east bank of the Wye. This may suggest that the river traffic was the accepted prerogative of the Welsh kingdom of Gwent, although the main reason for the dyke being built on this side of the Wye was probably as a measure against river-borne incursions into Mercia. If so, it was a highly sensible precaution.

VIKINGS

Towards the end of the eighth century longships from Denmark and Norway began raiding all around the coast of Britain and Ireland. Soon, these isolated Viking attacks turned into a wave of migration, and towards the end of the ninth century East Anglia and much of eastern Mercia were under Danish control. For a time, the Great Heathen Army was virtually unstoppable, and although King Alfred eventually managed to push the Danes back north of the Thames he was forced to accept the division of England. Ruling as king of the Anglo-Saxons, he held Wessex, Sussex, Kent and western Mercia. Elsewhere, in the north and east of the country, the Danelaw prevailed.

Soon afterwards, on the other side of the English Channel, Northmen sailed up the River Seine and took the French city of Rouen. From there they threatened Paris until the French king, Charles the Simple, ceded land to them in exchange for their agreeing to defend France against further Viking raids. Their leader, Rollo or Rolf, was baptised and became the first duke of Normandy.

During this chaotic period the Welsh borderlands were not immune to attack. In 914 a large Viking fleet raided along the south coast of Wales and into the Severn estuary. Arriving at Archenfield they seized the bishop of Llandaff and took him back to their ships. It appears that Archenfield was under English dominion at that time, and King Edward the Elder, Alfred's son, secured the bishop's freedom with a ransom of 40 pounds of silver. An English army made up of the men from Hereford and Gloucester then attacked and defeated the Viking raiders, who retreated along the south coast of the Bristol Channel. Their attempts to land were thwarted, as Edward had ordered defensive positions to be manned from Avonmouth to Cornwall, and many of the raiders were to die of starvation before the remaining few found refuge in Ireland.

The Anglo-Saxon part of Mercia was more or less independently governed by an ealdorman who had married Æthelflæd, Alfred's eldest daughter and sister to King Edward. When her husband died, Æthelflæd took over the reins of power and held the title of the Lady of the Mercians. It was entirely unprecedented in this period for a woman to govern, but it seems she was ideally suited to the task, and she governed well. She ordered the fortification of Mercian towns and was successful in recovering some Danish-held territory. During her seven-year rule she earned the respect of Mercians and Danes alike. It is clear that the Lady of the Mercians was not someone to be crossed lightly. In 916, a Mercian abbot was murdered during a Welsh raid. Just three days later, Æthelflæd's army made a retaliatory attack on the kingdom of Brycheiniog and captured the queen along with 33 of her attendants. The Mercians 'broke down Brecon Mere', a residence of the Brycheiniog royal family. This was the crannog on Llangorse Lake, a defensible artificial island. Although they are widespread in Ireland and Scotland, this is the only known crannog in Wales and England. Excavation carried out in 1989 showed that parts of the crannog had been destroyed by fire.[2]

The crannog on Llangorse Lake

King Edward and his sister, Æthelflæd, consolidated their hold over southern England and Mercia, and made significant advances into Danish territory. But it was Edward's son, Æthelstan, who in 927 annexed York and Northumbria, becoming the first king of all England. He then summoned the four Welsh kings to Hereford where they reluctantly acknowledged Æthelstan as their overlord and agreed to pay him an annual tribute of 20 pounds of gold, 300 pounds of silver and 25,000 oxen, along with as many trained hunting dogs and hawks as he might require. The River Wye was formally designated as the border between England and Wales. Later, the Welsh kings aided Æthelstan in invading Scotland. After this incursion, Æthelstan's coinage bore the title REX TO[TIUS] BRIT[ANNIAE] – king of all Britain.[3]

Towards the end of the tenth century the problem of Viking raids again intensified. In 991 King Æthelred was persuaded to buy off Danish invaders with a payment of over three tonnes of silver. This only encouraged further incursions, and for the next two decades Danish armies bled the English of silver. Æthelred was forced to raise ever-increasing amounts of Danegeld, the tax needed to pay his army and placate the enemy's demands. In a desperate bid to counter Danish settlement, on St Brice's day, 13 November 1002, Æthelred ordered the massacre of all Danes 'who had sprung up like weeds among the wheat' in those parts of England still under his control.

Historians are divided in their opinions of Æthelred's rule. His nickname 'the Unready' has nothing to do with his preparedness but is a pun on his name, which was derived from the Old English for 'noble council'. His epithet is actually *unræd*, meaning 'no council', so it seems he was sarcastically being called something along the lines of 'Noble advice – no advice'.

In 1013 Æthelred was forced into exile by the Dane, Sveyn Forkbeard, who placed himself on the throne of England. When Sveyn died the following year, the leading English noblemen elected to recall Æthelred, rather than accept Sveyn Forkbeard's son, Cnut, as the king. Æthelred subsequently regained control of much of the country. However, the situation was complicated by his son, Edmund Ironside,

A penny of King Æthelred minted at Hereford by the moneyer Leofgar

attempting to establish independent rule in the Danelaw. The return of Cnut, with a Danish army backing his own claim to the throne, brought further chaos. Æthelred held on until his death in 1016, after which Cnut and Edmund Ironside fought over the kingdom and then agreed to divide it between them. Within a year Edmund too had died and Cnut was declared king of all England.

At this time, Mercia was governed by King Æthelred's son-in-law, Ealdorman Eadric, called 'Streona', meaning the Acquisitive because of his appropriation of church property. During the Anglo-Danish wars this grasping and perfidious man had changed sides on a number of occasions. The wise Cnut showed great statesmanship by allowing Eadric Streona to keep the earldom of Mercia until the country was settled – then had him executed.

Cnut (or Canute) the Great was to rule an empire that stretched across the North Sea, including not only England and part of Scotland but also Denmark, Norway and part of Sweden. Between 1017 and 1035 Cnut consolidated his rule of England and attempted to bring about reconciliation between the Danes and the English. Although he was already married to an English noblewoman, Ælfgifu, he now married Emma, the Norman widow of Æthelred the Unready and he appointed Godwin, a powerful Saxon nobleman, to the militarily and symbolically important earldom of Wessex. This extended across the south of

A penny of King Cnut minted at Hereford by the moneyer Leofgar

England from Cornwall to Kent, roughly the same territory held by Alfred the Great. Cnut's marriage to Emma and the elevation of Godwin were to have crucially significant consequences for the future of England and, in particular, its border with Wales.

The succession to the throne of England was a complex issue during this period because of the number of rival candidates. After Cnut died, he was succeeded first by Harold Harefoot, his son by his English wife Ælfgifu, and then by Harthacanute, the son he had with Emma. Emma also had an older son, Edward, by her previous marriage to Æthelred, but Cnut had exiled him to prevent rivalry with his own sons. When Harthacanute died childless in 1042, Emma had sufficient leverage with both the English and the Danish nobility to bring Edward back from his exile in Normandy and have him crowned king. This remarkable woman had been married to two kings of England and had given birth to two more.

EDWARD AND THE GODWINSONS

The new king, Edward, known to us as the Confessor, was noted for his piety and was destined to be declared a saint. However, one of his first acts as king was to appropriate all his mother's treasure, because she had given him so little in the time before there was any prospect of his becoming king. This was done with the ready assistance of Earl Godwin, who had retained all the influence he had gained under Cnut and his sons. Edward then appointed Godwin's eldest son, Sweyn, to be earl of the shires of Hereford, Gloucester, Somerset and Oxford. Soon after, he took Godwin's daughter, Edith, to be his queen and he appointed Godwin's second son, Harold, to be the earl of East Anglia. Now in the possession of three earldoms covering virtually the entire south of England from the Welsh border to the Wash, Godwin and his six sons were by far the most powerful family in all England.

A penny of King Edward minted at Hereford by the moneyer Leothnoth

Sweyn Godwinson was a difficult man who seems to have caused problems wherever he went. Presumably with thoughts of making a bid for the crown, he claimed to be the son of King Cnut, although his mother vehemently denied this. It is likely that the only thing that saved him from execution was Edward's need to stay on the right side of the Godwin family.

Wales at that time was dominated by two rival kingdoms. Having taken charge of his earldom, Sweyn allied with Gruffydd ap Llewelyn, king of Gwynedd and Powys in the north, to mount an attack on Gruffydd ap Rhydderch, the king of southern Wales. Sweyn apparently achieved his objectives and was given hostages in the hope of ensuring peace in the future. On his way home he celebrated this successful outcome by ravishing the abbess of Leominster. For such a heinous crime, King Edward, ever an enthusiastic benefactor and defender of the Church's institutions, had Sweyn exiled. His earldom was divided between his brother Harold and a cousin, Beorn, who held the earldom of Middle Anglia. Sweyn stayed in Flanders for a time and then went on to Denmark. He soon found himself in some kind of trouble there, so returned to England and pleaded with King Edward to be reinstated. His brother Harold and cousin Beorn opposed this, as they were unwilling to give up what they had gained from his banishment. Sweyn was permitted to leave but came back again and hoodwinked Beorn into accompanying him to his ships on the pretext of their going to the king to plead his case again. Arriving at the ships, Beorn was abducted by Sweyn's men and then murdered. For this, the king and all the army declared Sweyn to be a *nithing*, a term of utter contempt, but Sweyn, now an outlaw, had already left again for Flanders.

In the same year, 1049, Gruffydd ap Rhydderch, saw the opportunity to take his revenge for Sweyn's raid on his kingdom. He procured the help of Irish Vikings who sailed up the River Usk in a fleet of 36 longships and then crossed the Wye to burn and plunder in Gloucestershire. The local people who attempted to oppose them were aided by a force led by Aldred, the bishop of Worcester, who 17 years later, as Archbishop of York, was to crown William the Conqueror at Westminster.

The disputed Welsh border was a perpetual problem, with Herefordshire and Welsh-speaking Ewyas and Archenfield being areas of particular contention. Here, where the gap in Offa's Dyke left the border ill-defined, King Edward tried out an innovative solution. During his exile in Normandy, he would have been aware of the effectiveness of the castles that the Normans were starting to build. On his return to England, Edward had brought many of his Norman friends with him and now he granted some of them land on the border and permitted them to build castles, the earliest to be seen in England. The first of these was built by Osbern Pentecost in the eastern part of Ewyas, later to be called Ewyas Harold. The English were not used to castles and resented this European influence. The Anglo-Saxon Chronicles reported, 'The foreigners had then built a castle in Herefordshire in Earl Sweyn's province, and inflicted every injury and insult they could upon the king's men thereabouts.' [4]

In 1050 Sweyn Godwinson was allowed to return again but soon there was an incident that opened up a rift between the Godwin family and King Edward. Count Eustace of Burgundy had paid a visit to Edward's court in Gloucester, and on his return journey home his men imposed themselves on the townsfolk of Canterbury and demanded accommodation. A fight ensued and soon turned into a pitched battle, resulting in a number of fatalities among both the townsfolk and the Burgundians. Eustace fled back to Gloucester and complained to the king, blaming the people of Canterbury for the affray. Edward ordered Earl Godwin to make a punitive assault on the town, but Godwin believed that the Burgundians had been to blame and refused to attack the people of his own earldom. A council meeting was called, and Godwin demanded that Eustace and his men be given into his hands and also the 'French' who were in the castle. Edward was advised by the Norman faction in court and backed by the other English earls, who doubtless would have wished to see the power of Godwin's family curtailed. Godwin's demands were refused and there was a stand-off between the forces of Godwin and his sons, and those of the king, which came near to outright conflict. Eventually, calm minds prevailed and both parties were persuaded to meet at a second council in London. Again, the two sides of the dispute arrived in force ready to do battle. This time Godwin and his sons decided to avoid further confrontation and slipped away during the night. Next day they were all declared outlaw. Godwin,

Sweyn and his younger brothers, Tostig and Gyrth, headed for safety in Flanders, while the other brothers, Harold and Leofwine, went over to Ireland.

With the Godwin family absent, Edward continued his policy of allowing Normans to build castles on the frontier with Wales. Richard FitzScrob erected a motte and bailey called Richard's Castle on the border between Herefordshire and Shropshire. When Gruffydd ap Llewelyn, the king of north Wales, raided the Leominster area in 1052, he had to fight against both the local people and 'Frenchmen' from the castle.[5]

Meanwhile, the Godwin family were preparing their comeback. Sweyn had gone on a penitential pilgrimage to Jerusalem and died on his way back, probably to the relief of his family. Godwin assembled a fleet at Bruges and made his way to the south coast of England where he was met by Harold, who had brought ships from Ireland. Together they sailed east to Kent and into the Thames estuary, gathering men and ships as they went. Edward had his ships and a land army waiting for them at London but neither side had the will to fight their own countrymen. A council was called to negotiate a peace, and Godwin and his sons were reinstated to their earldoms. The Norman faction, who had spread discord between the king and the Godwin family, were now in total disarray and found themselves outlawed. The archbishop of Canterbury and two other bishops who had replaced Anglo-Saxons fought their way to the coast and took ship back to Normandy. Osbern Pentecost abandoned his castle at Ewyas Harold and fled north to Scotland, where he joined forces with Macbeth, only to die at the battle of Dunsinane. Richard FitzScrob, however, was permitted to remain, as he was a friend of King Edward and had proved his use during the recent Welsh attack. Richard retained his castle after the Conquest and it was inherited by his son, Osbern.

In 1053, Godwin died and the earldom of Wessex passed to Harold Godwinson. Harold's earldom of East Anglia passed to Ælfgar, son of the earl of Mercia. Cross-border raiding continued unabated, so the English decided that the brother of the Welsh king, Gruffydd ap Llewelyn, should die because 'he did harmful things'. His head was delivered to King Edward, who was holding court at Gloucester, on Twelfth Night. Within months Welsh forces killed a large number of the English guard at Westbury. The chronicles don't say if this was Gruffydd ap Llewelyn attacking Westbury in Shropshire in revenge for his brother's death, or Gruffydd ap Rhydderch attacking Westbury near Gloucester. Soon after this, the confusion of having two King Gruffydds came to a decisive end. In 1055 the forces of Gruffydd ap Llewelyn defeated and killed his southern rival Gruffydd ap Rhydderch, and so, for the first time in its history, Wales was united under a single ruler.[6]

In the same year Ælfgar, the new earl of East Anglia, was convicted of treason and exiled from England, though according to the chroniclers he was blameless. He went to Ireland, where the Viking settlements were always a ready source of mercenaries, and raised a fleet of ships. Landing in north Wales, he joined Gruffydd ap Llewelyn who, now he was ruler of all Wales, was a force to be reckoned with, and together they marched on Hereford. At this time Herefordshire was part of the earldom of Ralph de Mantes, the nephew of King Edward and grandson of Æthelred the Unready. Ralph's men met the invaders two miles outside the town. He and his Norman officers elected to fight on horseback but the English troops were not accustomed to cavalry warfare and a rout ensued. It was said that Earl Ralph and the other Normans fled the field first, which earned him the nickname Ralph the Timid. The Irish and Welsh army now entered Hereford and stormed the minster in search of booty. The priests who tried to prevent them were killed and after the minster was ransacked for valuables, it was fired along with much of the town.

King Edward ordered an army to be recruited from across the country and assembled at Gloucester. Under Harold Godwinson's command, they followed Gruffydd's retreating forces back into Wales and 'encamped beyond Straddele'. Straddele, a corruption of the Welsh *Ystrad Dwr*, is the old name for the Golden Valley, beyond which lies the Welsh territory that later became Ewyas Lacy. Harold took part of his army back to Hereford where they repaired the city defences with a wide ditch, an earth embankment and gates. The rest of the army was ordered to remain in Wales and prepare for a Welsh attack. The Welsh attack failed to materialise and the English forces eventually withdrew, but Ælfgar's show of force had been enough to have him reinstated to his earldom in East Anglia.[7]

It is normal practice for an armed force waiting in enemy territory to dig in, making use of any existing fortification. This temporary advance of Harold's army into Wales,

The embankment at Longtown

ANGLO-SAXONS AND VIKINGS IN THE WELSH BORDERLANDS   103

provides the best explanation for what was revealed by the excavation on Longtown Castle Green – the massive enhancement of a Roman fort, resembling the rampart of an Anglo-Saxon *burh*, but without any obvious signs of a long-term occupation.

Two other locations have been suggested as the site of the English encampment – Snodhill in the Golden Valley and Mouse Castle near Hay-on-Wye. However, Snodhill was sometimes known as the Castle of Straddele, so could hardly be described as being 'beyond Straddele'. On the other hand, Mouse Castle is some distance north of the Golden Valley, overlooking the Wye. As neither of these sites shows any evidence of occupation by an Anglo-Saxon army, the Longtown rampart remains as the most likely candidate for the encampment of Harold's army.

Leofgar, Harold Godwinson's chaplain, was now appointed bishop of Hereford. He was clearly of a military persuasion, and kept his moustaches while a priest, although that was in contravention of canon law. This affectation may have been to imitate or flatter his patron, as Harold can be seen sporting the most exuberant moustaches in his portrayal on the Bayeux Tapestry. After his consecration, Bishop Leofgar immediately set out for Powys, along with Ælfnoth, the sheriff of Hereford, to campaign against King Gruffydd. This turned out to be another disaster for the people of Hereford. The campaign ended in a battle at Glasbury-on-Wye where both Leofgar and Ælfnoth were killed along with many of their men. Harold Godwinson had to come to the rescue of the defeated English army and agree peace terms with Gruffydd, who was persuaded to swear allegiance to King Edward.

Following the death of Ralph the Timid in 1057, the control of Herefordshire and Gloucestershire was added to Harold's huge earldom of Wessex. The border was not to remain at peace for long. Earl Ælfgar was expelled from England a second time and again resorted to an alliance with Gruffydd to persuade King Edward to reinstate him. This time they had the support of a fleet of Vikings from Norway, led by Magnus, the son of the Norwegian king, Harald Hardrada. The chronicler of Worcester who recorded these events, was apparently bored with goings-on along the Welsh border. He simply wrote, 'it is tedious to tell how it all happened.'[8]

Early in 1063, Harold Godwinson took measures to end the constant threat of Welsh raids on his earldom. With a small, mounted force, he made a surprise midwinter attack on Rhuddlan, King Gruffydd's capital on the River Clwyd in North Wales. Gruffydd managed to escape but Rhuddlan was burned along with some of Gruffydd's ships. The following spring Harold took a raiding fleet around Wales, while his younger brother Tostig overran the country with a land army. The Welsh, realising that their position was untenable, killed Gruffydd and sent his head to Harold as a peace offering. As demonstration of a job well done, Harold took the head to King Edward, along with the figurehead from Gruffydd's ship. Later, Harold went on to marry Gruffydd's widow, Ealdgyth. For just eight years Wales had been a unified country, but with Gruffydd's death it once again disintegrated into a number of smaller kingdoms.[9]

Harold's moustaches (*photograph © Mariana Ruiz Villareal*)

Describing Harold's campaigning a century later, Gerald of Wales wrote that, 'He advanced into Wales on foot, at the head of his lightly clad infantry, lived on the country, and marched up and down and round and about the whole of Wales with such energy that he left not one that pisseth against a wall.'[10]

It appears that Harold was able to extend his earldom into the Welsh kingdom of Gwent. A folk memory of this resulted in the row of three megaliths at Trellech becoming known as Harold's Stones. They reputedly mark where three Welsh chieftains fell in battle. In fact, the stones were almost certainly erected in the Bronze Age. Having conquered and apparently pacified the country, Harold decided to build a lodge in Gwent where he could invite King Edward to join him in hunting. The site he chose was at Portskewett on the Severn estuary, just west of the River Wye. He gathered together the necessary labour and construction materials but the project was abandoned when Caradog, the son of the former king of Gwent, Gruffydd ap Rhydderch, killed most of the workers.[11]

Harold's Stones at Trellech (*photograph © Nessy, CC BY-SA 4.0*)

Earl Harold would surely have taken his revenge on Caradog but his destiny led him elsewhere. King Edward's health had gone into decline and within a year he was dead. Harold Godwinson was offered the crown of England, but he immediately faced invasion threats from two rival claimants.

10

William FitzOsbern and the Norman Conquest

Stark man he was and great awe men had of him
William of Poitiers

Most of the English, sighing for their ancient liberties, were plotting for the purpose of recovering them
Orderic Vitalis

KING EDWARD HAD no direct heir so his succession was always going to be disputed. The Norman chroniclers later asserted that Edward had promised the throne of England to Duke William of Normandy and that Harold Godwinson had sworn an oath on holy relics to support William's claim. This event is shown on the Bayeux Tapestry.

Harold's oath to Duke William (*photograph © Myrabella CC0 1.0*)

On the other hand the Anglo-Saxon Chronicles say that on his deathbed, Edward named Harold as his successor. Both stories may be true. Based on their bloodlines neither of them had a particularly convincing claim to the throne. Perhaps Edward favoured William for a time because of his own association with Normandy, only later coming to realise that the English would never willingly kneel before a Norman, and that Harold was the only man who would be able to hold the country together. When Edward died, Harold was the man on the spot and was quickly crowned king in January 1066. King Harold immediately began to make preparations to repel an invasion from Normandy.

In Normandy, Duke William needed to assess the level of support he might have for a bid to take the English throne. One of his key advisors was the *dapifer* or high steward, William FitzOsbern. The two Williams were second cousins and longstanding friends. As high steward, William FitzOsbern was closely involved in the governance of Normandy, with responsibilities including financial, administrative and military matters. His father, Osbern, had been high steward before him and the guardian of the young William who, as a child, inherited the dukedom of Normandy.

William FitzOsbern was a strong advocate of the invasion of England and was probably well-informed of English affairs. His younger brother, called Osbern like their father, was chaplain to Edward the Confessor and would have been ideally placed to pass intelligence back to Normandy.

A council of the magnates of Normandy was summoned to determine what support there would be for an invasion. The barons were indecisive, with some in favour of Duke William's bid but others expressing reluctance to take part in a risky foreign venture. The barons proposed that William FitzOsbern should speak for them all. Instead of telling the duke of their uncertainty, he announced that every one of them would offer twice what his duty obliged him to do. He personally pledged 60 ships towards the invasion fleet in an attempt to shame the other barons into giving their full support. Duke William then spoke to each of the barons individually giving them little option but to give their backing for the invasion.[1]

INVASION

Duke William made his preparations and gathered his ships at Dives-sur-Mer on the coast of Calvados. The force included not only Normans but also Flemings, Bretons and contingents from other parts of France. The fleet was ready to sail by early August but a persistent wind from the north prevented their putting to sea. When a break in the weather eventually allowed them to embark, the storms soon returned and they only managed to move further up the coast, where they put in to Saint-Valery at the mouth of the Somme. Meanwhile, Harold's forces waited along the south coast of England with their fleet stationed at the Isle of Wight. By early September their supplies were running out and, since there was no sign of a Norman fleet, Harold decided that he could safely disband the army and send his ships along the coast to winter in the Thames at London.

Within days a Scandinavian fleet, led by Harald Hardrada, the king of Norway, landed without warning on the northeast coast of England. With him was Tostig, Harold's renegade younger brother, who had been expelled by his own people from the earldom of Northumbria and was looking for restitution. Harold was forced to reassemble his army and march north. The invaders were defeated at Stamford Bridge, not far from York on 25 September. Both Tostig and Harald Hardrada were killed, but Harold's difficulties were far from over.

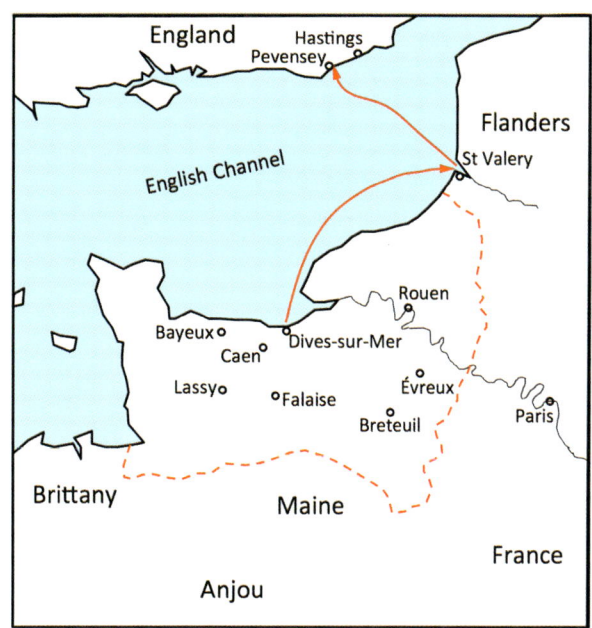

Normandy and the route taken by the invasion fleet

Three days later, the storms in the Channel having abated, Duke William's invasion fleet arrived at Pevensey on the south coast. Harold's depleted army now faced an exhausting 300-mile march to confront them.

Harold died at Hastings on 14 October. The battle lasted most of the day and there were set-backs on both sides, which suggests that the opposing forces were fairly evenly matched. Perhaps if the Norman fleet had not been delayed by the vagaries of the weather or if Harold had not been compelled to fight his brother Tostig and Harald of Norway, the battle might well have gone the other way and the subsequent history of Britain and northern Europe would have followed a very different trajectory. As it was, at Hastings England lost both its leader and the cream of its military might.

In London, on hearing of the death of Harold, the magnates and leading churchmen elected Edgar the Ætheling, the grandson of Edmund Ironside, to be king. But as William's army approached, support for Edgar melted away, leaving the way open for Duke William to be crowned at Westminster on Christmas Day. Initially, William made some efforts to work with the remaining Anglo-Saxon leadership; however, before long, nearly the whole ruling class of England had been replaced by the Normans and their allies.

When King William returned to Normandy in the spring of 1067, taking Edgar and a number of English earls with him to discourage any possibility of rebellion, he left England in the charge of two vice-regents. These were his half-brother, Odo, and the high steward, William FitzOsbern. Odo was bishop of Bayeux and one of the most important Norman commanders. He is portrayed in the Bayeux Tapestry as an arresting figure on horseback, in helmet and chain mail, wielding a huge club and rallying the troops. Odo had been given the earldom of Kent, with responsibility for guarding the eastern approaches to England. He also held numerous manors across 22 counties and was the wealthiest man in all England after the king. During King William's absence the two vice-regents had all but absolute power and the Anglo-Saxon Chronicles say, 'they built castles widely throughout this nation, and oppressed the wretched people.'[2]

Bishop Odo brandishing a club at Hastings. The Bayeux Tapestry ironically describes this as a baculu, meaning his bishop's staff of office (*photograph © Mariana Ruiz Villareal*)

One of the earliest castles to be built was within the city of Winchester. This was Alfred the Great's capital and therefore of huge symbolic significance for the English people. King William placed it under the control of his steward, William FitzOsbern. The grandest of the early castles, bigger even than the Tower of London and incorporating Roman building materials, was at Colchester, the provincial capital of Britain under the emperor Claudius. It seems that William was not only using castles to ensure the military security of his new domain but also to give an impression of continuity between his rule and earlier iconic regimes.

Although the main English forces were defeated, rebellions soon broke out across the country, from Durham to Exeter and from Cambridgeshire to the Welsh border.

Eadric, a nephew of Eadric *Streona*, the treacherous ealdorman of Mercia under King Æthelred, held out against Norman rule. From his lands in the north of Herefordshire and south Shropshire he waged a guerrilla campaign. In 1067, assisted by Welsh marauders, he pillaged as far as the River Lugg. When confronted by the garrison of the castle at Hereford Eadric retreated into the forests. Because of his hit-and-run tactics, the Norman chroniclers gave him the epithets *sauvage* and *silvaticus* meaning 'wild' and 'of the woods'.[3]

Two years later, Eadric the Wild and a force from Cheshire and Wales, lay siege to Shrewsbury. William FitzOsbern, who was temporarily governing York in the wake of a rebellion there, was ordered to go to Shrewsbury's relief. By the time he arrived, the town was burning and Eadric, along with his supporters, had again disappeared into the woods. William FitzOsbern and his men then had to continue their march south to help quell yet another uprising at Exeter.[4]

In 1070, King William led a retaliatory campaign into Wales and built castles at Chester and Shrewsbury.[5] This became the usual Norman response to rebellion – first bring in a punitive force to eliminate or disperse the insurgents and then construct a castle to impose order on the area.

It appears that King William had no immediate ambition to conquer Wales but he was well aware of the perpetual problems of the unsettled frontier. He decided to create three powerful earldoms along the border, centred on Chester, Shrewsbury and Hereford. These three cities were the most important commercial centres in the border area. They controlled the main navigable rivers and the old Roman roads that carried trade and military traffic into the west midlands of England. Chester, on the River Dee, had a circuit of Roman walls. Shrewsbury's security came from being almost entirely circled by a loop of the River Severn. Hereford on the River Wye had its Saxon defences but was less secure than the other two cities.

The king needed to put the border earldoms in the hands of experienced soldiers with a track record of working together. William FitzOsbern and Roger de Montgomerie had fought together on the right wing of the Norman army at Hastings, which included the contingent of fighters from Flanders.[6] King William put Gerbod the Fleming in charge of Chester, granted Shrewsbury to Roger and appointed William FitzOsbern to the earldom of Hereford.[7]

As the king's trusted deputy, William FitzOsbern was also given extensive territories corresponding to much of the vast earldom that had been held by Harold Godwinson, including the Isle of Wight. This meant that he not only had responsibility for defending the Welsh border but also for overseeing a huge stretch of coastline. During the early years of the eleventh century it had been a favourite strategy of Viking fleets to take over the Isle of Wight and use it as a base for raiding along the south coast of England. William FitzOsbern is attributed with building Carisbrooke Castle to secure the island and no doubt stationed part of his fleet there.

THE DEFENCE OF HEREFORD

Determined that Hereford would never again be pillaged and burned, Earl William developed a strategy to deter the Welsh princes from taking any further advantage of the disorder following the Norman invasion of England. He set about building a chain of castles to control the main incursion routes into Herefordshire.

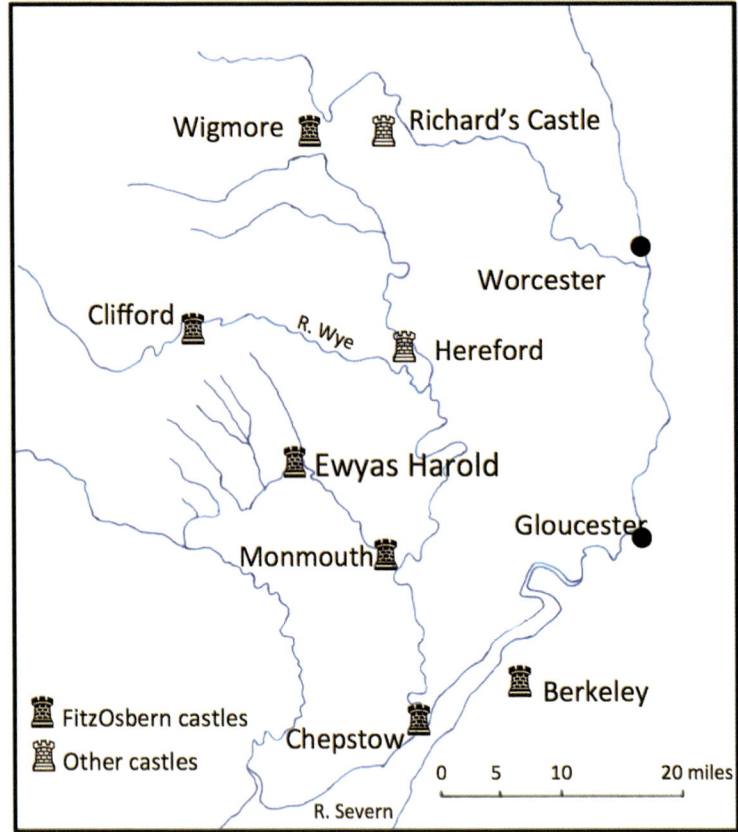

William FitzOsbern's castles protecting Hereford

Wigmore Castle, in the north of the earldom, was built between the Rivers Lugg and Teme, on the approach to Hereford along Roman Watling Street and near to the area that had been pillaged by Eadric the Wild. This was supported by Richard's Castle, built before the Conquest and still in the hands of King Edward's friend, Richard FitzScrob or his son, Osbern.

Earl William built Clifford Castle on waste land, possibly only recently taken from the Welsh, in order to command the approach to Hereford from the west, along the Roman road following the River Wye.

South-west of Hereford, Earl William re-fortified Osbern Pentecost's pre-Conquest castle at Ewyas Harold, which controlled the route to Hereford from South Wales and guarded the fertile lands of the Golden Valley.

To the south of Hereford, castles were built at Monmouth, where the River Monnow joins the Wye, and at Chepstow where the Wye enters the Severn. These two castles secured the river crossings used by the Roman roads leaving Gwent towards Gloucester and controlled the river-borne supply line to Hereford. They protected the important economic resources of the Wye Valley and the Forest of Dean – including iron working, timber, fisheries and millstone quarries – as well as the excellent hunting grounds beloved of the Norman aristocracy. Together with Berkeley Castle in Gloucestershire, Chepstow also oversaw the upper reaches of the Severn estuary and the seaborne approach to Gloucester.

Encroaching into Gwent and perched on a sheer cliff on the west side of the Wye, Chepstow Castle was clearly of particular importance to William FitzOsbern. While most early Norman castles were of timber, only later rebuilt in stone, Chepstow appears to have been built of stone from the outset, like King William's castles at London and Colchester. The oldest part, the Great Tower, is actually a magnificent Norman hall, 90 feet long and 30 feet wide internally, with two storeys over an undercroft. It was substantial enough for the Marshal brothers to add two more storeys in the thirteenth century. It makes use of Roman bricks and yellow sandstone, probably brought from Caerwent, the Roman town of *Venta Silurum*. The entrance was on the first floor, making it immune to attack by battering ram. The doorway has a splendid round arch and tympanum decorated with chip-carved saltires. The squared stones of the tympanum are set diamond fashion, in pink mortar made from crushed Roman tiles. The upper hall is accessed by a stairway in the thickness of the wall. The windows of both the upper and lower halls were on the secure eastern side, overlooking the Wye. The massive beams of the upper floor were capable of supporting a stone floor and a central hearth. Two walls are lined with round-arched alcoves, which probably provided sleeping places for the most honoured guests. While the Great Tower was readily defensible for its time, and obviously had an important military purpose, it smacks of being something of a vanity project. It has been argued that it may have been built by King William himself as an audience chamber, yet there is no record of his ever visiting Chepstow, and the Domesday Book clearly records that it was built by Earl William. Was William FitzOsbern setting out to prove that he could succeed where Harold Godwinson had failed and build a hunting lodge, fit for the king, inside Welsh territory?[8]

It is a remarkable achievement that all these castles were being built (if not completed) in the first five years after the Conquest. Each was carefully sited to counter specific threats and together they provided a strong defensive ring around William FitzOsbern's earldom of Hereford. He presumably consulted and had the benefit of intelligence from the Normans who had been in England during King Edward's reign, especially Richard FitzScrob who by now had nearly two decades' experience of living on the border.

Left: William FitzOsbern's Great Tower at Chepstow. *Right:* The tympanum incorporating Roman bricks

The area around a castle, known as a castlery, was effectively a military zone that was managed to provide the needs of the garrison of knights and foot-soldiers. Their primary roles were firstly deterrence and secondly 'holding the fort', in the event of an attack, until a relieving army could be deployed. The earls and senior barons held their land directly from the king as tenants-in-chief, in exchange for military service. To meet their obligations they in turn granted portions of land, known as *fees* or *fiefs* to vassals who would serve as knights. A knight's service normally meant providing an armoured and mounted warrior for 40 days per year, with squires and all necessary equipment. Knights might be employed in action or simply in garrisoning castles. This hierarchical arrangement for provision of military service in exchange for land became known as the feudal system.

In 1071, King William ordered William FitzOsbern across the Channel, to assist the queen in the defence and governance of Normandy. Baldwin, the duke of Flanders, had died, and the succession of this province bordering Normandy was disputed. Both Normandy and the king of France gave their backing to Baldwin's nominated heir, his second son, Arnold. But Baldwin's eldest son, Robert, had returned from banishment to claim his inheritance with an army of Frisians and the support of the Holy Roman Emperor. Uncharacteristically, William the Conqueror's finest military commander made a serious error of judgement. Back on his home territory after the rigours of the Welsh border, it seems that William FitzOsbern may have been in a holiday mood. 'Earl William joined the king with only ten men-at-arms, and rode with him gaily to Flanders, as if he was only going to a tournament.' When Robert's forces made a surprise attack, the king of France and his army were put to flight and the great William FitzOsbern was killed.[9]

11

Walter de Lacy I and the castles of Ewyas

The Normans built castles throughout the land and they oppressed the poor folk and wearied all England with their erections
                                                            Anglo-Saxon Chronicles

IN HIS DEFENCE of Herefordshire, William FitzOsbern had the assistance of another notable man – Walter de Lacy. Writing about 60 years after the Conquest, Orderic Vitalis recorded that King William granted

> the county of Hereford to William Fitz-Osbern, high steward of Normandy, giving him the charge, in conjunction with Walter de Lacy and other tried soldiers, of defending the frontier against the Welsh, who were breathing defiance. Their first expedition was a bold attack on the people of Brecknock in which the Welsh princes, Rhys, Cadogan and Meredith, with many others, were defeated.[1]

Walter de Lacy and his brother Ilbert de Lacy were two knights who became exceptionally wealthy and both founded highly influential dynasties on the borders of England. In Normandy, before the Conquest, the de Lacy brothers and their father, Hugh, were not great landowners nor members of the upper echelons of the aristocracy, although they were well connected. They held the village of Lassy in Calvados from Odo, the militant bishop of Bayeux, for a fee of two knights' service. This meant that in time of conflict Hugh was required to provide two fully armed and mounted men to fight on Odo's behalf. Odo is said to have pledged 40 ships towards the invasion fleet and may have actually provided 100. To fill them he would have called up a large contingent of his tenants owing knights' service, so it is not surprising that two of the de Lacy family are recorded as being at Hastings. It is unclear whether these were Hugh de Lacy and one of his sons, or the two de Lacy brothers (*see Appendix 2, p. 218*). However, very soon after the Conquest, Ilbert and Walter were both in England, but there is no record of Hugh, so it is likely that the two de Lacys who took part in the battle were Walter and Ilbert, leaving their father to look after the Normandy estates.[2]

Either at Hastings or when engaged in putting down later rebellions, the two brothers must have fought well, perhaps performing some outstanding service, because their rapid rise in fortune was truly remarkable. They were closely attached to King William's two vice-regents, with Ilbert de Lacy continuing to serve Bishop Odo in the north of England, while Walter's future was with William FitzOsbern on the Welsh border. (This book is concerned with Walter and his descendants but a brief summary of events concerning Ilbert's family can be found in Appendix 4, *see p. 228*).

As earl of Hereford and the southern Marches, William FitzOsbern granted huge amounts of land to Walter de Lacy. Walter also held manors as tenant-in-chief directly from the king. Some of these came from the estates previously owned by King Edward, Queen Emma and Harold Godwinson, which after the Conquest automatically became the property of King William.

THE DOMESDAY BOOK

We can get a fair assessment of the extent of Walter's holdings from the Domesday Book. In the winter of 1085 William the Conqueror ordered a survey of his kingdom. He instructed his commissioners to go out to every village and record how much land was farmed, who held it and what it was worth, both before the Conquest and at the time of the survey. The survey was intended to record lawful ownership for all time and so became known as the Domesday Book. It records the property held by Walter's son, Roger de Lacy, but since Walter died only a year before the Domesday Book was collated, it is reasonable to assume that nearly all Roger's holdings were previously held by Walter.

Much of the land owned by the de Lacys was strategically placed along the Welsh border in Shropshire, Herefordshire and Gloucestershire. The defence of these vulnerable frontier holdings was funded by more secure and lucrative properties away from the border in Worcestershire, Oxfordshire and elsewhere. In Herefordshire alone the de Lacy holding amounted to around 90 manors (detailed in Appendix 3, *see p. 220*). Walter also held land in the castleries of Clifford, Ewyas Harold and Chepstow, and would have been obliged to help defend these castles if they came under attack.[3]

Many of the de Lacy properties were sublet to tenants, who would either provide income or alternatively knight's service. The Domesday Book doesn't say how many of the de Lacy tenants were men-at-arms with a duty to fight on his behalf, but with so much property susceptible to cross-border raiding, he must have been able to raise a sizeable mobile fighting force at short notice. In the recently annexed territories of Archenfield and Ewyas, where indigenous Welshmen worked the land, rental could be paid in honey and livestock, as was customary under Welsh law.

The tenants' names indicate that about two thirds of them were Normans and only one third English or Welsh, giving an indication of how much land had been appropriated and reallocated to the invaders. Where tenure had continued from King Edward's time, it was sometimes drastically reduced. The wealthiest of the landholders before the Conquest had been an English nobleman called Edwy Cilt, who held 35 hides, valued at around £27. At the time of the Domesday Book, Edwy's son, Alwin, was left holding only five hides, worth £2.

Within the castlery of Ewyas Harold, the de Lacys had four ploughs equating to around 240 acres of land, worth 20 shillings a year. The Domesday Book also records a landholding in Ewyas that was beyond the castlery. This is the first known reference to Ewyas Lacy: 'Roger also has land called Ewias within the boundary of Ewias. This land does not belong to the castlery nor to the hundred. From this land Roger has 15 sesters of honey, 15 pigs when the men are there and hears their pleas.'[4]

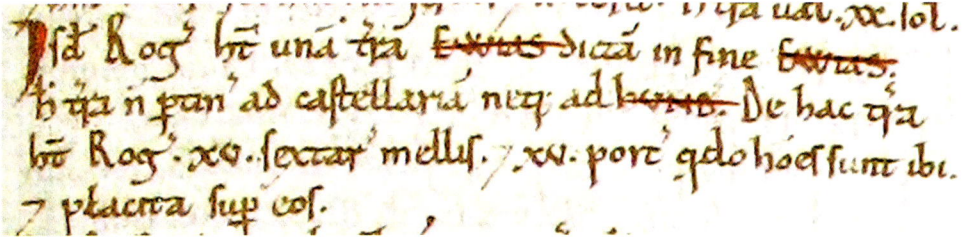

The entry for Ewyas in the Domesday Book

This entry is very unusual for the Domesday survey, for several reasons. No specific settlement is named. There is no information on the amount of land farmed. The name of the previous holder isn't given, nor that of any tenants. And importantly there is no assessment of its value, either before or after the Conquest. In fact the entry is so vague that it is unlikely that the king's commissioners ever went there, in which case, Roger might have under-reported its true value. On the other hand, in spite of lacking the usual details, this short paragraph conveys a great deal of information.

This block of land was outside both the castlery of Ewyas Harold and the hundred, meaning an administrative area of the county of Herefordshire. This tells us that before the Conquest it was a part of Wales. That Roger hears his tenants' pleas means that he was now the sole legal authority in the area and his tenants had no recourse to either the English or the Welsh justice systems.

The comment *'when the men are there'* has been interpreted as meaning that the population was nomadic. But nomads don't keep beehives or pigs, and they don't usually pay rent of any kind. It is more likely that the local Welsh population practiced transhumance, dividing their time between a *hendre* or winter farmhouse situated in the valley (as in Ponthendre) and a *hafod* or summer farmhouse used when they drove their stock up to the hills for the summer grazing. If Roger was understating the value of his holding, he may have been suggesting to the Domesday commissioners that it just wasn't worth an inspection visit, as they might not find anyone there.

The rent of 15 sesters of honey was equal to about 14kg. Before sugar was known in Britain, honey was a highly valued commodity. The Domesday Book says that according to the custom of Archenfield if anyone conceals one sester of honey from the customary due and this is proved, he pays five. Although there is no indication of the extent of this land holding in Ewyas, it is possible to get an idea of its size by looking at other land entries in the Domesday Book, where rent was paid in honey. In these areas of Wales only recently occupied, the cultivated land was traditionally measured in *carucates* or ploughs, rather than the English hide, and in the Herefordshire region a plough was equivalent to half an English hide or roughly 60 acres.

LOCATION	SESTERS OF HONEY	PLOUGHS
Caerleon	4	3½
Ewyas castlery	2	1
Ewyas castlery	7	6
Howle	18	11
Strangford	2	2
Wormelow	1	½
TOTAL	34	24

The honey rent per plough varied from one to two sesters, with an average of around 1.4 sesters. On this basis, Roger's 15 sesters of honey would be the rent from about 10.6 ploughs, so this holding was perhaps equivalent to 636 acres, roughly a square mile of cultivated land.

Feeding the ten or eleven plough teams, usually with six oxen to a plough, would have required extensive pasture and meadowland. Other cattle and sheep would also need grazing and fodder. The additional rental of 15 pigs suggests a herd of perhaps ten times that number, requiring a substantial acreage of woodland for its pannage of acorns and beech mast. It is clear that soon after the Conquest, the de Lacys were defending a large and valuable landholding within Wales. Ewyas Lacy was one of the earliest Marcher lordships, a more or less independent social, political and economic unit with its own laws and customs, and no assessment for tax.

Medieval ploughing from the Luttrell Psalter (*photograph* © *The British Library Board: MS 42130 f11*)

There were no maps showing the boundaries of the territory of Ewyas Lacy but by the time of the Domesday Book it probably included the entire upper catchment of the River Monnow and its tributaries, the Olchon and the Escley. At its northernmost extent, Roger (and presumably Walter before him) held Cusop from the king. To the east, Ewyas Lacy shared a boundary with the lordships of the Golden Valley and the castlery of Ewyas Harold. To the south, Roger held from Henry de Ferrers three churches, a priest and 32 acres of land paying two sesters of honey. The three churches were probably those at Llancillo, Rowlestone and Walterstone. These were originally all within the castlery of Ewyas Harold but were later transferred to Ewyas Lacy. To the west, the de Lacys controlled the valley of the River Honddu, known as the Vale of Ewyas.

WALTER'S CASTLES

There is no record that Walter de Lacy built castles, but he could hardly have been expected to carry out his commission to defend the border without them. The Domesday Book, usually so informative, is unhelpful with regard to castles, naming only four in the whole of Herefordshire. These are the two pre-Conquest castles of Richard's Castle and Ewyas Harold, and William FitzOsbern's castles at Wigmore and Clifford, which must have been built before his death in 1071. The Domesday Book makes no mention of Hereford Castle, which was certainly already in existence by 1067 when Eadric the Wild led his attack on its garrison, and it may well have been first built by Ralph the Timid some years before the Conquest. Clearly, the Domesday Book does not provide a comprehensive record of early castles. There are over 60 castle mottes in the county of Herefordshire and it is implausible that none of these was built along the troubled Welsh/ Herefordshire border in the 15 years between 1071 and 1086.[5]

In spite of the lack of documentary evidence, in view of the Normans' predilection for castles, it has to be assumed that the second greatest landholder in the county, in possession of numerous vulnerable border properties and a significant territory actually within Wales, was a castle builder. If we accept this assumption, it is possible to construct a reasonable hypothesis for the development of Ewyas Lacy, which explains why there is an unfinished castle at Ponthendre, little more than half a mile away from the castle at Longtown that later became the *caput* of Ewyas Lacy.

The subjugation of Ewyas Lacy would have begun from the pre-Conquest castle of Ewyas Harold, re-fortified by William FitzOsbern. Walter de Lacy held land and houses there, and there can be little doubt that it was he who advanced into Welsh-held Ewyas to build the motte and bailey at Walterstone – Walter's town.[6]

Siting his new castle on relatively flat ground suggests that Walter was minded to establish a borough there, though Walterstone was never to develop into anything beyond a village. The high motte was thrown up using the earth and stone from a very deep and wide ditch. While there is plenty of stone visible on the motte, there is no sign of any built structure, so it was presumably only ever topped with a timber tower.

Walterstone motte

The crescent-shaped bailey to the east of the motte would have housed a garrison. From here Walter could venture further into Welsh territory and also send advance warning to Ewyas Harold in the event of an attack from Gwent or Brycheiniog. Doubtless, the castles of Ewyas Harold and Ewyas Lacy would have been mutually supportive and they were near enough to provide reinforcements to each other if ever the necessity arose. The question is, what happened next?

A glance at the map shows that once Longtown Castle was founded, a castle at nearby Ponthendre would be completely pointless. Therefore, the Ponthendre earthworks must have been built before Longtown Castle was established. That then raises the questions of when was Ponthendre constructed and why wasn't it built at the more strategically advantageous site of Longtown?

Longtown had been the site of a Roman fort that had been reinforced by Harold Godwinson's army only a decade before. With the country in turmoil in the years immediately after

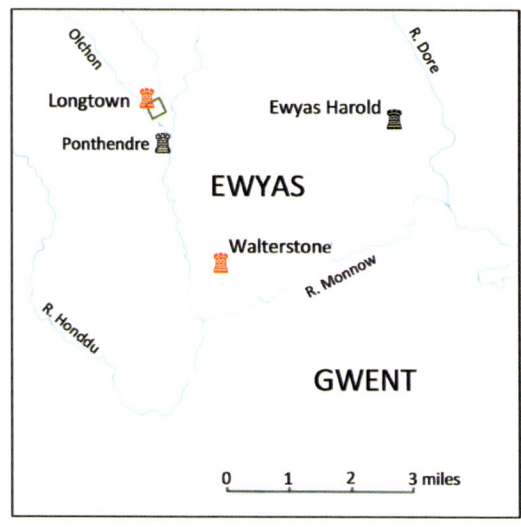

The early castles of Ewyas

120   THE MARCH OF EWYAS

the Conquest, it would be remarkable if a strategic site such as this were not occupied and defended. We cannot be sure who the occupants were but they were probably local Welshmen, perhaps reinforced by an advancing force from Brycheiniog and maybe even including English troops retreating before the Norman advance. The only certainty is that in those troubled times the fort at Longtown must surely have been occupied by a force hostile to the Normans. This would have posed a serious military threat to both Walter de Lacy's castle at Walterstone and William FitzOsbern's at Ewyas Harold.

Walter must have been faced with a difficult choice. He could either eliminate the threat, with the risk of heavy casualties, or else try to contain it. William FitzOsbern and Walter de Lacy had been charged with defending the border. In the early years after the Conquest the Normans had to contend with numerous English uprisings and foreign invasions. They were frequently overstretched and it is easy to understand why Walter might have preferred a policy of containment rather than taking an aggressive stance against the Welsh occupying a well-defended position.

This would account for the decision to start building a motte and bailey castle at Ponthendre, on the northern boundary of Clodock, guarding the road from Longtown where it crosses the Olchon Brook. However, our excavations proved that this castle was never completed. The occupants of the Longtown fort certainly would not have appreciated a castle being built just over half a mile south of their position and were doubtless 'breathing defiance'. The Normans' response to any opposition was invariably draconian. This may have been the impetus for William FitzOsbern and Walter de Lacy's attack against the people of Brycheiniog, mentioned by Orderic Vitalis. Clearing the fort at Longtown would have been a sensible preliminary to this action, so as not to leave a hostile force behind their lines.

Having driven the Welsh out, Walter could now utilise the rampart at Longtown to build a new and more easily defended castle, while preventing its re-occupation by hostile elements. A tall motte was raised on the north-west corner of the rampart to take advantage of the groundwork already completed by the Romans and the Anglo-Saxons. It is likely that most, if not all, of the earth and stone used to build the motte came from cutting through the rampart in two places and then digging a circular moat linked with the rampart ditch (*see plan, p. 55*). Another ditch was then cut from the motte moat to near the southern entrance of the rampart where it again joined the rampart ditch, isolating the western third of the embanked enclosure to make an inner bailey. The motte would then have been topped with a timber tower, probably surrounded by a wooden palisade. The embankment around the three sides of the bailey would also have had a palisade whose ends joined the palisade around the top of the motte. A gateway was installed approximately midway along the eastern side of the bailey. It was then necessary to make two further openings through north and south sides of the rampart to allow the roadway to pass alongside the castle. These were probably gated.

With the newly created territory of Ewyas Lacy now safely triangulated by the three castles of Ewyas Harold, Walterstone and Longtown, the uncompleted castle at Ponthendre would have become an irrelevance that could be safely abandoned.[7]

Castle building in Ewyas did not stop with Longtown. Two more motte and bailey castles were sited between Ewyas Harold and Walterstone. Another two were added to the west of Walterstone, at Tre-fedw and Pen-y-Clawdd, guarding the entrance to the Vale of Ewyas. Together they form a chain of six castles, on average only one and a half miles apart from each other, marking the southern border of Ewyas. Apart from Ewyas Harold, there is no record of when any of these small castles was built. It is possible that they were all constructed at different times, but their location and closeness to each other strongly suggest that they were intended to be an integrated frontier defence system along the border between Ewyas and the Welsh kingdom of Gwent.

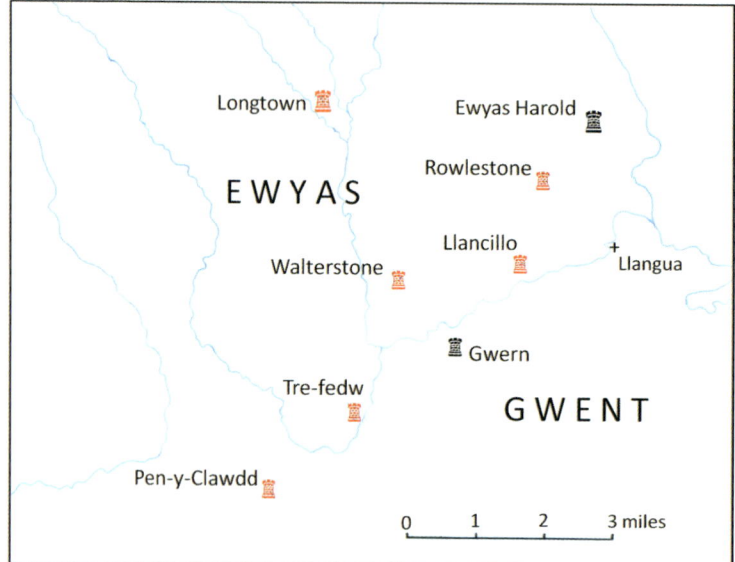

Left: The Ewyas/ Gwent border. The de Lacy castles are shown in red

Below: The small motte at Tre-fedw with the Skirrid in the background

According to the Book of Llandaff, at the time of the Norman Conquest, Ewyas was ruled by Rhydderch ap Caradog of Gwent. Ewyas and Ystradyw in Breconshire are quaintly described as 'the true sleeves of Gwent', as if these separate entities were seamlessly joined like the sleeves of a tunic or mail shirt. After Walter de Lacy tore Ewyas away from Gwent, it is logical that Gwent represented the main threat to his new territory. Anchored at one end by William FitzOsbern's castle of Ewyas Harold, this chain of new castles would have been manned by Walter's tenant knights and men-at-arms.[8]

The kingdom of Gwent did not survive for long after the Conquest. By the time of the Domesday Book, there was already a Norman castle at Gwent's administrative centre of Caerleon, tenanted by Turstin FitzRolf, King William's standard-bearer at Hastings. This indicates that Gwent had collapsed to Norman encroachment by 1086 and was no longer a viable military force. But the eastern part of Gwent had capitulated much earlier. William FitzOsbern's castles at Monmouth and Chepstow had encroached on Gwent territory and, before 1071, he granted land to a newly founded religious house at Llangua on the Gwent side of the River Monnow, south of Ewyas. This suggests that the small motte of Gwern Castle across the river from Walterstone was probably built by one of William FitzOsbern's knights.[9]

With Gwent under Norman control, there would no longer have been a requirement for such a concentration of military force along the border. It is therefore reasonable to conclude that the string of de Lacy castles was built during the first five years after the Conquest.[10]

Four of the castles have high mottes, but Rowlestone and Pen-y-Clawdd have low mottes of around 4m and 2.5m respectively. The raising of these mottes may have been terminated before reaching their planned heights, when Gwent was annexed. The resulting low mottes may then have been used for fortified houses rather than castles.

Although the threat from Gwent had diminished, the southern boundary of Ewyas still retained some of its importance. It flanked a section of one of the routes that could potentially be used by an army coming out of south Wales towards Hereford and the Midlands. For this reason, the castle of Ewyas Harold was rebuilt in stone and probably remained in use until the fourteenth or fifteenth century. At Llancillo, a tenant of the de Lacys replaced the timber tower on the motte with a polygonal stone shell keep, probably in the twelfth or thirteenth century. It is not known how long the other fortifications in the defensive chain along the southern border of Ewyas Lacy remained in use but in all likelihood they were soon abandoned.

There are no similar lines of defence along the other boundaries of Ewyas Lacy. The north was protected only by Mouse Castle and a possible ringwork or fortified house in Cusop. Mouse Castle is a motte and bailey with a stunning view over a lengthy stretch of the Wye Valley and a direct line of sight to the castles at Clifford, Hay and Clyro. A double embankment on the eastern side suggests that the castle probably used the earthworks of a small Iron Age fort. The side of the five-metre high motte appears to have been quarried in later times, perhaps as a source of road stone, so it is possible that it was originally higher than it is now. There is no record of who built Mouse Castle. It may have been Walter de Lacy or his son, Roger, although the location on a natural hill overlooking the river valley is typical of the sites favoured by William FitzOsbern. The name Mouse Castle apparently comes from the Welsh *llygod* meaning mice, a confusion with *llygad,* which means an eye and signifies the castle's important role as a lookout over the Wye Valley. The embanked area would have been capable of housing a sizeable garrison under the command of one of the de Lacy's knights.

The eastern boundary of Ewyas Lacy, abutting the settled Golden Valley with its castles at Urishay, Snodhill and Dorstone, had no need of serious defences. Only at Bacton is there a low motte that may have been raised only for a fortified house. In 1086 it was held by a de Lacy tenant called Gilbert. Gilbert is a common enough name but it is one used by the de Lacys, so he may have been a junior member of the family.

The western boundary of Ewyas was ill-defined, with no fortifications at all. Having soundly beaten the forces of Brycheiniog (although without annexing any of their territory), it seems that Walter felt that the difficult terrain was defence enough. This was to cause serious problems in the future, as it left Llanthony Priory in the Vale of Ewyas vulnerable to frequent raiding during the next two centuries.

LORD OF EWYAS

No doubt the local Welsh people would have resented being coerced into building castles for their new lord, but in time they may well have come to appreciate the relative security and stability that they brought. With their military and organisational superiority, the Normans were probably seen as offering the best chance of deterring the incursions of both Anglo-Saxon and Welsh marauders. The Welshmen of neighbouring Archenfield, which had been laid waste by King Gruffydd of Powys in the time of King Edward, appear to have preferred first English and then Norman rule to that of their own countrymen. The Domesday Book relates that when the sheriff of Hereford took an army into Wales, the Welshmen of Archenfield by custom formed the vanguard and, on their return, the rearguard. Clearly, they could be trusted to perform these very important roles.[11]

There is perhaps an insight into Walter's relationship with his new tenants in the fact that even though he chose to build the castle at Longtown, the ancient parish church at Clodock retained its status. It also kept its Welsh dedication to Saint Clydawg even though he would have meant nothing to the de Lacys. It seems that the de Lacys were reluctant to disturb the *status quo* and wanted to avoid causing unnecessary offence to the local population.

After the death of William FitzOsbern, Walter de Lacy had a new overlord. Earl William's estates were divided between his two sons. The eldest son inherited the family lands around Breteuil in Normandy. His second son, Roger de Breteuil, inherited the earldom of Herefordshire, though with neither the exceptional powers held by his father, nor the confidence of King William. Roger was dissatisfied with his lot and in 1075, while celebrating the marriage of his sister Emma to Ralph Guader, the earl of Norfolk, he and the groom plotted to depose King William. Ralph, who was part-Breton, persuaded other Bretons to join the revolt and, in time-honoured tradition, the Danes were invited to send a fleet to support the uprising. Earl Waltheof of Northumbria was initially part of the plot but soon had second thoughts and confessed all, first to the archbishop of Canterbury and then to William, who was in Normandy.

After the wedding Earl Roger returned to Hereford to marshal his forces. Walter de Lacy now faced the stark choice of either backing his sworn liege lord or maintaining his loyalty to King William. He wisely chose the latter option. When Earl Roger and his troops set out to join up with those of Earl Ralph, they were prevented from crossing the River Severn by the bishop of Worcester's militia, supported by Walter de Lacy and his men-at-arms. Meanwhile, near Cambridge, the other rebel army under Earl Ralph was met by a superior Anglo-Norman force under Bishop Odo, who was looking after the kingdom during King William's absence. Ralph fled to Brittany and the Revolt of the Earls collapsed. Regardless of their rank, those rebels who were taken captive had their right foot hacked off.

When the Danish fleet arrived, they soon realised that things weren't going to plan. Not wanting to go home empty-handed, they sailed north and sacked York Minster before returning to Denmark.

On the king's return to England, Roger de Breteuil was summoned to court and arrested. The seditious son of William's faithful steward and commander was then stripped of his earldom and sentenced to life imprisonment. He wasn't to regain his freedom until after King William's death. The Bretons who had taken part in the conspiracy were put on trial. Some were exiled, while many were blinded. Earl Waltheof, who had warned William about the plot against him and hadn't actually taken part in the fighting, was beheaded. He was the last of the Anglo-Saxon earls who had held on to their positions under Norman rule and the only one to be executed.[12]

Walter de Lacy, a tried and tested soldier, had demonstrated his loyalty to King William by taking up arms against his own overlord. In the aftermath of the rebellion, Walter might have been a candidate to replace Roger de Breteuil as earl of Herefordshire, but instead King William allowed the earldom to lapse and distributed its lands and castles among a number of notable barons, thereby preventing any one of them from becoming too powerful. Walter may have been rewarded with some of Roger's lands and he became tenant-in-chief from the king for those lands he had previously held from the earl.

Walter de Lacy held land in each of the castleries of Ewyas Harold, Clifford and Chepstow, and so should have been a clear candidate to receive at least one of the castles built by William FitzOsbern. The probable reason that he received neither the earldom nor even one of the castles was because he was already in possession of a substantial power base along the border. With the removal of Roger de Breteuil, Walter de Lacy was now the wealthiest and most powerful man in Herefordshire. It seems likely that by that time, as well as having castles in Ewyas, Walter would have already founded castles to defend his lands around Weobley and Ludlow. The location of the major de Lacy castles strongly suggests that they were sited to complement those built by William FitzOsbern to defend Hereford.

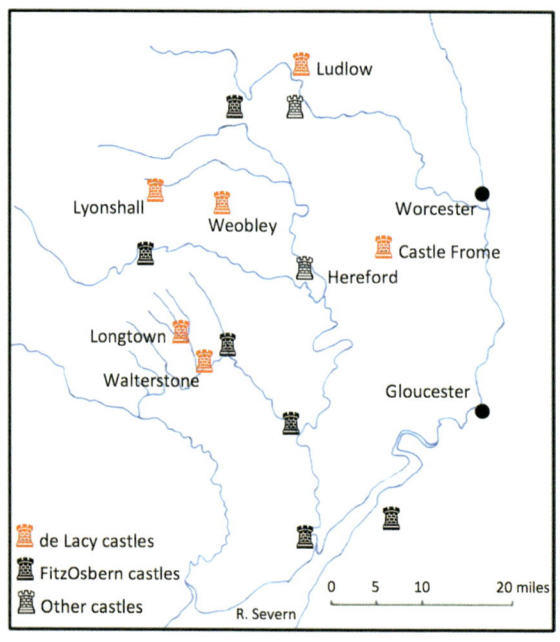

The principal de Lacy castles in the southern Marches

Walter de Lacy was not only concerned with defence. Before 1081 he took part in a concerted attack by all the most important Marcher lords, striking deep into Welsh territory. His knights joined the men of the earl of Shrewsbury, the earl of Chester and Robert of Rhuddlan on a plundering raid that went as far as the Llŷn Peninsular on the north-west coast of Wales. When properly undertaken, campaigns such as this could be very profitable and they also served to demonstrate the Norman's military superiority over the Welsh, while exploring the possibilities of permanent conquest.[13]

The arms of Walter de Lacy (taken from The Ludlow Castle Heraldic Roll, Logaston Press, 2019. Photograph © Friends of Ludlow Museum)

Approaching old age after a lifetime of warfare, like many Normans, Walter gave consideration to his spiritual wellbeing. He donated his manor of Lea to the church of St Peter in Gloucester and enrolled his son there as a novice monk. He endowed St Peter's in Hereford with the manor of Priors Frome and land in Ocle Pychard. He was enthusiastically involved with building a church or churches in Hereford, dedicated to St Peter and to St Guthlac, possibly a single foundation with a dual dedication. Ironically, Walter met his untimely end in 1084 or 1085, not in battle with the Welsh, but by falling from scaffolding while inspecting the building work at his church in Hereford.[14]

12

Roger de Lacy – rebel

*The chiefs … who had the custody of the castles, treated the natives,
both gentle and simple, with the utmost scorn*

Orderic Vitalis

O<small>N</small> W<small>ALTER'S DEATH</small>, Roger de Lacy inherited his father's vast estates and became by far the biggest individual landowner in Herefordshire, outdone only by the king and the Church. This brought him the revenues from around 90 manors with over 200 hides. At around 120 acres to the hide, that amounts to some 25,000 acres of ploughland. He also received additional income from the rental of burgesses in the towns, valuable fisheries on the River Wye and 14 mills. Some of these paid a rental of eels caught in the millstreams. At Weobley, Roger enjoyed the privilege of having his own hunting park.[1]

Roger and his tenants kept over 200 slaves, both male and female, spread across many of his manors in Herefordshire. This was quite normal for the time, and even the manors belonging to the Church were often worked by slaves. The Anglo-Saxons, Welsh, Danes and Normans were all involved in slavery, and raiders routinely took captives as booty to sell as slaves. It was another century before the practice of slavery was discontinued and the slaves were absorbed into the general population of serfs, still tied to the land and with limited customary rights but not liable to be sold.

In spite of his having a huge landholding, Roger had no lucrative boroughs. Perhaps Roger considered Ewyas Lacy to be too isolated for planning a new town there and it appears that his interests lay further north, focused on his holdings around Weobley and the manor of Stanton Lacy in Shropshire. It is likely that Roger would have continued his father's programme of castle-building to secure his inheritance. A large castle was developed at Weobley, probably originally founded by Walter, but nothing remains except for its slighted earthworks. These have not been dated but Weobley appears to have been a substantial fortification and became the de Lacy *caput* or headquarters in northern Herefordshire. A market town grew up around the castle, which in subsequent years developed into a borough.

When the Domesday Book was written in 1086, the centre of de Lacy wealth in Shropshire was around Stanton Lacy. Here Roger had enough land for 50 ploughs, about 3,000 acres. This flourishing community had a church with two priests, two smiths, two mills and 28 slaves. Near here the de Lacys built the most important of their castles at Ludlow, on a promontory protected by a bend in the River Teme. Although its foundation cannot be precisely dated, it is one of the earliest castles in the Welsh Marches to be built in stone, rather than timber. It was probably begun by Walter de Lacy and then continued by Roger and his brother Hugh. A planned town grew up around the castle in the twelfth century and it was walled and gated in the thirteenth.[2]

Roger was certainly a powerful and ambitious man. With the knights' fees and income from his properties around Ewyas, Weobley and Ludlow, he could raise a considerable fighting force in times of trouble, and it was not long before trouble arrived.

William the Conqueror died in 1087, leaving three sons. The eldest of these, Robert Curthose, inherited the dukedom of Normandy. The nickname, 'Curthose', or short stockings, was given to him by his father and it seems to have stuck. Next in line was William, called Rufus for his red hair or complexion. He inherited the crown of England. The youngest son, Henry, received a large sum of cash. If Robert was disappointed with his inheritance and thought he was entitled to England as well as Normandy, he was forestalled by William Rufus who quickly took control of his new kingdom. This left the Norman barons with a difficult problem. Most of them had land and castles in both Normandy and England, and now owed loyalty to two liege lords who could soon be at war with each other. They needed to consider where their best interests lay.

REBELLION

A plot soon developed to depose William Rufus and reunite England and Normandy under Robert Curthose, the Conqueror's eldest son. This appears to have been instigated by Bishop Odo and his brother, Robert the count of Mortain. They were both half-brothers of William the Conqueror, uncles to Robert Curthose and William Rufus, and enormously influential with the barons on both sides of the channel.

In 1088 they declared open rebellion against William and were supported by many barons across the whole country. The rebels fortified their castles and began pillaging the estates of the king and those who remained loyal to him. The Northumbrians, as ever, were quick to join the uprising. Under their earl, Robert Mowbray, they raided as far south as Bristol and Bath, while the bishop of Durham harried the north. William, the count of Eu in Normandy and lord of Hastings, attacked and burned Gloucester and the king's estate at Berkeley.[3]

Meanwhile, Roger de Lacy 'wrested Hereford from the king' and then joined a coalition of other Marcher lords who backed Robert Curthose. These included Roger de

Bishop Odo and Robert of Mortain sitting either side of King William as shown on the Bayeux Tapestry (*photograph © Myrabella CC0 1.0*)

Montgomery the earl of Shrewsbury, Ralph Mortimer of Wigmore, Osbern the son of Richard FitzScrob, Bernard de Neufmarché of Snodhill and Robert of Rhuddlan who held North Wales. They marched on Worcester, determined to take the city and loot the minster. The Norman barons may have been generous in their donations to the Church, but when it came to the necessities of paying their armies they showed little if any compunction about robbing a neighbour's churches. The elderly Bishop Wulfstan, who in William the Conqueror's time, with help from Walter de Lacy, had thwarted Roger de Breteuil's rebellion, took refuge in the castle. He told his household that they would come to no harm and sent them out to help the garrison and citizens of Worcester confront Roger de Lacy and his confederates. It is difficult to explain how the experienced and battle-hardened soldiers of the Marches came to be so comprehensively beaten. Florence of Worcester says that they were stricken by an affliction that rendered them blind and enfeebled. Robbed of their senses they were unable to defend themselves or run away and were easily taken captive by the bishop's men. It would appear that Bishop Wulfstan had, for a second time, thwarted an uprising from the Marches.[4]

Although the threat from the Marches evaporated, the rest of the country was still in turmoil. In the south-east of England Bishop Odo pillaged the king's lands to stock his castles in Kent where he and his accomplices meant to take a stand to await the arrival of Robert Curthose with Norman reinforcements. However, in Normandy, the duke was taking his time mustering the army and preparing an invasion fleet. An advance force set sail, but it was intercepted by the English fleet and returned to Normandy.

William Rufus offered land and treasure to those Normans who would support him, and to the English he promised 'the best law that has ever been in this land.' Many of the English gave William their backing, preferring their independence, albeit under a Norman king, to subservience to Normandy itself. Profiting from this support, William advanced into Kent at the head of a largely English army. The castle at Tonbridge quickly surrendered and the army moved on to Odo's castle at Rochester. Here they learned that Odo had fled to Pevensey where he would be nearer to a landing by the expected Norman fleet. The siege of Pevensey lasted for six weeks until eventually, with their supplies exhausted and no sign of relief from Normandy, Odo and his supporters were forced to surrender. Peace terms were negotiated and Odo agreed to deliver up his castle at Rochester, which was still holding out. He travelled there under escort but when the defenders saw him they sallied forth, overpowered his guards and took him into the castle. William Rufus and his army now had to lay siege to Rochester. They built two forts to prevent anyone escaping. The defenders, packed into the confined space of the castle, were greatly troubled by a plague of flies that bred in the amassed dung of men and horses. Eventually, they could bear it no longer and surrendered.

The English besiegers wanted to hang Odo for the outrages he had inflicted on the country. William Rufus was also minded to execute the leaders of the rebellion but his advisors persuaded him to treat the rebels with clemency, so that they would give him their support in the future. Bishop Odo swore that he would never oppose

William again and his life was spared, but he was stripped of his English lands and permanently exiled to Normandy. William Rufus had little option but to pardon Roger de Lacy and the other rebellious Marcher barons, as collectively they controlled and maintained order along virtually the entire length of the Welsh borderlands.

With the rebellion behind them, the Marcher lords turned their attention to Wales. Roger de Montgomery, Ralph Mortimer, Ralph Tosny of Clifford and others advanced into Radnorshire. Roger de Lacy was ideally positioned to expand his territory westwards. Gwent was no longer a threat and his father, Walter, with William FitzOsbern had beaten the men of Brycheiniog in battle. But now it was Bernard de Neufmarché who took control of Brycheiniog and built a castle at Brecon. Strangely, there is no indication that Roger de Lacy made any attempt to move further into Wales and it is possible that the king had ordered him not to do so.[5]

William Rufus himself campaigned in Wales, which meant taking an army through the Marches. This show of force was perhaps aimed as much at the troublesome Marcher lords as at the unruly Welsh. It is not recorded which of them accompanied the king. The campaign was not a success. Faced with a fearsome but slow-moving royal army, the Welsh employed hit-and-run tactics, making use of the terrain and the weather. When opportunities arose they picked off men and horses or robbed the baggage train before disappearing again into the hills and the mist. 'Before the onslaught of the *Saes*, the *Cymru* melted like the snow. At night they came back like the ice, to nip the finger and the toe.'[6]

In 1095 Roger de Lacy was implicated in another conspiracy to replace William Rufus, led by Robert Mowbray, the earl of Northumbria, and William d'Eu. It began when Mowbray seized some merchant ships. When the owners took their complaint to the king, he summoned Mowbray to court to explain himself. Mowbray refused to attend and began plotting with others to depose William Rufus and replace him with his cousin, Stephen of Aumale. The king acted quickly. He took an army north and trapped Mowbray in his castle at Bamburgh. Perched high on a crag overlooking the North Sea, Bamburgh was virtually impregnable. Rather than attempting to storm the castle, William Rufus ordered Bamburgh to be blockaded with a counter-castle. It was named *Malvoisin*, meaning 'Bad Neighbour'. After a while, Mowbray managed to evade the blockade and fled to Newcastle. In the fighting that took place there, Mowbray was wounded and taken prisoner.

Hugh Montgomery, the earl of Shrewsbury, was involved in the uprising, and in his absence the Welsh took the opportunity to take his castle at Hen Domen and killed many of his men. In response, William Rufus once more took his army into Wales and campaigned as far as Snowdonia, but the Welsh again refused to engage and William had to withdraw having lost both men and horses.

Bamburgh was still being held by Mowbray's wife and his steward, so the king ordered Mowbray to be taken there and threatened to put out his eyes unless the castle yielded. Having handed it over, the steward bought his freedom by naming other conspirators. Roger de Lacy was accused but how he was involved is not recorded. The chronicler William of Malmesbury wrote, 'The same accusation involved many innocent and honourable men.'[7]

With Mowbray in captivity, the revolt quickly crumbled. William Rufus was in no mood to extend clemency to those implicated in revolt a second time and imposed harsh penalties on the perpetrators. Robert Mowbray was imprisoned for life and his earldom transferred to his brother. William d'Eu faced trial by combat and lost. Subsequently he was blinded and castrated. Hugh de Montgomery, the earl of Shrewsbury, kept his estates but had to pay an enormous fine of £3,000, several million pounds in today's money. Roger de Lacy was stripped of his lands in England and Wales, and was exiled for life. The honours of Ewyas Lacy, Weobley and Ludlow were bestowed on his younger brother, Hugh de Lacy.[8]

William Rufus showed great political skill and expediency in sentencing the rebels. Robert Mowbray was a hostage for the good behaviour of the north. The critically important defence of the Welsh Marches remained intact. The harsh fate of William d'Eu was an example to anyone else who might consider insurrection.

Roger de Lacy went to Normandy where he took service with Robert Curthose. By 1102 he had become commander of Robert's knights but he developed a bad reputation. In 1119, during a conference between King Henry I and Pope Calixtus on the future of Normandy, Henry remarked how, 'Roger de Laci … and other miscreants oppressed the Normans … domineered over the bishops, the clergy and the whole defenceless people.'[9]

13

Hugh de Lacy I – a nobleman of noble behaviour

Here in Llanthony let them rather turn their minds towards the promise of eternal bliss
Gerald of Wales, 1191

After Roger was expelled from England, his huge landholding was granted by King William to his younger brother, Hugh de Lacy, who had 'faithfully kept his fealty' during the rebellion. Unlike his brother, it seems that Hugh kept a low profile and little is recorded about him or his actions during his two decades or so as lord of the honours of Ewyas, Weobley and Ludlow. He and his wife Adeline had no sons but they raised a daughter called Sybil.[1]

In 1097, tired of unrest in the Marches, William Rufus took another army into Wales, according to Florence of Worcester, 'vowing that he would exterminate the whole male population'. Several of the Marcher lords would have been required to ride with William's army and provide men, but if Hugh played any part in the action it was not recorded. The campaign lasted most of the summer, with the Welsh retreating before the English army and refusing to engage in battle, but picking off men and horses whenever the opportunity arose. Realising that he was not achieving his objectives, William returned to England and ordered more castles to be built along the border.[2]

Although little is known of Hugh's life, momentous events were happening in the world around him. In the same year as Hugh was granted the de Lacy lordship, Pope Urban II called on Christians in western Europe to go to the aid of the Byzantine Empire that was losing ground in Anatolia to Turkish invaders. Robert Curthose, the duke of Normandy, decided to joined the First Crusade. Being desperately short of cash he raised the finances needed by handing Normandy over to his brother, William Rufus, in exchange for a loan of 10,000 marks. Bishop Odo of Bayeux, the tenant-in-chief of the de Lacy lands in Normandy, set off in Robert's company but died en route at Palermo in Sicily.

Arriving in Anatolia, the crusaders pushed back the Turks to relieve the pressure on the Byzantines. They then fought their way along the east Mediterranean coast to Palestine. In 1099, after a debilitating siege lasting five weeks, they finally captured

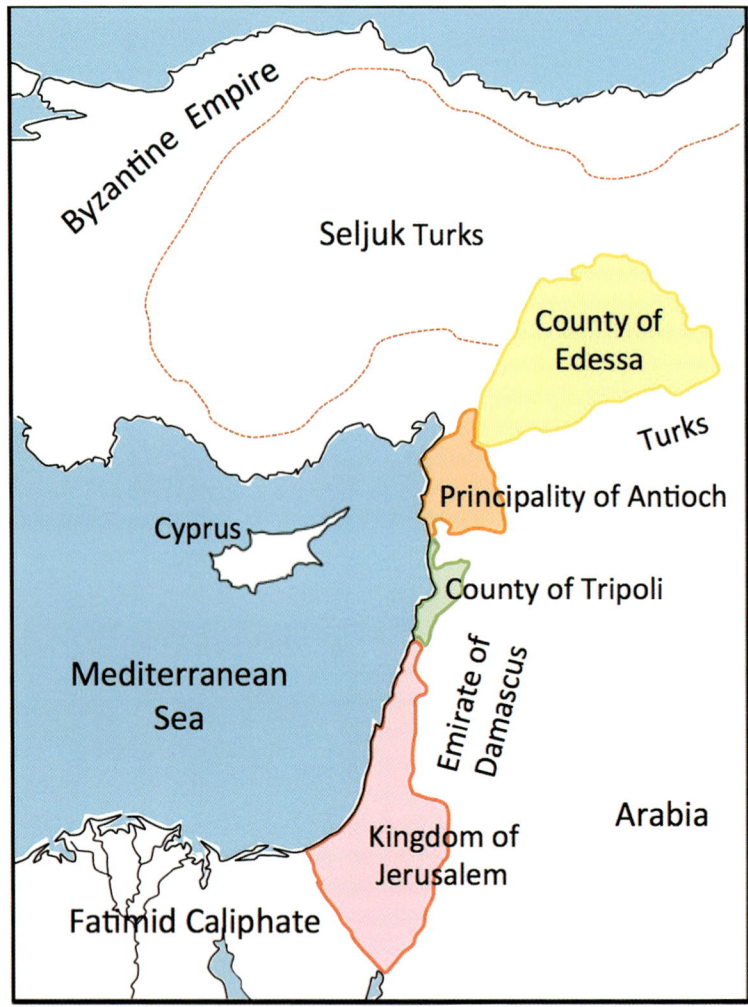

The Crusader states

Jerusalem, which had been under Muslim rule since the seventh century. The victory was celebrated with a bloody massacre of the Muslim and Jewish inhabitants. By the end of the First Crusade, four Christian states had been established, stretching from northern Mesopotamia to the Red Sea, centred on the cities of Edessa, Antioch, Tripoli and Jerusalem.

Robert Curthose distinguished himself during his four years crusading, but rather than carve out a territory for himself in the East, he preferred to return home to recover the duchy of Normandy. While Robert was on the return journey in 1100, his brother William Rufus died in an accident or possibly an assassination, while hunting in the New Forest. Walter Tirel, the skilled bowman whose arrow had killed William, fled the scene and escaped to France.

The death of William Rufus (*drawn by A de Neuville, 1895*)

On hearing of the king's death, his younger brother, Prince Henry, was quick to claim the throne before his elder brother, Robert Curthose, could arrive back from Jerusalem and make his own bid for the crown. Presented with this fait accompli, the barons with land in both England and Normandy again had the problem of owing military service to two masters in contention with each other. Robert Curthose disputed Henry's right to the crown and launched an unsuccessful invasion of England. Henry responded by invading Normandy but he too was forced to withdraw. Henry led a second invasion of Normandy in 1106. When the armies of the two brothers met at the Battle of Tinchebray, Robert's forces were soundly defeated and Robert was taken captive. The kingdom of England and the duchy of Normandy were now reunited under the rule of King Henry I, the youngest of William the Conqueror's sons. The unfortunate Robert Curthose was left languishing in captivity for the next 28 years, until his death at Cardiff Castle in 1134.

Hugh de Lacy appears to have taken no active part in the hostilities between Robert and Henry. He is best known for his enthusiasm in supporting churches and ecclesiastical foundations. At his *caput* of Weobley, he rebuilt the parish church of St Peter and St Paul in stone. Some ashlar quoins embedded in the angle between the thirteenth-century south aisle and the chancel of the present church are probably all that remains of Hugh's twelfth-century building.[3]

Hugh gave generously to the Benedictine abbey of St Peter in Gloucester. His father, Walter, had been buried in the chapter house, and Hugh's younger brother, also called Walter, spent his life there, having entered the abbey as a novice monk and eventually rising to the position of abbot. Hugh's donations included the church or churches of St Guthlac and St Peter that his father had founded in Hereford. The splendid abbey church of St Peter in Gloucester still stands. After the dissolution of the monasteries, it was re-designated as Gloucester Cathedral.[4]

Later, Hugh's interest was dominated by the priory of Llanthony, which he founded in his own domain of Ewyas Lacy. Gerald of Wales related how the priory began. William, one of Hugh's knights, was with Ernisius, the queen's chaplain, in a remote part of the Honddu Valley, perhaps hunting the deer that abounded on the slopes. They came across a ruined chapel, reputed to have once been the home of Saint David, and decided that they would give up their worldly lives and settle there, dedicating their days to poverty and prayer. They built a simple church dedicated to John the Baptist, who was their exemplar, having led an ascetic life in the wilderness, surviving on locusts and wild honey. According to Gerald, for a time they cleared no land for farming and the valley remained an impenetrable wood, where the two of them lived as hermits.[5]

After a time Ernisius invited others to join them and, with Hugh de Lacy's patronage, a religious foundation was established with some 40 canons following the Augustinian rule. Gerald reported that in the early years they prayed that their foundation would never be embarrassed by a wealth of possessions, and they were deeply distressed when

The Honddu Valley

Llanthony Priory today

Hugh and others began to endow them with land and church benefices. Among Hugh's first gifts were the Ewyas Lacy churches of Walterstone, Rowlestone and Llancillo. To these he added several other churches and land from his manors around Herefordshire and Gloucestershire.[6]

Llanthony thrived under Hugh de Lacy's patronage and protection. The embanked precinct extended over around 16 hectares with entry controlled by a gatehouse. The canons enjoyed the benefit of an infirmary, a dovecot and fishponds. Eventually, because of the generous donations the abbey received, its church was to become one of the most impressive medieval buildings in the Marches.

Unlike his troublesome brother, Hugh was apparently a good man. One of the canons of Llanthony, writing about the founding of the priory, said, 'He was indeed a noble man by birth and even more noble in his behaviour, most highly renowned among the leaders of the land, most merciful to the poor and the oppressed', surpassing even his father's acts of generosity and devotion.[7]

The ruins of Llanthony Priory in 1807

Hugh de Lacy's personal life was either so uneventful, or simply so unrecorded, that it is not even known with any certainty when he died. His death occurred sometime after 1108 and before 1121.[8]

14

Pain, Anarchy and Gilbert de Lacy

'I now attempt to give a clue to the mazy labyrinth of events and transactions that occurred in England in 1141
Unknown author of the twelfth-century *Gesta Stephani*

Pain FitzJohn was not from one of the great aristocratic families. His one-eyed father, John Monoculus was a relatively minor landholder, seemingly descended from a Norman moneyer. Pain entered royal service, possibly first as a page and then chamberlain to King Henry I. He gained the king's favour and in 1115 was rewarded with marriage to Hugh de Lacy's daughter and heiress, Sybil. As a result of this advantageous match, most of the de Lacy lands came under his control after Hugh's death.[1]

King Henry also granted Pain valuable lands in eastern Gwent and Lincolnshire. He soon rose to be one of the most powerful men in the Marches, holding a number of castles including Ludlow, Weobley, Caus, Bridgnorth and presumably Painscastle. He was appointed sheriff of both Hereford and Shrewsbury and held the position of *justiciar*, hearing legal cases on behalf of the king. He was an acquisitive man and, along with other magnates, was twice admonished in papal bulls for misappropriating property belonging to the see of Llandaff – once in 1119 by Pope Calixtus II and again in 1128 by Pope Honorius II.[2]

Miles, the hereditary constable of the royal castle at Gloucester, was another rising man under King Henry. Henry had advanced Miles by giving him the daughter of Bernard de Neufmarché in marriage, which brought him the territory of Brycheiniog as a dowry. Both Pain and Miles were secretaries and privy counsellors of Henry. The two men were close associates, and it was said that they 'raised their power to such a pitch that from the Severn to the sea, all along the border between England and Wales, they involved everyone in litigation and forced services.'[3]

Writing half a century later, Gerald of Wales related a strange tale of how one day his great uncle, Gruffydd ap Rhys ap Tewdor was riding past Llangorse Lake accompanied by Pain and Miles. Miles was ribbing Gruffydd about his claim to noble blood and said that there was an old legend that if the rightful ruler of Wales ordered the waterfowl on the lake to sing, they would obey him. Gruffydd replied that since Miles was the present ruler he should try. The birds failed to respond and again kept their silence when Pain tried his luck. Then Gruffydd dismounted and prayed aloud that the birds should acknowledge his descent from the five princes of Wales. Immediately all the birds began beating the water with their wings and singing with one accord. Pain and Miles hurried back to the court and recounted to the king what they had seen. Henry expressed no surprise and said, 'It is we who hold the power, and so we are free to commit acts of violence and injustice against these people, and yet we know full well that it is they who are the rightful heirs to the land.'[4]

Llangorse Lake

In 1135, King Henry died in Normandy from a fever, supposedly brought on by eating the flesh of lampreys against his doctor's orders. His only legitimate son and heir had drowned 15 years earlier in the loss of the White Ship. Henry had then declared that, were he to die without a son, it was his wish that his daughter, Matilda, would succeed him. Matilda, also known as Maud, had been the child bride of the Holy Roman Emperor. Although widowed, she still liked to style herself the Empress. King Henry had required his nobles to swear an oath that they would give her their backing. However, on hearing of Henry's death, his nephew Stephen of Blois, rushed to England and seized the throne, promising strong and stable government. Impressed by his decisive action, most of the barons and bishops put aside their commitment to Matilda and gave Stephen their support. He was a grandson of William the Conqueror and besides the Norman magnates were far from enthusiastic about having a female ruler, especially one who was now married to the count of Anjou. Anjou was the French province immediately to the south of Normandy, and the Angevins were uneasy neighbours and rivals of the Normans.[5]

The Welsh saw the uncertainty following Henry's death as an opportunity to regain much of the territory they had lost to the Normans. A bloody battle broke out in Gower. Richard de Clare, the lord of Cardigan was ambushed and killed in the Grwyne valley, on the edge of Ewyas Lacy, a few miles south-west of Llanthony. This triggered an invasion of his lands in the west of Wales where the Flemings that King Henry had planted there came under attack from dispossessed Welshmen. The rout was such that when the bridge over the River Teifi broke under the weight of men fleeing the battle, others continued to cross the river on the mass of human corpses and drowned horses. Richard de Clare's younger brother, Baldwin, was sent into Wales to attempt the recovery of Cardigan but, faced with a united Welsh front, he got no further than Brecon. A force led by Robert FitzHarold, the lord of Ewyas Harold, managed to garrison Carmarthen for a while but he soon had to withdraw. Meanwhile, Richard de Clare's widow was stranded in Cardigan Castle, which managed to hold out until Miles of Gloucester led an expedition to rescue her and escort her back to England. It would be years before the Normans recovered their dominance of the south and west of Wales. Only a substantial royal army could have saved the situation in Wales, but Stephen was occupied putting down a revolt in the south-west of England. He also had to contend with an invasion of the north of England by the Scots, as well as mounting a defence of Normandy, which was threatened by attack from the Empress Matilda and her husband.[6]

Matilda and Geoffrey of Anjou (*picture modified from public domain images* © J.C. Plummer 2019)

Pain FitzJohn had attended the new King Stephen's court and he was present at the three-month-long siege of Exeter. During his absence, Ewyas Lacy was affected by the unrest in Wales and depredations were made on Llanthony Priory. Most of the canons withdrew to the safety of Hereford and then to Gloucester, where Miles founded a daughter priory for them, Llanthony Secunda. The new foundation soon rivalled the

Top: Cardigan Castle and bridge over the River Teifi, 1786. *Bottom*: The Ruins of Llanthony Secunda, 1784

parent abbey, but Gerald of Wales was far from impressed with the materialism of the new priory. He said, 'Let the bustling and active take up their residence in Gloucester, leaving this other foundation for men of contemplation. There in Gloucester men strive for earthly possessions, but here in Llanthony let them rather turn their minds towards the promise of eternal bliss.'[7]

Following the Norman retreat from south Wales, control of the southern Marches was once again of crucial importance. King Stephen confirmed most of the land holdings Pain FitzJohn had received from King Henry, but awarded him Archenfield in exchange for eastern Gwent. This gave the Crown direct control over the strategically important corridor between south Wales and Gloucester. Subsequently, three imposing stone castles were built there – Grosmont, Skenfrith and the White Castle at Llantilio.

The White Castle (*photograph © Crown copyright (2020) Cadw, Welsh Government*)

Pain had no male heir, so he arranged a marriage between his daughter, Cecily, and Miles's son, Roger, which would have united their extensive estates along the Welsh border into one huge Marcher power bloc. But, in 1137, Pain was killed before the marriage could be formalised. While countering a Welsh raiding party, his head was pierced by a spear. After Pain's death, King Stephen confirmed the marriage contract between Roger and Cecily, but Roger was not yet of age to take possession of his legacy. For the time being, his father, Miles of Gloucester, probably had effective control over the de Lacy lordship. However, it appears that Sybil, Pain's widow, initially retained the custody of Ludlow, before she was married to Joce de Dinan, the man who subsequently held the castle.[8]

Around this time, the upheaval in England drew in another contender for the wealth of the de Lacys. It was Gilbert, the son of the exiled Roger de Lacy. Born around 1110 and raised in Normandy, he had inherited Roger's Norman estates. He is described as being a prudent man, far-sighted and exacting in all military matters. It is not clear when he began campaigning to recover the de Lacy properties in England and Wales. It is claimed that he was at court within weeks of King Stephen taking the throne, although, with no powerbase in England, it seems unlikely that he would have ventured to challenge such a pre-eminent magnate as Pain FitzJohn while he was still alive. The de Lacy who witnessed a charter of King Stephen's in 1136 was more likely to be Ilbert de Lacy of Pontefract than Gilbert.[9]

Who controlled the castles of the Marches and elsewhere was to be a matter of the utmost importance for Stephen, because the following year 'the abominable madness flared up.' The unrest of the first three years of Stephen's reign escalated into a full-scale civil war that historians have dubbed the Anarchy.[10]

Geoffrey de Talbot, who was Gilbert de Lacy's cousin, seized Hereford Castle and held it against the king. Gilbert may have been with him at this stage, but it was not recorded. Meanwhile, in Normandy, Robert, the earl of Gloucester and illegitimate son of King Henry, renounced his allegiance to Stephen and declared his support for his half-sister, the Empress Matilda. Soon, across England, castles were fortified against the king, and their custodians declared for the Angevin cause. After a month-long siege, the defenders of Hereford Castle surrendered, but by then Geoffrey de Talbot had already left for the de Lacy *caput* of Weobley. When Weobley came under siege, Geoffrey responded by burning the Welsh suburb of Hereford, south of the Wye. He then withdrew to Earl Robert's castle at Bristol. From there, he and Gilbert de Lacy were reconnoitring the defences of Bath, prior to an assault, when Geoffrey was captured by the bishop of

A statue of King Stephen at York Minster (photograph © Allan Harris on Flickr)

Bath's men. The bishop was inveigled into a parley with Geoffrey's supporters, who then threatened to hang him unless Geoffrey was released. Geoffrey's release then led to King Stephen questioning the unfortunate bishop's loyalty.[11]

In the Welsh Marches, once Hereford and Weobley were again under royal control and garrisoned by forces loyal to the king, Stephen turned his attention to Shrewsbury, where the sheriff who succeeded Pain had declared for the empress. After another month-long siege the castle was stormed and Stephen, in a fit of pique, hanged several of the surviving defenders.[12]

King David of Scotland was an uncle of the Empress Matilda and supported her cause. The uprising in the west of England and the Marches presented him with an opportunity to advance into Northumbria and Yorkshire. Ilbert de Lacy of Pontefract was a notable commander of the local forces that managed to defeat the Scots. King Stephen then took his own army north into Scotland to force a more lasting peace settlement.

In 1139, Stephen and his army returned to the Marches where Ludlow, the strongest of the de Lacy castles, was holding out against him. In his entourage was the king of Scotland's son, Henry, who had joined Stephen's campaign partly as an honoured guest, having been made earl of Northumbria as part of the peace deal, and partly as hostage for his father's good behaviour. This young man 'was pulled off his horse by an iron hook, and nearly taken captive, but the king himself bravely rescued him from the enemy.' Some historians maintain that the hook was a grappling iron swung from the battlements of the castle, but in all likelihood it was simply a billhook or other hooked pole arm wielded by a foot-soldier. The renowned warrior, William Marshal, who later became earl of Pembroke and Chepstow, suffered a similar indignity as a young and inexperienced knight when he was nearly unhorsed by a Flemish infantryman with a hook. In later centuries, pole arms were widely adopted by infantry as an effective measure against armoured horsemen.[13]

Realising that Ludlow was too strong to be taken by force, Stephen had two siege fortresses built nearby and then, having manned them, departed towards London. In his absence, the garrisons of these two fortresses came to blows with each

The keep/gatehouse at Ludlow. In later years the entrance to the castle was repositioned alongside the keep
(*photograph © Sam Saunders, CC BY-SA 2.0*)

other. Whether this was because of rivalry as to who should be the first to attack the castle, or a tournament that got out of hand, is not clear, but Stephen was obliged to return to Ludlow and 'settle all things peaceably'. Whether that meant the castle capitulated or the siege was abandoned is not stated.[14]

The two chroniclers who wrote the accounts of the siege of Ludlow left out one very important detail. They omitted to say who was holding Ludlow against the king. In spite of the lack of evidence, distinguished historians have confidently asserted that the castle was held by: -

    i.   Gilbert de Lacy who had somehow taken possession but then escaped before the garrison surrendered,
    ii.   ature FitzJohn's widow, Sybil, before she was remarried, or
    iii.   Joce de Dinan after he married Sybil.[15]

There is little basis for the first of these assertions, as neither of the chroniclers of the siege mention either Gilbert de Lacy or the surrender of Ludlow. It seems equally unlikely, though not impossible, that a widow would be inclined to hold out against a lengthy siege by the king's army. That leaves only Joce de Dinan, who was certainly known to be holding Ludlow a year later when King Stephen gave the earldom of Hereford to the earl of Leicester. Leicester appears to have been offered all of rebel-held Herefordshire but Stephen excluded the fiefs of Mortimer, Richard's Castle and Braose, which were still to be held directly from the Crown. These were the fiefs in the north of the county that had remained loyal to Stephen. Also excluded from the new earldom was the fee of 'Godso de Dinan which before was Hugh de Lacy's'. There was a peculiar caveat that 'If the Earl of Leicester could so deal with the said Godso as that he himself should be willing to hold the fee aforesaid under the Earl – that the King fully allows.' This points to Joce having managed to negotiate exceptional terms for himself to end the siege of Ludlow the year before. As it turned out, Leicester had little impact on the situation in Herefordshire and soon retired to his estates in Normandy.[16]

It is usually assumed that the marriage of Sybil to Joce had been arranged by King Stephen himself, or at least had his sanction. However, it is not impossible in those troubled times that it was Miles of Gloucester who arranged the marriage in order to look after the widow of his close friend, Pain, while ensuring that one of the most important castles under his control was properly defended. There is no backstory for Joce or Godso de Dinan, but four decades earlier, when Hugh de Lacy granted the priory of St Guthlac to Gloucester Abbey, one of the knights witnessing the charter was Gotse, Hugh's *dapifer* or steward. The similarity of the names suggests the possibility that Joce/ Godso/ Gotse may have been the son or grandson of one of Hugh de Lacy's senior household knights, who would presumably have served Pain FitzJohn and now owed allegiance to Miles of Gloucester. Admittedly, the similarity of names is not much to go on, but this proposition would explain the mystery of how an otherwise obscure knight came to be the custodian of one of the strongest and most important castles on the Marches.[17]

It seems certain that Miles had already abandoned his support for Stephen when, later that year, Matilda and her half-brother, Earl Robert of Gloucester arrived in England. Stephen besieged them in Arundel but, after Robert slipped away, Stephen showed great chivalry, if not necessarily sound judgement, by giving Matilda safe conduct and an escort to join her supporters at the rebel stronghold of Bristol. She then moved to Gloucester where she made the castle her residence. Miles, as sheriff of Gloucester, was now her protector and senior military commander, second only to Earl Robert himself. Matilda rewarded him with the Forest of Dean and other properties that linked his estates in Gloucestershire with his Marcher lordships of Brycheiniog and Ewyas. Miles now moved on Hereford and used the cathedral as his fortress while he attempted to take the castle. The king's army came to Hereford's relief but then retreated, presumably to deal with problems elsewhere in the country. Miles's next attempt to take the castle was aided by Geoffrey de Talbot, who stabled his horses in the cathedral and mounted catapults on the tower, putting them in range of the castle. The citizens of Hereford were horrified to see the cemetery of St Guthlac's church dug up to make siege works that were dotted with corpses of the recently buried. After the castle eventually fell, Miles appointed Geoffrey as the new castellan, but within months he was mortally wounded when Earl Robert's troops were ambushed on their way to attack Bath.[18]

John Speed's map of Hereford showing the cathedral and castle

The Angevin party now held much of the west of England, with a chain of secure bases in Bristol, Gloucester and Hereford. Supported by Welsh mercenaries, they were able to take the war to Stephen. In 1141 the king was captured at the Battle of Lincoln and was incarcerated at Bristol. Matilda soon took control of the royal treasury at Winchester and proceeded to Westminster for her coronation. This could have brought an end to the civil war, as Matilda now held all the key cards, but she played her hand badly. Her imperious behaviour and demands for money offended the citizens of London, resulting in her being driven from the city by an angry mob before the coronation could take place.[19]

For his help in her bid for the throne, Matilda rewarded Miles of Gloucester with the earldom of Hereford, the charter being witnessed by, among others, Gilbert de Lacy. In revenge for her humiliation in London, Matilda had Stephen put in irons. Her army, led by Robert of Gloucester, Miles and the king of Scotland, now laid siege to the bishop of Winchester's castle. The engagement was inconclusive until a relieving army from London overwhelmed Matilda's forces. In the ensuing rout, many of the barons only escaped by discarding their armour. Earl Robert was captured while fighting a rearguard action to ensure Matilda's safe retreat. With the chief military leader of the Angevins now held by Stephen's supporters and the king held by the Angevin party, the only possible outcome was a prisoner exchange. Stephen and Robert were both released, which allowed the civil war to drag on for several more years.[20]

Subsequent military action was now mainly concentrated around the Thames Valley and the east of England. With Miles of Gloucester and his son, Roger, now firmly in control of most of Herefordshire and the southern Marches, Robert of Ewyas Harold switched sides and worked for Miles as his household constable. The position of the two rival contenders for the Ewyas Lacy estates – Gilbert de Lacy and Joce de Dinan – is unclear. They seem to have been mainly concerned with furthering their own ends.[21]

Miles's position as a major military commander left him short of money, so he attempted to recoup by taxing the churches in his earldom and attacking church property. This resulted in his excommunication by the bishop of Hereford. On Christmas Eve in 1143, Miles took time off from the fighting to go hunting in the Forest of Dean, where he was accidentally struck by an arrow and died excommunicate. His titles and rights passed to his son, Roger, who also inherited his father's role as an important commander of Angevin forces.[22]

The war now lapsed into an uneasy stalemate. Robert, earl of Gloucester and leader of the Angevin forces, died in 1147, and the following year Matilda returned to Normandy, leaving it up to her teenage son, Henry, to continue the conflict and pursue his own claim to the English throne. Many of the participants in the civil war left England to join the Second Crusade. This was an attempt to recover the County of Edessa, a crusader state in upper Mesopotamia, which had recently fallen to the Turks. The two main armies from France and Germany fought separately and, without any unified leadership, the venture was a disaster. The crusader armies suffered terrible losses and failed to recover Edessa. The only success came from a contingent of knights from England, Normandy and elsewhere, which had opted to travel to Edessa by sea rather than overland and, while en route, helped the kingdom of Portugal to wrest Lisbon from the Moors.

At the same time as the civil war was being fought in England, Matilda's husband, the count of Anjou was taking control of Normandy, castle by castle. Once he had gained overall mastery of the dukedom he ceded it to his son, Henry, who was only seventeen. Young Henry was then able to use Normandy as a base for launching his bid for the English crown. His early campaigning in England seems to have been ill-prepared and largely ineffectual. In 1147 he came with only a few knights and insufficient funds to pay off his mercenaries. Neither his mother nor Robert of Gloucester would advance him the money he needed, so bizarrely it was King Stephen who agreed to bail him out, against the advice of his nobles. Whether this was another foolhardy gesture of chivalry or a sensible and inexpensive way of removing a troublesome irritant is a matter of conjecture.

It would be some time before Henry eventually showed himself to be a capable military commander and a match for Stephen. Henry's one great advantage was that those barons with land in both England and Normandy were reluctant now to oppose him for fear of losing their Norman property. The war rumbled on until Stephen's eldest son and designated successor died. At last, in 1154, a truce was agreed whereby Henry was adopted as Stephen's son and heir. Later that year, Stephen died and Henry became the first Plantagenet king of England, with an empire stretching from the Scottish border to the Pyrenees. Part of the Marches briefly rose in revolt, with Hugh Mortimer of Wigmore and Roger FitzMiles of Gloucester holding out against Henry, but with nobody enthusiastic for further bloodshed, peace was soon restored.[23]

A silver penny of King Stephen minted at Hereford by the moneyer Edpine. The bulbous nose suggests it may be a better likeness than the idealised depiction at York

Historians have expended much time and ink in debating whether 'anarchy' is in fact the appropriate term for the time of the civil war. There was certainly suffering and immense hardship in some parts of the country. Medieval armies, foraging off the land, often left famine and devastation in their wake, even when not following deliberate 'scorched earth' policies. But for most of the period, government continued in those areas that remained loyal to either Stephen or the Angevins. Both parties operated mints and circulated coinage. Charters were issued and chroniclers wrote their histories. Some churches were robbed, commandeered or burned by combatants, but the Church prospered. During King Stephen's reign, 120 religious houses were founded in England and Wales, more than in the entire previous century. In Herefordshire, Robert of Ewyas Harold founded the Cistercian Abbey Dore in 1147. Later, according to Gerald of Wales, the venal denizens of the abbey, hoping for further gain, made Robert's widow a monk on her deathbed. The Herefordshire School of Romanesque Sculpture flourished during this period and the work of its masons can be found in Hereford Cathedral and numerous churches across the county.[24]

Romanesque carvings at Rowlestone Church

It was against this background that Gilbert de Lacy was pursuing his claims to the de Lacy estates. During the early stages of the civil war, he doesn't seem to have had much success with either Stephen or Matilda. However, as time went on, he did eventually manage to recover the bulk of the de Lacy holdings including Ewyas Lacy, Weobley and Ludlow, although it is far from clear how and when. Odd snippets of information hint at his progress, but they are open to different interpretations.

It has been argued that Gilbert's claim was accepted by many of his feudal tenants soon after he came to England. The fact that he was able to take an active part in the war does suggest that he had the backing of at least some of the tenant knights of the de Lacy domains. Between 1143 and 1148, Gilbert came to Llanthony 'and took by seignory all the things that belonged to the Canons [of Shobdon], and caused their wheat to be carried away, worth a great sum of money.' On face value this would indicate that he was in control of Ewyas Lacy, but alternatively he may have been plundering assets still under the control of one of his rivals. By 1145 Gilbert had taken Mansel Lacy from William de Braose. This implies that he probably had control of the important castle at Weobley by then, as it lies between Mansel Lacy and the Braose castles of Kingsland, Eardisland and Pembridge. Certainly, by around 1148 Gilbert had regained enough of his inheritance for Roger FitzMiles to enter into a formal alliance with the new earl of Gloucester, aimed at dispossessing Gilbert of lands that Roger considered were rightly his.[25]

In 1150 King Stephen had attacked Worcester but failed to take the castle and made no further advance into Herefordshire or the Marches. Roger FitzMiles was then in control of Worcestershire, and around that time he seized four of Gilbert's knights from where they had taken sanctuary in a churchyard and held them to ransom. Whether Gilbert and his knights were fighting for either King Stephen or the Empress Matilda is not clear, though in June 1153 he was in the company of Matilda's son, Henry.[26]

Gilbert had definitely regained the de Lacy estates in Herefordshire before 1154/5 because it was then that he donated the churches at Clodock and Weobley to Llanthony Priory.[27]

It is not known exactly when Gilbert recovered Ludlow and the Shropshire manors from Joce de Dinan. At some time between 1148 and 1154 Joce still held Ludlow Castle and was conducting a feud from there with Gilbert's ally, Hugh Mortimer. The strange *History of Fulk Fitz-Warine* may contain a flawed memory of how Gilbert finally ousted Joce and took control of Ludlow. This romance, complete with a cast of giants, monsters and fair damsels, conflates the lives of two or three different Fulks, but appears to include some genuine historical elements. It begins with an account of a dispute between Joce of Ludlow and 'Sir Walter de Lacy, who then sojourned much in Ewyas'. If there is any truth in the story, the author is clearly incorrect in the name. The de Lacy referred to must be Gilbert, who was the grandson of one Walter de Lacy and grandfather of another. In the romance, Fulk is a ward of Joce, sent to him to be educated. Following a skirmish, they overcome de Lacy and one of his knights, and imprison them in Ludlow Castle. A serving lady who tends their wounds falls for de Lacy's knight and helps them to escape by means of a rope of knotted sheets. Fighting continues between de Lacy and Joce until, while Joce is away gathering troops for an attack on Ewyas, the besotted damsel is tricked into allowing de Lacy's men into the castle. Realising that she has been duped, she runs her lover through with his own sword and plunges to her death from a window. Subsequently, when Joce attempts to retake Ludlow, he is captured by de Lacy's reinforcements brought in from Wales. Now it is de Lacy's turn to hold Joce prisoner, until Fulk petitions King Henry, who orders Joce's release.[28]

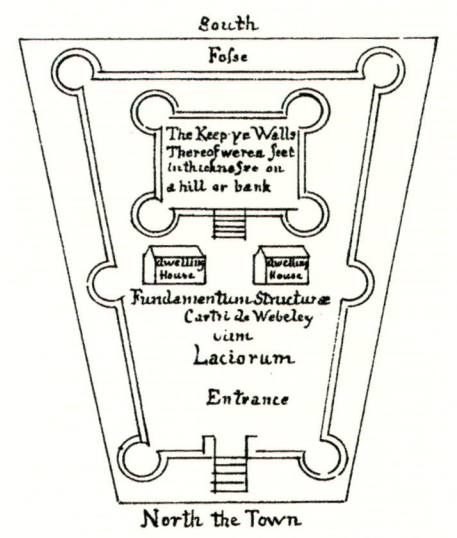

A plan of Weobley Castle by Silas Taylor, 1655

There is no way of telling if this story has any basis of truth, but Joce did eventually relinquish Ludlow to Gilbert de Lacy. By 1157/8, Gilbert was in possession of the bulk of the de Lacy estates with King Henry's approval and favour, because he was excused a tax on his lands in Herefordshire, Shropshire and Gloucestershire at a time when Henry was gathering revenue for war on Wales. Presumably, in spite of his father's rebellion, Gilbert's entitlement through the direct male de Lacy line was seen as taking precedence over the rights Joce had gained by marriage to the female line. It appears that King Henry compensated Joce for his loss of Ludlow with the grant of royal demesne land in Berkshire.[29]

It may have been the failure of the Second Crusade that sparked Gilbert's interest in the Templars, or it may have been remorse for the part he had played in the civil war. The military order of the Knights Templar had been founded after the First Crusade, to protect and assist the stream of pilgrims visiting Jerusalem. Individually, the Knights were sworn to poverty, but as an organisation the Templars came to control huge assets. Gilbert donated some of his Gloucestershire properties to the Templars, including land and buildings at Holford, Winchcombe, Quenington and Guiting (later Temple Guiting). Gilbert also built a Templar chapel within the bailey of Ludlow Castle. Typical of Templar churches, it has a circular nave and, although it is not a defensive structure, it is capped with crenellations giving it the appearance of a round keep.[30]

The Templar chapel at Ludlow Castle

In Herefordshire there were two other round Templar churches, one at Hereford itself and the other at Garway. It is not known who built them, but Gilbert possibly had some influence.

Around 1158, Gilbert relinquished control of all the de Lacy estates, which he had fought so long and hard to recover, and handed them over to his eldest son, Robert. Having divested himself of his personal fortune, he was able to become a member the Order. In 1160, he witnessed a treaty between Henry II and King Louis of France, signing as a Templar. He is last heard of in 1163, commanding a group of Templars escorting pilgrims on their way to Antioch and successfully defending them from an attack by the forces of Nur Al-Din, the Muslim ruler of Damascus and Aleppo.[31]

In view of the momentous happenings that beset the country during this period, the restoration of Gilbert de Lacy's lordship in the Marches might be seen as a relatively parochial matter, but the actions of his successors had repercussions that affect the politics of the British Isles to this day.

15

Hugh de Lacy II – governor of Ireland

At the creek of Baginbun
Ireland was lost and won,
Lost by the Irish and won by the Welsh
    The Annals of Thady Dowling

Hugh de Lacy first appears in the records in 1155 as a minor knight in Shropshire, possibly working in the service of the Mortimer family. Although there is evidence that he may have been in control of Ewyas Lacy by the late 1150s, it was only by the mid-1160s that he inherited the main de Lacy estates from his elder brother Robert, who had either died or left England to join his father as a Templar. At some point shortly after his succession, Hugh received a charter from Henry II, confirming the manors of Stanton Lacy, Ludlow, Weobley and Yarkhill.

The *cartae baronum* of 1165–66, an audit of English knights' fees owing to their tenants-in-chief, lists Hugh as having 58 fees. This does not include Ewyas Lacy which, lying in Wales, was outside Exchequer control.[1]

It perhaps says something of Hugh's character that, no sooner had he gained his estates than he was immediately in dispute with the See of Hereford. This concerned the number of knights' service owed by Hugh to the bishop for the manor of Holme Lacy. This dispute continued until 1177, when Hugh was finally forced to admit two knights' service instead of the one he had claimed. Hugh was also fined on at least two occasions for assarting – unauthorised clearing of woodland for agriculture – fines that it appears were never paid. These actions show that Hugh was looking for ways to increase the value of his lordship.[2]

THE INVASION OF IRELAND

His fortunes were to improve dramatically in 1171 when he accompanied Henry II on his expedition to Ireland. This expedition had originally been planned to exert Henry's authority over his wayward subject, Richard de Clare, who was claiming the kingship of Leinster through his marriage to the late king of Leinster's daughter. Richard was the earl of Pembroke and lord of Chepstow Castle. He later became known as Strongbow, probably a mistranscription or perhaps a deliberate pun on Striguil, the old name for Chepstow.

Strongbow and the later invaders and colonisers of much of Ireland are usually referred to as Anglo-Normans but this ignores the large contingent of knights and their attendants recruited from Wales and the Marches. Notable among Strongbow's forces was a camp-follower called Alice of Abergavenny. After a battle in which her lover had died, she took an axe and beheaded 70 Irish prisoners before pushing their bodies over a cliff into the sea.[3]

The Normans had created the Welsh Marches as an expedient to protect newly-conquered England from attack by the unconquered Welsh. The customary independence of the Marcher barons that resulted from this policy had been a persistent problem for the English Crown. It seems that Henry was determined to retain direct control over his barons in Ireland so that the same thing would not happen again. Before the expedition could take place, however, Strongbow surrendered Dublin and his castles to the Crown by way of reconciliation.

Not one to pass up an opportunity, Henry nevertheless decided to proceed with his plan, which may have been for territorial expansion all along. Hugh de Lacy's knights, supported by a large contingent of foot-soldiers recruited from the able-bodied men of Ewyas and Herefordshire, would have formed a significant part of Henry's army. It is thought that the unusually large outer bailey of Ludlow Castle may have been created for marshalling and preparing Hugh's forces before they left for Ireland.[4]

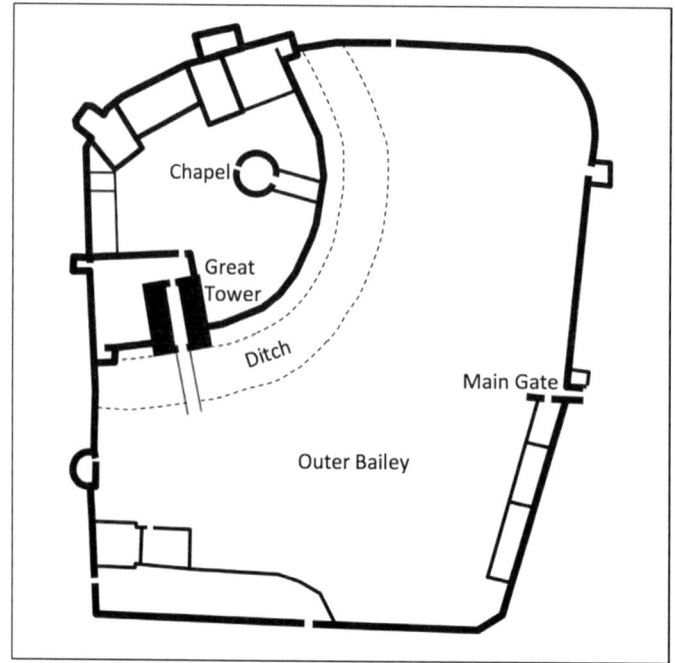

A plan of Ludlow Castle

154 THE MARCH OF EWYAS

While in Ireland, Henry received the submission of nearly all of the local kings, with the notable exception of the king of Connaught and High King of Ireland, Rodry O'Connor (Ruaidri Ua Conchobair), who refused to submit. Henry spent the winter planning a move against O'Connor, but in the spring of 1172 he was called back to England and Normandy to deal with the fallout from the murder of Thomas à Becket, which had taken place the year before. Placating the Pope and making suitable reparations was something he had to do in person. Before leaving, Henry placed the defence of Dublin in the hands of his trusted lieutenant, Hugh de Lacy, and also granted him licence to annex the kingdom of Meath for a fee of 50 knights. This was a shrewd move as Meath covered a large portion of central Ireland, half of which was under the control of O'Connor; the other half held by the equally hostile Teirnan O'Rourke (Tigernan Ua Ruairc). Hugh would have to fight to gain control of his new lordship. Trouble started in the summer of 1172, when Hugh moved his army west, building castles and garrisoning them with his knights.[5]

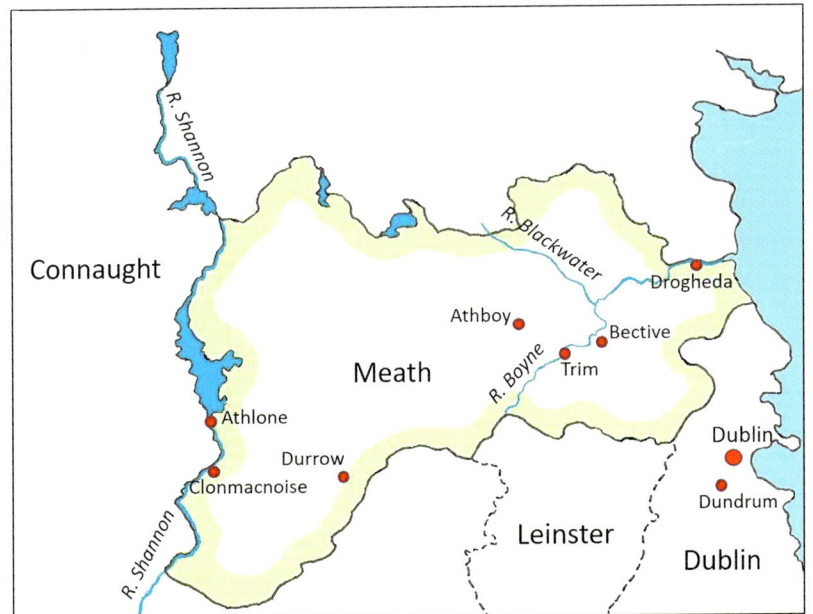

Meath after the Norman invasion, showing the major towns and castles

On a hill outside Athboy, Hugh met a small contingent of O'Rourke's forces under a flag of truce. Accounts differ as to what happened, but according to Gerald of Wales:

> O'Rourke ... the one-eyed villain, meditating treachery ... beckoned to his friends to come up with all speed. He was hastening with long strides, his face pale with revenge and his axe raised, towards those who were engaged in the parley, when Maurice Fitzgerald, being on his guard and having watched all that had taken place, ... now drew [his sword] and rising up, warned Hugh de Lacy also to stand on his defence. The traitor then made a desperate stroke at Hugh,

HUGH DE LACY II – GOVERNOR OF IRELAND   155

but it fell on the interpreter, who, faithful to his lord, thrust himself forward to shield him, and cut off his arm, giving him a mortal wound. Maurice now called aloud to his friends to make a hasty retreat, while sword encountered battle-axe, and Hugh de Lacy, being twice felled to the ground, was saved by Fitzgerald's prowess. Meanwhile, the Irish rushed in greater numbers from the valleys at the traitor's signal ... and there would soon have been an end to Maurice and Hugh, had not Gryffith and his small band rode up at full speed ... O'Rourke, seeing them coming, thought that it was time to seek safety in flight and was in the act of mounting a horse ... when Gryffith, putting spurs to his own, ran his spear through both O'Rourke and the horse he was mounting. There were slain with him three of his followers ... His head was cut off and afterwards sent to the King of England; and the rest of the Irish fled in confusion ... the English pursuing them without respite and making great slaughter amongst them.[6]

Gerald tells us that Gryffith was Maurice FitzGerald's nephew and son of the constable of Pembroke Castle. His mother was a daughter of Rhys ap Tewdor, the last king of Deheubarth, so Maurice and Gryffith were both Norman-Welsh, as indeed was Gerald himself.

The death of O'Rourke removed a major obstacle and opened up vast swathes of Meath to further colonisation, which Hugh was not slow to capitalise on. He took his army north and west, while O'Rourke's mangled corpse hung upside down outside Dublin.

Unfortunately, Hugh's Irish aspirations suffered a setback in 1173, when he was required to take part in Henry's wars in Normandy. O'Connor, taking advantage of his continued absence in 1174, led a combined Irish force through Meath with the intention of taking Dublin. The situation was only saved by Strongbow, who arrived from Leinster with his army in time to strengthen the Dublin garrison. In 1175, Hugh returned to Ireland to reassert his authority in Meath with a campaign of terror and violence – 'Durrow and the whole of Meath, from Athlone to Drogheda, was laid waste by the foreigners.'[7]

Peace was eventually restored in October 1175 with the Treaty of Windsor, in which O'Connor was recognised as High King of Ireland, but with King Henry as his overlord. Limits to Norman expansion in Ireland were agreed in return for Irish recognition of English lordship of Meath and Leinster. O'Connor was even promised English military help if needed. Secure in his Irish possessions, Hugh returned to England, where his estates had been long-neglected.

As ever, there was trouble in the Welsh Marches. Henry, the son of Miles of Gloucester, had been killed by the Welsh and his nephew, William de Braose, inherited Brecon and Upper Gwent. In revenge for his uncle's murder, de Braose invited the local Welsh princes and other nobles to Abergavenny Castle at Christmas in 1175, ostensibly for peace talks, but then had them slaughtered by his men. De Braose became known as the 'Ogre of Abergavenny' for instigating the massacre. His action resulted in a deterioration of the already bad Anglo-Welsh relations that ultimately led to the destruction of Abergavenny Castle seven years later.

The ruins of Abergavenny Castle

In Ireland the following year Strongbow died, leaving something of a power vacuum in Leinster. To improve and consolidate good administration, Henry convened a council at Oxford in May 1177, at which all the barons who held lands in Ireland were made to pay homage to his son, John, as Lord of Ireland. Hugh de Lacy was given governance of Meath and a large part of northern Leinster – in all about one third of colonised Ireland. The other two thirds were controlled by two other governors – part of Henry's strategy of preventing any one baron from becoming too powerful. At the same time, Henry took control of Ludlow Castle to limit Hugh's power in England.

From 1177, Hugh's attention was firmly focussed on Ireland, with his English, French and Marcher estates administered by trusted subordinates. His family was most likely based in Dublin, at least while Hugh was on campaign. After her death some time before 1180, his first wife, Rose of Monmouth, was buried there. It is worth pointing out that Hugh's three surviving sons, Walter, Hugh and Gilbert probably spent many of their formative years in Ireland. An eldest son, Robert, known from two existing records, presumably died young, and certainly before 1186.[8]

With his new powers, Hugh embarked on a major castle-building programme, in order to consolidate his grip on his enlarged province. This was exactly the strategy that had been used by the Normans in the Welsh Marches. His castle and town at Drogheda, for example, controlled a major strategic crossing of the River Boyne, while Dundrum Castle controlled the approach to Dublin from the south.

Hugh's centre of operations was at Trim on the River Boyne, where he and his son, Walter, built what would become the most impressive castle in Ireland. Uniquely, the

Hugh's motte at Drogheda, now topped by a nineteenth-century Martello tower
(*photograph © Tommyxx CC BY-SA 4.0*)

square keep was reinforced with a square turret midway along each wall, making it immensely strong. The curtain wall of the large bailey is strengthened by both square and D-shaped towers.

As Hugh worked his way west, it was perhaps inevitable that he would come up against the forces of O'Connor, the High King and supposed ally since the Treaty of Windsor. In fact this seems to have been Hugh's intention, as he went on to attack and plunder Clonmacnoise, the ecclesiastical centre on the Shannon, and traditional burial place of O'Connor's family. Outraged, O'Connor appealed to Henry who seems to have done little to intervene. Perhaps recognising the weakness of his position, O'Connor shrewdly solved his problem with Hugh by offering him his daughter's hand in marriage. As a further inducement Hugh would be paid a tribute from the coffers of Connaught. Marriage into the Irish royal house would further legitimise Hugh's position, so he agreed. The marriage took place in 1180 and led to an immediate quarrel between Henry and O'Connor. The last thing Henry needed was an alliance between the most powerful Norman in Ireland and his Irish counterpart. Hugh appears to have escaped Henry's wrath as, after a short recall to England, he returned to Ireland in 1182 as sole governor. With his Connaught alliance, he was now the most powerful man in Ireland.

Hugh spent the following years extending his influence in Ireland and building more castles, not just in Meath, but throughout Leinster and into the contested western areas beyond. Always, he was pushing at the boundaries, forging alliances and controlling, through favours, those who could be useful to him.

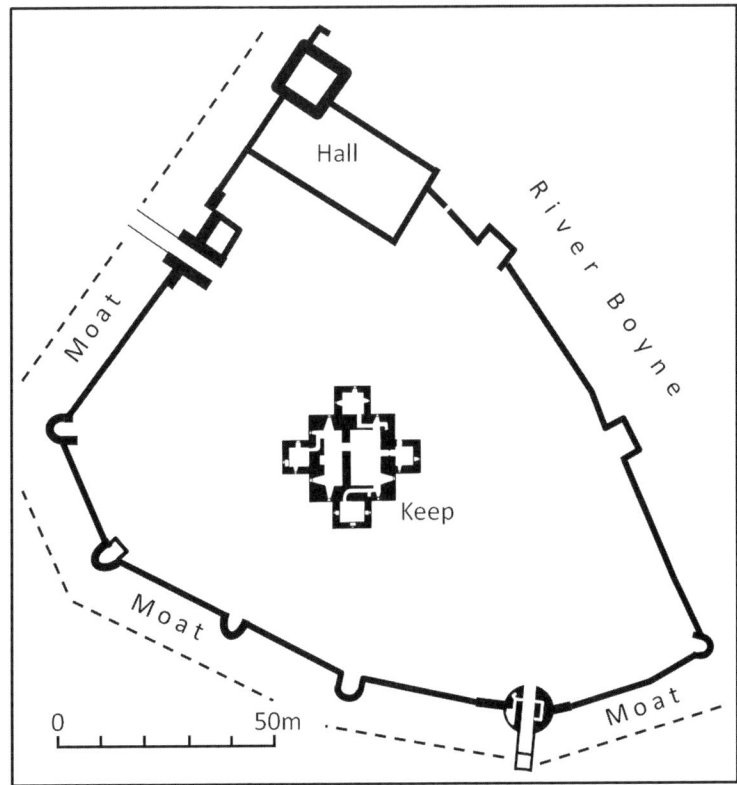

A plan of Trim Castle

King Henry had installed Hugh de Lacy in Ireland because of his concerns regarding Strongbow's pretensions to kingship. Now he had even more reason to be worried by Hugh's ambitions. Inevitably, as his power and wealth grew, rumours began to circulate that Hugh's aim was to break with Henry and forge his own kingdom in Ireland. As William of Newborough reported:

> Amongst the barons of the English king in Ireland, Hugh de Lacy caused most anxiety to the crown. After the death of Richard de Clare, he had settled upon him vast estates and was given the management of the king's dominions, becoming so rich and powerful that he was feared by friends and foes alike. It seemed that he held more in Ireland than the King of England himself, as much as to rival God, and that he was preparing to have a royal crown placed upon himself, or so it was said. Summoned by the king to explain his unfaithfulness, he disobeyed, thus giving credit to the popular presumption.[9]

To counter this perceived threat, in 1185 Henry sent his young son, John, to re-establish regal authority and be crowned as king of Ireland. In this mission Prince John failed abysmally, and went home in disgrace the following year, complaining bitterly of Hugh de Lacy's refusal to recognise his overlordship.

As it turned out, Henry's problem with Hugh was resolved in an unexpected way. In 1186, while inspecting his newly completed castle at Durrow, Hugh was approached by a youth carrying a concealed axe, one Gillagan O'Mala. Drawing his axe, O'Mala quickly decapitated Hugh with a single blow, to the astonishment of Hugh's companions. He escaped into a nearby wood and was never apprehended. It seems likely that this assassination was a revenge attack by disaffected Irish nobles, although Hugh's robbing of stone from the venerated nearby church of St Columba to use on his castle, is thought by some to have been a motive. When King Henry heard the news of Hugh's death he is reported to have been filled with joy.

Hugh's corpse was buried at Durrow, but nine years later his body was reinterred at Bective Abbey in Meath, while his head was buried in St Thomas's Abbey, Dublin. Following a further decade of dispute between the two abbeys, his head and body were eventually reunited and laid to rest beside the remains of his first wife, Rose of Monmouth.

So ended the life of perhaps the most remarkable individual of the whole de Lacy dynasty – a man who had completely transformed the family's fortunes by dint of his own energy and forceful personality. We are fortunate to have Gerald of Wales's own description of Hugh, whom he must have met at some point during his time in Ireland in 1183 and 1185:

Gerald's depiction of Hugh de Lacy (*photograph © Courtesy of the National Library of Ireland, Ms 700*)

He had a dark complexion, with black sunken eyes and rather flat nostrils, and he had a burn on his face from some accident which much disfigured him, the scar reaching down his right cheek to his chin. His neck was short and his body hairy and very muscular. He was short in stature and ill-proportioned in shape. If you ask what were his habits and disposition, he was firm and steadfast, as temperate as a Frenchman, very attentive to his own private affairs, and indefatigable in public business and the administration of the government committed to his charge.[10]

Gerald added a portrait of Hugh to his manuscript, even showing the burn on his face.

16

Walter de Lacy II – last of the dynasty

*The lofty pine is oftenest shaken by the winds, high towers fall with a heavier crash
and the lightning strikes the highest mountain*

Horace, *c*.66 BC

WHEN HUGH WAS killed in Ireland, his eldest surviving son, Walter, was still a minor and too young to inherit the de Lacy estates. As was the custom of the time, until Walter came of age, his lordship was commandeered by the Crown. Between 1186 and 1190, the royal accounts known as Pipe Rolls for Herefordshire 'in Wales' record that Ralph of Arden, who as sheriff of Hereford was acting as administrator, had £47 per annum from the 'farm' or income of the lands of Hugh de Lacy. Of this amount, £37 was spent on the custody of '*castelli de Ewias et Novi Castelli*' – the Castle of Ewyas and the New Castle. The remaining £10 was used on the custody of Weobley Castle.[1]

Clearly, there were two operational castles in Ewyas Lacy during this period, and historians usually assumed that the Castle of Ewyas was at Ponthendre and the New Castle was at Longtown. However, from our excavations, we now know that the motte and bailey castle at Ponthendre was not completed so cannot have been the Castle of Ewyas. For a time, we thought that the Castle of Ewyas must refer to the first Ewyas Lacy castle at Walterstone. But there is an alternative possibility. Only two of the castles of Ewyas Lacy are known with certainty to have been rebuilt in stone. These are Longtown and Llancillo. Since Longtown was the Ewyas Lacy *caput*, it was presumably the first to be upgraded, and in later years it certainly became known as the Castle of Ewyas. That leaves the strong likelihood that the stone shell keep at Llancillo was the New Castle mentioned in the Pipe Rolls.

DIVIDED LOYALTIES

Walter de Lacy had his inheritance restored when he came of age in 1189, just after Richard I came to the throne. Walter quickly took steps to share his estates in Normandy with his two brothers, Hugh and Gilbert, but retained overall control of those in England, Wales and Ireland. Establishing his authority in Ireland, however, proved far from easy. In the three years since his father's death, the political situation in Meath had changed. Prince John, as effective overlord in Ireland, had undermined de Lacy control by granting away some estates and putting his own favourites in positions of power. Meanwhile, Irish incursions ate away at the fabric of Norman Meath.

Restitution for Walter may have been possible through King Richard's influence over his brother, but for the fact that Richard was away on crusade, risking his own crown in an unsuccessful bid to recover the kingdom of Jerusalem, which had recently fallen to the forces of Saladin. In 1192, on his way home, Richard was captured in Austria and famously spent over a year in captivity. Prince John reacted by orchestrating a revolt against Richard, in collaboration with the king of France. This proved unsuccessful and the vestiges of rebellion were quickly quelled upon Richard's return in the spring of 1194. Walter de Lacy was quick to show his loyalty to Richard and was rewarded with a charter confirming his lordship of Meath, an action that eroded John's authority as overlord in Ireland.

Walter returned to Ireland in the spring of 1195 with full royal authority and quickly began to reverse many of Prince John's changes. With John de Courcy as co-justiciar, Walter arrested Prince John's previous justiciar, Peter Pipard. He also took steps to block John's grant of Connaught to another Norman noble, William de Burgh, which had dispossessed the O'Connors, leading to major unrest in Munster. Walter, showing some of the diplomatic skills of his father, met the O'Connors in Athlone, where an agreement was reached recognising the O'Connors as rightful kings of Connaught, in return for peace in the region.

The Great Seal of King Richard I
(*photograph* © *Selbymay CC BY-SA 3.0*)

Unfortunately, Walter's plans were soon to be thwarted, as John became reconciled to Richard and resumed overall control of Ireland. Walter and John de Courcy were soon replaced as justiciars, but Richard made sure that there would be no retribution dealt out by his brother. John sent the following directive to his men in Ireland:

> Know that, at the request of King Richard, my brother, I have remitted to Walter de Lacy and all his heirs the animosity, anger and ill will I had conceived against them … I have restored to the aforesaid Walter all his rights in Ireland for 2,500 marks … Wherefore, I order that you regard him and all his men as my faithful men and that you maintain, protect and defend them.[2]

After this fine, which was to be the first of several inflicted on Walter, his relationship with Prince John began to improve. In June 1195, John issued his own charter recognising Walter's tenure of Meath, while Walter in turn accepted some of the changes John had made prior to 1190. William de Burgh was confirmed in his grant of Connaught, but as a conciliatory gesture, de Burgh in turn granted a third of the province to Walter's brother Hugh. This, together with grants of land by John to Walter between 1195 and 1197, began to extend de Lacy control north towards Ulster and west to Limerick.

While de Lacy relations with John were improving, those with King Richard appear to have faltered. In 1195, Walter's lands in Normandy were confiscated and a fine of 1,000 marks imposed, possibly for Walter failing to support Richard's war in Normandy. Affairs in Ireland, together with disturbances in the Marches from the Welsh under Rhys ap Gruffudd, may have taken all of Walter's attention at the time. By 1197, the fine was still unpaid, so Richard increased the penalty by also confiscating Walter's English lands, including Ludlow Castle. The situation was only retrieved on payment of the enormous sum of 3,100 marks, equivalent to millions today, whereupon Walter's lands were restored to him.[3]

Norman control in Ireland by 1205

RELATIONS WITH THE DE BRAOSE FAMILY

When King Richard died in 1199, the complications of having two overlords in different countries were removed from the de Lacy brothers. Being on good terms with King John, expectations were probably high. One of the first of the king's acts to benefit the de Lacys was to sanction Walter's marriage to Marjory, daughter of William and Maud de Braose, which took place in 1201. The de Braose family had become increasingly powerful in and around the southern Marches. William de Braose, the fourth lord of Bramber in Sussex, had inherited the lordships of Radnor, Brecon and Abergavenny from his mother, a daughter of Miles of Gloucester. Under King John, he was granted a charter for 'all the lands and holdings he could acquire from enemies in Wales to add to his lordship of Radnor.'[4]

Further estates in Herefordshire and Shropshire were added to the de Braose family holdings with the appointment of William's son, Giles, as bishop of Hereford. William also became custodian of the three castles, Grosmont, Skenfrith and White Castle for a period after 1205. A favourite of King John, he was also granted the honour of Limerick in Ireland. Whether or not this latter action was a bungled attempt by John to shift the power politics in Ireland, it led to unrest amongst the resident Norman hierarchy.

The de Lacy brothers might have reacted with alarm to the increasing power of the de Braose family in the Welsh Marches and in Ireland, but with the new alliance created through Walter de Lacy's marriage, arrangements would be made which benefitted both families. By 1203 the de Lacy lands in Normandy and England, including Ewyas Lacy, were being administered by de Braose, while the de Lacys looked after the Braose holdings in Ireland.

These arrangements were initiated with King John's approval and the de Lacys continued to prosper. When John de Courcy, lord of Ulster, who had been co-justiciar with Walter in 1195, fell foul of King John in the early 1200s, it was Walter and Hugh de Lacy who were sent to apprehend him. De Courcy, an ambitious and impetuous man, operating for much of the time as a warlord outside the king's writ, was eventually defeated and relieved of his lordship. The de Lacy brothers were first rewarded with lands in Ulster and Connaught, but the following year Hugh, who had captured de Courcy, was granted the lordship of Ulster and then made earl of Ulster. De Courcy, having been expelled from Ireland, returned the following year with a Norse army provided by his brother-in-law, the king of Man, but was again defeated and imprisoned.

By 1206, de Lacy prestige in Ireland had never been higher, but things were about to change. As a result of a series of disastrous military campaigns, by 1204 King John had lost all his lands in France. This had a major impact on the royal treasury, which could only be rectified by increasing taxation on his remaining subjects. John started to put pressure on his barons to extract more revenues, partly for use in a campaign to regain his French possessions. At the same time, John began to scheme secretly with his Irish justiciar, Meilar FitzHenry, to retake for himself some key possessions granted to his Irish barons, such as Limerick and part of northern Leinster. Taking Limerick put the king at odds with both William de Braose and the de Lacys, while his action in Leinster also placed him in conflict with the great William Marshal, his army commander in France and lord of Leinster, through marriage to Strongbow's daughter.

William Marshal's effigy in the Temple Church, London (*photograph courtesy of Rupert Willoughby*)

Early in 1207, Walter de Lacy, defending the de Braose interests in Limerick, came to blows with the justiciar. Soon after, William Marshal's forces were also in conflict with the justiciar in Leinster. In May, King John reprimanded the barons for acting against his interests, thus admitting his complicity. Nevertheless, Walter and Marshal were quick to submit to the king, confirming him as overlord. Walter remained with the king during the rest of 1207, distancing himself from the Irish conflict in Limerick, which was carried on by Geoffrey de Marisco, on behalf of William de Braose. As a result, the de Braose castles in Wales and the Marches were seized and garrisoned by the king.[5]

At the end of 1207, matters between the king and his Irish barons were settled at a council at Woodstock, which led to new charters for Walter and William Marshal. William de Braose, despite failing to submit and absenting himself from Woodstock, also appears to have settled with the king. However, dissatisfied with the outcome and encouraged by his wife, Maud, who refused to give up her eldest son as a hostage, de Braose rebelled again in 1208, attacking his occupied castles in Wales and burning the town of Leominster. Failing to gain any support, and with a royal army approaching, de Braose and his family were forced to flee to Ireland. Now outlawed, they should have been given up to John's authorities, but instead they were sheltered, first by William Marshal, then by Walter de Lacy.[6]

During 1209, Walter appears to have continued a working relationship with King John, despite harbouring the fugitive de Braose family. However, there is some evidence that during this period the de Lacys were involved in negotiating a treasonable pact with the king of France to overthrow King John. If King John heard rumours to this effect, it could explain the drastic action he took against his Irish and Marcher barons in 1210. Raising the vast sum of 66,000 marks from the Jewish moneylenders of England, John assembled an army for an expedition to Ireland. Hearing of this, both William Marshal and William de Braose were quick to return to court and throw themselves on John's mercy. While Marshal demonstrated his loyalty by joining the expedition, de Braose was permitted to remain in Wales. After a show of force in Wales during May, the army embarked for Wexford towards the end of June.[7]

With Marshal and de Braose reconciled to King John, the focus of royal ire was now directed at the de Lacys and their followers. Walter could also have submitted, but how much did John know of the de Lacy's treachery with France? For whatever reason, he left it too late. Forced eventually to surrender, to avoid all-out war, Walter was stripped of his lands and banished. After a triumphal tour of Meath, John then turned his attention to Hugh de Lacy and Maud de Braose, holding out in Ulster. The royal army was sent north, but by the time it arrived at Hugh's castle of Carrickfergus, the fugitives had escaped to Scotland. However, their problems did not end there. De Braose's wife and eldest son were soon captured by the earl of Carrick in Galloway and returned to England, where they were held in a dungeon and deliberately starved to death. Hugh de Lacy escaped north to find shelter with the lord of Lennox, before finding his way to St Andrews and a ship to France.

EXILE AND RESTITUTION

The de Lacy brothers were reunited in exile at the monastery of Saint-Taurin d'Évreux in Normandy, which had a long association with the de Lacys and to which they had granted endowments. They were to remain there three years during which the abbot of the monastery attempted to secure their reconciliation with King John. Meanwhile, in the absence of the two powerful barons, Ireland suffered further unrest. King John, having achieved his aim of obtaining a large portion of Irish wealth for his own use, found its secure retention more difficult. In Meath, the native Irish began to reassert themselves, coming into conflict with the settlers, while in Ulster the O'Neills showed a renewed willingness to act against King John. During this period the king was obliged to spend considerable sums building the keep at Athlone and manning and maintaining de Lacy castles across Meath, particularly the main castle at Trim.[8]

Trim Castle (*photograph courtesy of Phil Brown*)

By 1213, the political situation had changed against King John to such an extent that he could no longer ignore Walter de Lacy's war-hardened military experience. With a Welsh truce due to expire, rumours of a French invasion and increased disaffection amongst the English nobility, Walter was recalled to England. His English and Welsh lands, with the exception of Ludlow Castle, were restored on the provision of four hostages, including his son, Gilbert, and the son of John Pickard of Tretower.

Walter de Lacy's seal attached to a grant to Craswell Priory
(taken from The Ludlow Castle Heraldic Roll, Logaston Press, 2019. Photograph © Friends of Ludlow Castle)

The following year Walter was campaigning with King John in France. In April, he visited the remote abbey of Grandmont, where he appears to have been impressed by the austere life of the monks. He would later grant the Grandmontine order land in Ewyas to found a priory at Craswall. John was obviously pleased with Walter's loyal service in France, as he returned both the town and castle of Ludlow to him at the end of 1214.

By 1215, the king was in serious trouble. A faction of barons, in league with Llywelyn ap Iorwerth, was waging open rebellion in Shropshire. Walter, with a Marcher army loyal to the Crown, was sent to treat with the rebels and bring them to heel. Hostilities ceased temporarily with the signing of Magna Carta in June 1215. As a result of Walter's actions in supporting the king, his Irish lands were restored to him, with the significant exception of Drogheda. This was a shrewd move on the part of King John, as Drogheda was the main port for Meath at the mouth of the River Boyne. John could oversee river traffic coming to and going from the interior of Meath including

King John depicted with an appropriately unsteady crown (photograph © The British Library Board, Royal MS 14.vii f9)

WALTER DE LACY II – LAST OF THE DYNASTY

Walter's castle at Trim, thus retaining some control over Walter's affairs in Ireland. Drogheda was also important in the defence of the royal city of Dublin. In addition, the king imposed a fine of 4,000 marks but later rescinded it in return for Walter agreeing to remain in his service in England and hold the royal castle of Hereford. This Walter did, sending his half-brother William Gorm de Lacy to look after the family interests in Ireland.

SHERIFF OF HEREFORD AND WARDEN OF THE CENTRAL MARCHES

By the spring of 1216, Walter was with the king's army on the south coast, ready to repel a French invasion. However, the French force, commanded by King Philip's son, Prince Louis, managed to evade the royal army and moved north to take control of London. In the meantime, rebel barons including Henry de Bohun, earl of Hereford, and the two surviving sons of William de Braose, Reginald and Giles, the bishop of Hereford, continued to oppose the king in the northern Marches. The de Braose brothers, in particular, had reasons aplenty to hate the king after his treatment of their parents and elder brother. They seized control of their father's castles at Brecon, Hay, Radnor and Builth. Llywelyn had also captured Shrewsbury the year before and John was determined that the same fate would not befall Hereford, so he charged Walter with the refortification of his royal castle and strengthening of the town's defences.

Walter was appointed sheriff and castellan of Hereford Castle in August 1216 and, later in the year, after Bishop Giles's death, was granted custody of the vacant see. He had full authority as warden of the central Marches, to spend the royal income from the county in its defence against the Welsh and the French.[9]

Nothing of Hereford Castle now remains to be seen above ground. Even by 1536, when John Leland described it in his *Itinerary*, it was falling into ruin, although it had been 'one of the fairest, largest and strongest castles of England.' His description of its high, strong walls and great tower, together with John Speed's drawing of the castle in his county map of 1611, give us a glimpse of how it probably looked in the later thirteenth century, after the improvements of Walter de Lacy and others. On the motte, a tall central keep was surrounded by a high wall with semi-circular towers – ten according to Leland but only five or six in Speed's drawing. Speed was most probably correct, as it is hardly likely there would be room for ten towers on the Norman motte. The inner and outer baileys were both surrounded by high walls and water-filled ditches, the main gate from the town being accessed by a bridge of stone arches and a drawbridge.[10]

The political situation changed dramatically on 19 October 1216, when King John, on campaign in Norfolk, contracted dysentery and died. Walter de Lacy was amongst those present and named as an executor of the king's will. One of John's last acts, perhaps in a fit of remorse, was to confirm an endowment from Walter's wife, Margaret de Braose, for a priory of nuns at Aconbury to pray for the souls of her father, mother and brother, who had been treated so badly by the king.

An impression of Hereford Castle, c.1250 (*image courtesy of David Whitehead*)

Prince Henry was only nine years old when his father died, so the royalist forces under William Marshal, Walter de Lacy and others had to move quickly to ensure Henry's succession. Prince Louis and the rebel army controlled London and the risk was that Louis would have himself crowned king at Westminster Abbey. After rushed preparations, Henry was duly crowned at Gloucester Cathedral on 28 October by the bishop of Winchester, with the Pope's legate Guala in attendance.

With William Marshal acting as regent and 'Guardian of the Realm', steps were quickly taken to entice the rebel barons back to the royalist cause. A renewed and simplified version of Magna Carta was issued in November and favourable terms offered to the rebels. A truce was negotiated in the New Year, during which Prince Louis returned to France to raise reinforcements. During this lull in hostilities a number of rebel barons changed sides. However, it was only with the Battle of Lincoln in May 1217, that the fortunes of the royalists improved dramatically. During the summer, hundreds of barons abandoned Louis and returned to the royalist fold. These included Reginald de Braose, who finally submitted in June and, with Walter de Lacy's intervention, had all his father's inheritance restored to him,

A silver penny of King Henry III, minted at Hereford by the moneyer, Ricard

WALTER DE LACY II – LAST OF THE DYNASTY

including Limerick. The final act of the war came in August when the French fleet bringing Prince Louis's reinforcements was intercepted and soundly defeated at the naval Battle of Sandwich. A treaty was agreed at Kingston and the French troops sailed home.

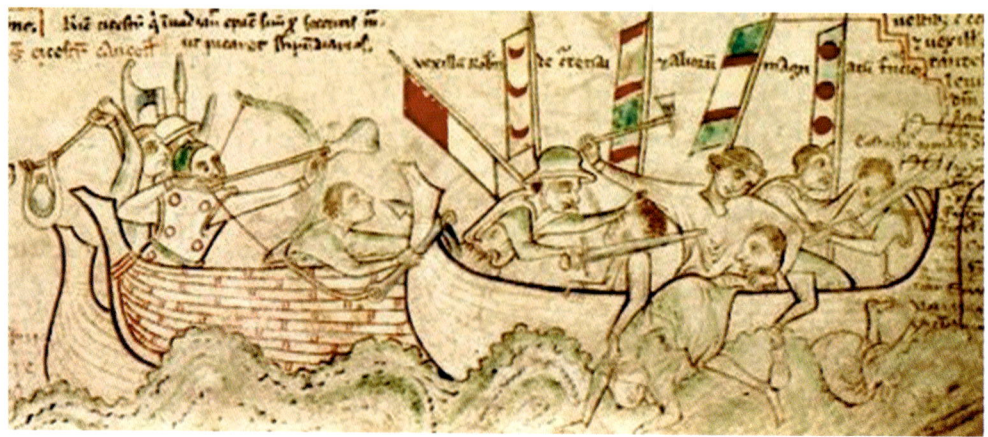

An early depiction of the Battle of Sandwich, by Matthew Paris
(*photograph* © *Parker Library, Corpus Christi College, Cambridge*)

While the French bid for the throne had been thwarted, Llywelyn ap Iorwerth continued to pose a threat along the Marches. As warden of the central Marches, Walter de Lacy was perhaps in the best position to negotiate a truce and this was duly achieved by the spring of 1218. Walter was tasked with escorting Llywelyn and the other Welsh nobles to pay homage to young King Henry at Worcester. Here, a treaty was negotiated which ensured that royal backing would not be given to any English incursions into Wales. The Welsh, in turn, would keep the king's peace. However, the marcher barons placed little trust in Llywelyn's intentions and the coming years would see building and refortification of castles all along the border. It was possibly during this period that Longtown Castle gained its cross-wall and gatehouse, in all likelihood using some of the Herefordshire royal revenues available to Walter.

During his time as sheriff, Walter was instrumental in bringing Jewish moneylenders to Hereford. This showed great foresight, given the demands that would be made on his financial resources by the young king in the coming years. Around the same time, Walter granted lands to the Grandmontine monks to build a priory at Craswall, in the north of Ewyas. This endowment, for the salvation of the souls of Walter, his wife and son, Gilbert, included 600 acres of land to the west and north of the priory. Additionally, the monks enjoyed substantial revenues from Walter's boroughs in Ireland.

Walter also gave a deed to the priory at Llanthony, conferring on them the absolute legal powers that he and the earlier de Lacys had in Ewyas. He authorised the prior and the canons to try the most serious offences committed in their estates, including murder, and urged that their court have its own gallows.[11]

Above: the remains of Craswell Priory today

Left: a cupboard and doorway within the south chapel at Craswell Priory

RETURN TO IRELAND

With the situation relatively settled in the Marches, Walter again turned his attention to his affairs in Ireland. His half-brother, William Gorm, had provided good service in looking after Walter's interests during the previous five years, despite the interference and malpractices of the then justiciar, Geoffrey de Marisco. As a reward, Walter decided to provide William with land to the north of Meath, in the province of Breifne. This was a region occupied by the O'Reillys and the de Lacys' old enemies, the O'Rourkes, who would both have to be forced into compliance. Walter first began building a castle at Athleague, a strategic site on the west bank of the Shannon, controlling a crossing and the flow of maritime traffic on the river. However, O'Connor's army from Connaught destroyed the castle before it was finished and it was only rebuilt by William Gorm in 1227.

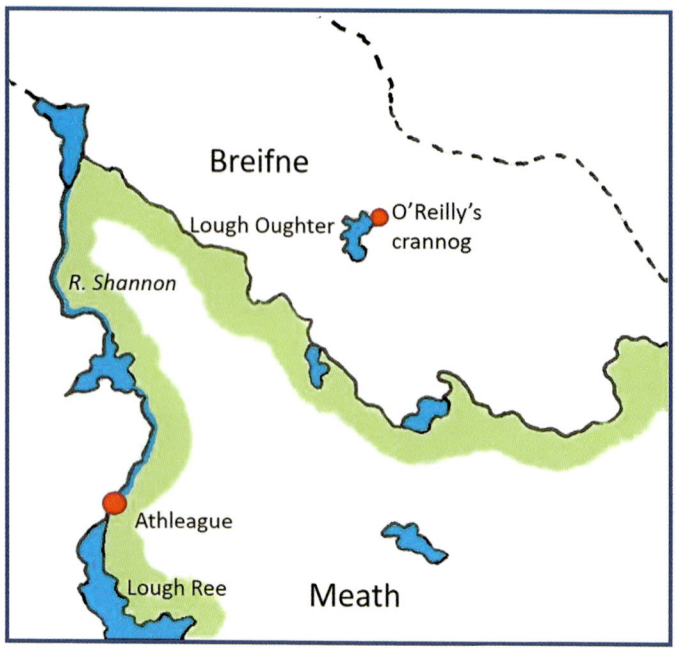

Part of Ireland showing Breifne, Athleague and Lough Oughter

Undeterred, Walter took his forces into Breifne and attacked the O'Reilly chieftain's crannog on Lough Oughter. The Irish annals record that hostages were taken and Walter 'obtained great power'. This artificial island must have been an impressive fortress, as William Gorm later made it his own base in Breifne.

THE RETURN OF HUGH DE LACY
In 1222, Hugh de Lacy returned to England from his exile in France, where latterly he had been with Simon de Montfort, fighting against the Cathar heretics in Languedoc. He immediately petitioned King Henry's government for the restoration of his lands in Ireland, but was offered instead a pension of 300 marks. Shunning this derisory offer, Hugh began making plans to retake his lands by force. Firstly, alliances were developed with Llywelyn ap Iorwerth and Earl Runulf of Chester. Hugh's brother, William Gorm, and Earl Ranulf's nephew both married daughters of Llywelyn. It is likely that Earl Ranulf, by aligning himself with the de Lacys, may have been hoping to re-establish control of the lucrative trade links between Chester and Ireland through

Drogheda, established when Walter was in charge of the port. The events of the following two years can perhaps be viewed against the backdrop of a power struggle for control of the Irish Sea and its trade. Since the de Lacy brothers' banishment in 1210, Drogheda and the Ulster ports had been in Crown control. With King Henry still a minor, effective control of the Irish Sea resided with the Marshal family, headed by William Marshal II since the death of his father in 1219. As earl of Pembroke, Marshal also controlled trade flow between the south Wales ports and Wexford. Having Hugh de Lacy active again in Meath and Ulster may have been seen by Marshal as a potential threat to his control of the northern Irish Sea trade and may have been one reason for his resisting the return of Hugh's estates in Ireland.

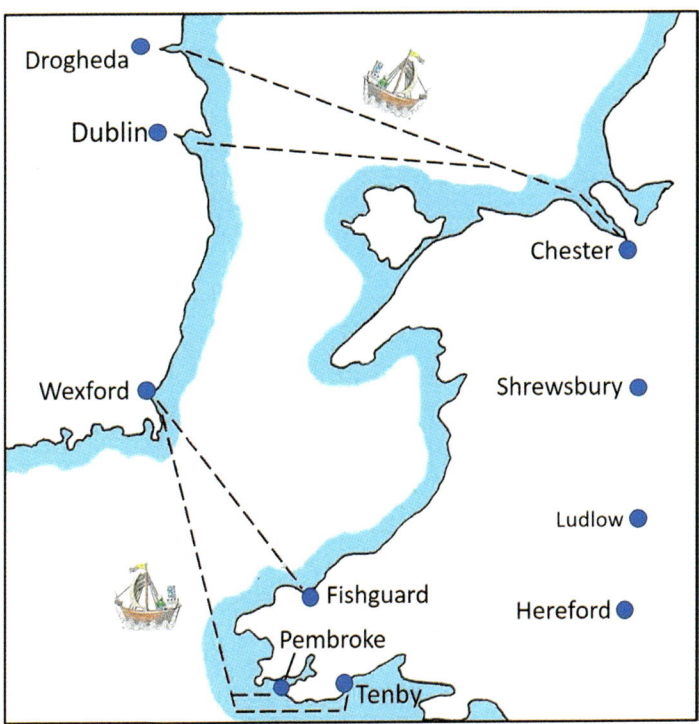

Irish Sea ports in the thirteenth century, and trade links with Wales

With tensions rising and fearing another war in Wales, King Henry's regency government, led by Marshal and Hubert de Burgh, offered Hugh all his Irish lands, with the notable exception of Ulster, a deal he declined to accept. Trouble broke out in the spring of 1223, when Hugh and Llywelyn captured some castles in Shropshire. Marshal responded by taking castles in south Wales that had been under Llywelyn's control. As hostilities continued over the summer, rumours of an impending invasion of Ulster spread and castles there held by the Crown were put on a war footing. By October, a truce was agreed with Llywelyn, and hostilities in Wales ceased. Hugh, perhaps disappointed with Llywelyn's capitulation, then crossed to Ireland and, with his brother William, raised a force of Walter's tenants and began ravaging those parts of Meath loyal to the Crown, even threatening Dublin. Walter himself took no active part in these events. He had even been with the government troops during the summer in their actions against Llywelyn. However, suspicions remained and in November 1223, Walter was deprived of his official positions in Hereford, which he had held for over seven years.

Hugh's warring in Ireland continued, with a move into Ulster to recapture his old earldom. By March 1224, the government's suspicions over Walter's involvement resulted in his being forced to surrender the castles of Trim and Ludlow and to go to Ireland to sort out his rebellious brothers. By the summer of 1224, Walter had retaken a number of castles held by the rebels and bizarrely was busy besieging his own castle of Trim when William Marshal arrived with his army. Trim was soon secured and the army moved on to Ulster where a peace was agreed with Hugh. No reprisals were taken against him, but, ironically, in 1225 Walter was fined 3,000 marks for the actions of his rebellious tenants in Meath. By 1226, Walter had been granted custody of Hugh's Irish estates and the following year King Henry III, now of age, restored these in full to Hugh. From that point until his death in 1242, Hugh de Lacy remained fully loyal to the Crown. However, relations between the de Lacys and the Marshals, which had always been good in the first William Marshal's time, never quite recovered. Had Hugh's lands been restored on his return in 1222, the war could easily have been avoided.

The period 1226–28 in Ireland was complicated by political changes in Connaught, during which the de Lacys and the Marshals were again at loggerheads. Walter de Lacy's son-in-law, Richard de Burgh, held a claim to Connaught from his father, William, whose land it had been during the time of King Richard. Since William's death in 1205, however, Connaught had been returned to the O'Connors. William Marshal II, in his role as justiciar of Ireland, was keen to preserve the status quo and avoid Irish unrest. However, it also seems likely that he would have been unwilling to sanction further empire building by the de Lacys or their relations. However, de Burgh's claim was upheld by King Henry and in June 1226, Marshal was replaced as justiciar by Geoffrey de Marisco, whose task it would be to depose the O'Connors and hand Connaught to de Burgh. As Marisco travelled through Leinster to Dublin to take up his post, Marshal's troops attempted to oppose his passage. Clearly working against the king's wishes, Marshal also advised the O'Connors to defy Marisco's directive. Aed O'Connor, the king of Connaught ignored a summons to Dublin and instead attacked and burned Athlone, killing the constable of the town. With this act, his fate was sealed. By May 1227, Richard de Burgh had been granted the whole of Connaught and the de Lacy forces from Meath were soon invading the province. By early 1228, Aed O'Connor had been killed – treacherously slain while suing for peace, if the Irish Annals are to be believed.[12]

WALTER DE LACY'S SON, GILBERT

Since losing his position as sheriff of Hereford, Walter was able to concentrate most of his attention on Ireland and ceded many of his responsibilities in the Welsh Marches to his only son, Gilbert. Now in his twenties, Gilbert is increasingly named in English charters and grants, and appears on the list of nobles called to arms in Henry's Welsh war of 1228. Gilbert may have had his base at Longtown Castle, as the honour of Ewyas Lacy was assigned to his wife, Isabel Bigod, as a dower. In 1230, however, Gilbert was killed while campaigning with the king's army in France. Unfairly to his grieving widow, Gilbert's lands were ruled to have been held of his father, so they eventually reverted to Walter. Gilbert was buried at Llanthony Priory. His death must have been a severe blow to his aged father, whose succession now depended on the fate of three young grandchildren, Walter, Margaret and Matilda. Isabel, Gilbert's widow, did not accept her dispossession of Ewyas Lacy, but appealed to King Henry for its return. In late 1233 the king found in her favour, but the honour was not immediately restored to her. Only in April 1234, after she had married John FitzGeoffrey, was Ewyas Lacy returned.[13]

THE 1230S: A DECADE OF REBELLION

During the 1230s, Walter was active in aiding King Henry quell a number of rebellions in both Ireland and the Marches. In 1231, the Marcher castles were put on a war footing, when Llywelyn ap Iorwerth rebelled again. Walter was ordered by Henry III to strengthen the garrisons of the border castles and prepare for siege. Once again the situation was defused by a truce, which Walter was involved in brokering.

A more serious uprising on the Welsh border started in 1233, but this time it was the barons who were involved. It is worth examining this rebellion in detail, as it is one of the few occasions in history when Longtown Castle is specifically mentioned. The catalyst for the confrontation appears to have been the removal of the English justiciar, Hubert de Burgh, on the advice of the unpopular bishop of Winchester, Peter des Roches. King Henry, perhaps unwittingly, destabilised the political situation in both Ireland and the Marches by placing unrivalled power in the hands of des Roches and his son, Peter de Rivallis. Hubert de Burgh, who fell out of the king's favour for alleged abuses of power, was deprived of all his lands and castles in the Marches, and their custody was granted to Rivallis. Hubert's nephew, Richard de Burgh, then justiciar of Ireland, was also replaced and ordered to surrender the royal castles in his control. Richard resisted and, as a consequence, forfeited his lands in Connaught. By 1232, Rivallis had been given financial control of Ireland and custody of many towns and castles. Not surprisingly, King Henry soon found himself faced with revolt from not only his own barons, but also the Irish in Connaught, hoping to exploit the situation.[14]

In February 1233, Richard Marshal, now earl of Pembroke after the death of his brother, William, came to court to remonstrate with the king over the many injustices being forced on the barons. Rebuffed by the king, Marshal left court determined not to

Clockwise from top left: Henry II, Richard I, Henry III and King John
(*photograph © The British Library Board: Royal MS 14.vii f9*)

let matters rest. In July, the king summoned his barons to a conference at Westminster, in order to address their concerns. Many, however, stayed away. Roger of Wendover describes how Marshal did attend, but then took flight to Wales on hearing of a plot against his life by Rivallis and his father. King Henry, angered by the failure of his conference, commanded the barons to meet him with his army in Gloucester, but when Marshal and his associates ignored this summons, the king, treating them as traitors, 'burnt their villages, destroyed their parks and warrens and besieged their castles.' Amongst those proscribed and banished was Walter de Lacy's son-in-law, Walter de Clifford. Marshal responded to these proscriptions by allying himself with Llywelyn ap Iorwerth, stipulating that neither should submit to King Henry without the agreement of the other. By August, the castles of both Hay and Ewyas were occupied by the rebels, forcing the king to act. Why Longtown Castle, in particular, was attacked seems puzzling, but may have had something to do with the bad feeling between the de Lacys and the Marshals in the recent past.[15]

By 1 September, the king and his army were at Hay-on-Wye. It would appear that the castle was back in royal hands. From Hay, a communication was sent to those occupying Longtown Castle, offering terms for surrender. The king then moved from Hay to Longtown and spent two days at the castle. We know that the rebels holding the castle put up a resistance, as later the treasury gave a loan of ten marks to John Talbot to cover the funeral costs of his cousin, William de Abetot, who was killed 'in the king's service in the siege of the castle of Ewyas in Wales.' The army then marched on to Abergavenny and on the following day to Usk, where Marshal's castle was also surrendered. By 10 September, Henry was back at his base in Hereford. At this stage, it appears that Walter Clifford and his men had capitulated, being offered safe conduct to make their submission. Where Walter de Lacy was during these events is not recorded, and it may be that he remained in Ireland during the entire Marshal rebellion.[16]

By early October, the king was back in London, after a show of force on the Welsh border and in Shropshire. On 9 October he held a conference of the barons during which some of the bishops urged him to make his peace with the rebels. However, learning that Marshal had retaken one of his Welsh castles, the enraged king ordered a muster of fully armed and horsed troops at Gloucester on 1 November. From Gloucester, the army moved to Hereford and then into Marshal territory where they found the countryside abandoned and stripped of available food supplies. The desperate army was forced to retreat to Grosmont Castle, where they suffered a surprise night attack from Marshal's forces on 11 November. The king's depleted army was forced to retreat first to Hereford, then Gloucester, but not before Henry had strengthened the border castle garrisons to repel attacks and withstand siege.[17]

Treasury records give details of the expenditure involved in garrisoning some of these castles:

A reconstruction of Grosmont Castle c.1230
(Image © Crown copyright (2020) Cadw. Illustration by Chris Jones-Jenkins, 1991, with modifications 2000)

> Liberate to Henry de Trublevill, for the use of the sixteen knights staying with him in the king's service in the Marches of Wales, each of whom has 2s. a day, and for the use of 45 serjeants staying with him in the king's service in the said parts, each of whom has 12d. a day, and for the use of 33 foot cross-bowmen, each of whom has 3d. a day, 153l. 9s. for their wages for 36 days, … and to him [Trublevill] 100 marks for this Michaelmas term, of the 200 marks yearly that he receives for the custody of the castles of Clifford, Hay, Ewyas and Usk. By Peter de Rivallis.[18]

With King Henry's withdrawal, Marshal and Llywelyn had free rein to attack at will the castles under royal control. On 25 November the rebels engaged a force outside Monmouth Castle and they appear to have gained the upper hand. During December, John of Monmouth took an army against Marshal, perhaps as a reprisal for the Monmouth skirmish, but was ambushed by the rebels and soundly defeated. Later in December Marshal and Llywelyn took a large force to Shrewsbury and burned the town. With his defeated and demoralised army, King Henry was powerless to stop these attacks. During December he was variously to be found at Hereford, Ledbury, St Briavels in the Forest of Dean and, by Christmas, Gloucester.[19]

Richard Marshal unhorsing an opponent before the Battle of Monmouth, by Matthew Paris
(*photograph © Parker Library, Corpus Christi College, Cambridge*)

In January 1234, the king issued further commands to the constables of the border castles, including Ewyas, Hay and St Briavels, to be on their guard against attack. At the same time, he issued a directive to the Irish barons to apprehend Marshal if he should come to Ireland. If they agreed to this, Marshal's estates in Ireland would be divided amongst them. Greedy for spoils, the barons took this as signal to attack and plunder Marshal's lands and castles in Leinster. Walter de Lacy was one of those involved, perhaps to his discredit. Word of these raids eventually reached Marshal, whereupon he took himself to Ireland, raised an army and by the spring had made progress in retaking some of his property.[20]

By March, the king was looking with apprehension towards another summer of war on the Welsh Marches. Money was allocated to the supplying and refortification of the border castles, including Ewyas and Hay, and commands sent out to that effect. It was about this time, however, that the king underwent a change of heart. According to Roger of Wendover, some of Henry's bishops, including Alexander, bishop of Chester, and Edmund, archbishop-elect of Canterbury, managed to persuade him that his problems stemmed from the bad advice he had been receiving from the bishop of Winchester and his son. As a result, des Roches and de Rivallis were summarily dismissed from court and their substantial assets seized.[21]

It is one of history's ironies that, while the scales were falling from Henry's eyes and he was ready to make peace with those still opposing him, Marshal was about to meet his doom. In April, the opposing Irish factions agreed to a truce and arranged a meeting to discuss their differences. Trusting his opponents, Marshal arrived at the rendezvous with a limited force, only to discover a full-scale army awaiting him, with Walter and Hugh de Lacy among its leaders. Forced into battle, he was mortally wounded and died a few days later on 16 April. When King Henry heard of his death sometime later, he reportedly 'burst into lamentations for the death of such a distinguished knight.'[22]

While Walter de Lacy's involvement in the death of Richard Marshal was arguably one of his less honourable acts, in mitigation, Marshal was officially a traitor, wanted dead or alive. With his death, the rebellion collapsed and the remaining rebels were accepted into the king's peace. The de Burghs, Hubert and Richard, had their lands and position restored.

As a postscript relating to Ewyas Castle, the Close Rolls record that on 30 April 1234, the king sent his emissary Drogo de Barentin to Hugh de Kinnersley and Hugh Milville, who were holding the castle, to plead for its release. We know they were rebels, as Drogo had been sent by the king at the beginning of the month to inform de Kinnersley that his lands were forfeit because of his support for Marshal, and would only be restored on his capitulation and payment of an unspecified fine. This must have been one of the last acts of the Marshal rebellion.[23]

THE FINAL YEARS OF WALTER DE LACY

Walter's last years were marked by further family tragedy, ill health and serious financial problems. He had incurred five major fines dating from King Richard's time through to 1225. These totalled nearly 14,000 marks, although 4,000 of this was later cancelled. The remaining 10,000 marks was a huge sum, equivalent to many millions today and in fact equal to around 40% of the entire annual income of the king's exchequer. There was no possibility of Walter repaying these debts in full and he was having to resort to the Jewish moneylenders of Hereford. By 1228, Henry was pressuring Walter for payment with the threat of requisitioning Trim Castle. Eventually, agreement was reached that Walter would pay 500 marks per annum, but this was later reduced to 400 marks and then 200 marks.[24]

The king's own demands on the moneylenders led them to call in Walter's debts, placing him under additional pressure. By 1234, the need for money forced him into offering William de Lucy the stewardship of his English lands and the position of hereditary constable of Ludlow Castle. Around the same time, Walter's wife became embroiled in a dispute with the Knights Hospitallers over the priory at Aconbury. The dispute lasted years, involving expensive litigation before the Pope found in her favour in 1237.

In 1239, Walter left Ireland for the last time and returned to his ancestral base at Ludlow. By then he was in his late sixties, blind and in poor health. He died in the early part of 1241, shortly after the untimely death of his grandson and heir, Walter. It was an ignominious end to a man remembered by the annals of Clonmacnoise as 'the bountifullest Englishman for horses, cloathes, money and goold, that ever came before his time into this Kingdome.'[25]

17

After the de Lacys

Some things change. Some stay the same
Chrissie Hynde

WALTER DE LACY's son, Gilbert, predeceased his father, leaving no male heir. As a result, the de Lacy holdings were divided between Walter's two granddaughters, Matilda and Margaret, sometimes called Maud and Margery. Matilda received the most important of the de Lacy castles, Ludlow and Trim. Margaret received the castle at Weobley and, after the death of her mother Isabel Bigod in 1250, Longtown Castle. In Ireland, the de Lacy holding of Meath was divided, with Matilda taking the eastern part and Margaret the western part. Unfortunately, they also inherited Walter's debts, which amounted to nearly £1,000 to his Jewish creditors alone. In Ewyas Lacy, many of the rights of the lordship, such as the income from courts, fairs and mills, were shared between the two heiresses. The descendants of both sisters continued to use the title of lord of the manor of Ewyas Lacy.

On her granddaughter's marriage, Matilda's inheritance passed to Roger Mortimer, who had already held huge estates in the Welsh Marches. Following a relationship with Queen Isabella and helping her depose her husband, Edward II, Roger was created first earl of March. Eventually, the Mortimer line joined with that of the Plantagenets. When Edward Plantagenet was crowned King Edward IV, his half share of the manor of Ewyas Lacy was subsumed into the Crown Estates.

Margaret's share of the manor was in turn inherited by significant power brokers like the Despensers, the Beauchamps and Warwick 'the Kingmaker', before coming into the possession of the Nevill family, who were the lords of Abergavenny.[1]

In the years after Walter de Lacy's death, war continued to break out sporadically between the Marcher lords and those parts of Wales still under the control of the Welsh princes, known as *Pura Walia*. In 1282–83 King Edward I took an English army, backed by Welshmen from the Marches, into north Wales and brought an end to Welsh independence. Following the conquest, much of what had been *Pura Walia* was run as a royal fiefdom. It was secured by a chain of immensely strong castles and walled towns populated by English settlers. The castles at Caernarfon, Harlech, Conwy and Beaumaris are some of the finest and most sophisticated examples of medieval, defensive architecture to be seen anywhere in Britain. Yet even these did not bring an end to warfare in Wales. There were significant Welsh rebellions in 1287–88, 1294 and 1316–18. In the last of these, Longtown Castle was ordered to be garrisoned with 30 men.

A few years later, in 1322, Ewyas Lacy and Ewyas Harold were required to provide a levy of 200 foot-soldiers to join King Edward II's forces in the north of England, who were defending against the depredations being carried out by the Scots under Robert the Bruce. It is not known how many ever returned to their homes.[2]

The division of the lordship of Ewyas Lacy was to cause problems for Roger Mortimer, the second earl of March. In 1359, there was a breakout from Roger's prison in Ewyas Lacy and many felons escaped. Roger transferred John de Boa, who was charged with assenting to the escape, out of Ewyas to his castle at Radnor to await trial. Each of the Marcher lordships maintained its own court and customs, and transferring a prisoner from one lordship to another was considered to be illegal. Roger was held to have acted with contempt towards the king but was pardoned when he petitioned that he held no castle in the 'land and lordship of Ewyas Lacy' in which to hold prisoners, as the castle there belonged to the other lord of Ewyas Lacy. He was granted a special licence to send felons from Ewyas to either of his castles in Radnor or Builth.[3]

The last serious attempt by the Welsh to recover their independence began in 1400 when Owain Glyndŵr raised his standard at Glyndyfrdwy in the Dee Valley. His ancestry included the bloodlines of three of the Welsh royal houses, which allowed his family and supporters to declare him to be Prince of Wales. Early in the rising, Glyndŵr and his supporters had some notable successes. His cousins managed to take Conwy Castle, but were unable to hold it for long and negotiated its surrender. Glyndŵr captured Sir Edmund Mortimer, the uncle of Edmund Mortimer, the child fifth earl of March, at the Battle of Bryn Glas. King Henry IV, fearful of the Mortimers and their claim to the throne, refused to allow a ransom to be paid. Sir Edmund responded by allying with the rebels and marrying one of Glyndŵr's daughters.

The revolt soon spread across Wales. Both local Welshmen as well as those living in England flocked to Glyndŵr's flag. The king's castles of Aberystwyth and Harlech fell to the rebels. There was much looting and burning of towns, and retaliatory expeditions by English and Marcher forces. Many of the Marcher castles, including Longtown, were garrisoned against the possibility of attack. There is no record of Longtown being directly engaged but in 1404 one of Glyndŵr's excursions was stopped at Campston Hill, two miles south of Walterstone, with 'great slaughter of Welsh.' Fighting also came to Abergavenny, Grosmont and Usk. The abbot of Dore Abbey was permitted to 'treat with the Welsh rebels for the greater safety of the abbey which is situated near them and is in great peril of destruction and burning.'[4]

Grosmont Castle. The rebels burned Grosmont but then suffered a serious defeat

Owain Glyndŵr was highly ambitious. He negotiated the Tripartite Indenture with Sir Edmund Mortimer and Henry Percy, the earl of Northumberland. Under this contract, once King Henry was deposed, Glyndŵr would rule all Wales as far as the Severn and the Mersey, pushing the border back much further than its position as defined by King Offa, 600 years earlier. England was to be divided across the Midlands, with Percy taking the northern part and Mortimer the southern.

Glyndŵr also formed an alliance with the French, who were harassing Henry's land and property in France. In 1405, the French landed 2,000 men at Milford Haven and together with Welsh forces they marched across south Wales and through Herefordshire. They were met by an English army near Worcester. After an eight-day stand-off, during which there were just a few skirmishes but no real engagement, both armies retired. The French returned home with 18 wagonloads of booty, most of which had been taken in Wales.[5]

In 1408, Aberystwyth was recovered by the English and Harlech fell the following year. Sir Edmund Mortimer died during the siege. Driven from his strongholds, Glyndŵr disappeared. He ignored pardons offered by the young King Henry v, and was rumoured to be hiding in Herefordshire with his daughter's in-laws, the Scudamores. He soon entered Welsh folklore as a national hero but after more than a decade of armies criss-crossing the country, burning and looting, the legacy of Glyndŵr's failed uprising was not liberation, but rather the impoverishment of the people of Wales. Certainly, many of the Marcher lordships were weakened by the disruption to payment of rents and taxes but the English administration continued to function.

In 1472 Edward IV created the Council of Wales and the Marches to administer the holdings of his young son, who had been invested as Prince of Wales. The Council sat at the old de Lacy castle of Ludlow. This meant that, until the abolition of the Council over two centuries later, Ludlow was effectively the capital of Wales.

The conquest of Wales and its pacification after Glyndŵr's defeat had taken away the *raison d'être* of the Marches. The Wars of the Roses brought many of the Marcher lordships under the control of the English Crown but some managed to hold on to their rights and privileges. It was not until the time of Henry VIII, the son of a Welshman, that the jurisdiction of the Marcher lords was finally abolished.

The preamble to the Law of Wales Act of 1535 compared the lawlessness of the Marches with the order of the English shires:

> And forasmuch as there be many and divers Lordships Marchers within the said County or Dominium of Wales … and being no Parcel of any Shires where the Laws and due Correction is used and had, by reason wherof hath ensued … manifold and divers detestable Murthers, brenning of Houses, Robberies, Thefts, Trespasses, Routs, Riots, unlawful Assemblies, Embraceries, Maintenances, receiving of Felons, Oppressions, Ruptures of the Peace, and manifold other Malefacts, contrary to all Laws and Justice; and the said Offenders thereupon making their Refuge from Lordship to Lordship, were and continued without Punishment or Correction.

Under this and subsequent Acts the remaining Marcher lordships lost their rights to try serious offences. All of Wales and the Welsh Marches came under county administration, with courts operating under English law and using the English language. The border between England and Wales was legally defined and Wales was entitled to elect members to the Westminster parliament.

The newly defined border followed the line of Hatterall Ridge, dividing Ewyas Lacy in two. The main part to the east of Hatterall Ridge became a new English hundred, a division of the county of Herefordshire. The lands granted to Llanthony Priory in the Vale of Ewyas became part of Monmouthshire. A peculiar exception to this division was the Futhog or *Fwddog*, a tract of wooded hillside to the west of Llanthony, presumably retained by the de Lacys and their successors as prime hunting ground. This was left as a small separate island of Herefordshire surrounded by Monmouthshire and Breconshire. It remained in isolation until its incorporation into Monmouthshire in 1852.

The Hundred of Ewyas Lacy, from a 1750 map of Herefordshire by Emanuel Bowen.
The Futhog is bottom left

AFTER THE DE LACYS

Henry's motive for harmonising the administration of England, Wales and the Marches was not just a matter of efficiency. The Marches could now be taxed. In 1540, for the first time the inhabitants of the Ewyas Lacy hundred were assessed for taxation. The first payment amounted to 70 shillings.[6]

Another of Henry's policies would have had an impact on the Ewyas region – the dissolution of the monasteries and other religious houses. Although the influence of Llanthony Priory had been greatly diminished during Glyndŵr's uprising, after which it appears to have come under the control of Llanthony Secunda in Gloucester, it was presumably still a factor in the local economy. Likewise, the suppression of Dore Abbey must have come as a great loss to Ewyas Harold. Craswall Priory, as an alien house, had already been suppressed in the fifteenth century.

The gilt copper alloy seal matrix of Roger, son of Huw de Ewyas, perhaps an official of Dore Abbey or Llanthony. The reverse bears the intriguing message, 'Have faith in me. I conceal secrets.'
(*Photograph © The Portable Antiquities Scheme: UID. 256258*)

THE DILAPIDATION OF LONGTOWN CASTLE

When the Hereford artist and traveller, James Wathen (nicknamed Jemmy Sketch) drew Longtown's keep in 1788, the upper part of the stair turret was still in place. However, the lower two thirds of the turret and the main wall as far as the entrance door is seen as a ragged-sided hole.

James Wathen's sketch of the keep in 1788, from the *Gentleman's Magazine*

By the same artist, the keep in 1804 (*photograph courtesy of Ron Shoesmith*)

When Jemmy Sketch returned in 1804 to draw the castle a second time, the upper part of the turret had fallen. The eastern end of the curtain wall is shown as a stump projecting from the side of the keep, while all that is visible of the western curtain wall is a large block of fallen masonry in the foreground. From the way that the upper part of the stair turret was hanging in the air so perilously unsupported in the earlier sketch, it seems unlikely that the initial collapse could have occurred very long before 1788. We can only speculate about the cause.

After Parliament had gained control in the Civil War, it was decided to slight or partially demolish a number of castles to prevent them from again being used by rebellious Royalist forces. In the southern Marches these included Goodrich, Raglan and Caerphilly. Although there is no record of Longtown being involved in the Civil War, it is not far away from known engagements. Early in the conflict a lethal skirmish took place at Ewyas Harold, when Welsh Cavaliers holding the village were surprised and routed by a troop of Roundheads from the army occupying Hereford at that time. Between the autumn of 1642 and the spring of 1643 the Royalists twice lost the city of Hereford to Parliamentarian forces and twice regained it. Then, in 1645, the Scottish army supporting the Parliamentarians laid siege to Hereford for nearly six weeks. They were over 12,000 strong and came with 'a very able traine of artillerie'. The ordinary soldiers were ill-supplied and, during the siege, parties of foragers roamed the county in search of food, livestock, horses and money. The church at Clodock and most of the parishes in the Golden Valley were robbed of their plate and other valuables.[7]

Writing in 1932, Alfred Watkins mentions a cannonball from Longtown Castle:

> Mr Arthur Ireland of Ewias Harold found this about 1865, close to the keep of the Castle at Longtown. It weighs 11lbs 2ozs [5kg], and has been given (through me) to the museum. From enquiries I have made in Longtown I hear of three or four similar cannon-balls having been found near the Castle. Then for twenty years I have heard the folk-tale of the spot (on the mountain above Oldcastle) where "so folk say", the cannon were planted to destroy the castle. Mr Ireland's version of this is that the guns were placed on "Money-Farthing" Hill. It looks as if some light on the date of the final destruction of the castle might result, if an expert could fix the period of these balls.[8]

If Longtown Castle came under artillery attack, then it is most likely to have been during the Civil War. This may also account for the musket and pistol balls found in the excavations on Castle Green. Oldcastle, at around two and a half miles from Longtown, and Mynydd Ferddin, at one and a half miles distance, are both well outside the effective range of accurate cannon fire during this period, so the details of Alfred Watkin's report can be dismissed as folk tales. A shot of around 11 pounds was fired from something like a demi-culverin with a four and a half inch bore, a very modest weapon compared with Roaring Meg, a 15½ inch mortar firing 200 pound explosive shells, employed by the Parliamentarians against the castles at Goodrich and Raglan. A few shots from a demi-culverin would be unlikely to cause wholesale damage to the walls of Longtown's keep but would certainly be capable of destroying wooden gates and forcing the surrender of a few defenders armed with only muskets. The castle might then have been slighted in the aftermath.

There is another more mundane possibility to explain the dilapidation of the castle. Like the rest of the country, Ewyas experienced a building boom in the sixteenth and seventeenth centuries, with many old, timber-framed buildings being replaced in stone. After his defeat at the Battle of Naseby, Charles I passed through Hereford and Abergavenny on his way to Raglan. During the journey, one of his officers with an interest in antiquities climbed to the top of the castle tump at Ewyas Harold and found 'not a vestige of wall above the ground'. The castle there had already all been entirely lost to stone robbers.[9]

Top: a Civil War cannonball found near Longtown. *Below*: Musket and pistol shot from Castle Green (*photograph by Chas Breton*)

In Ewyas Lacy, the curtain walls of Longtown Castle rising up the motte, acted as highly effective buttresses for the keep – but only as long as they were well anchored to the level ground at the base of the motte. If stone robbing removed their anchorage, then there was a risk that they could slide down the side of the motte. The western wall was keyed into the stair turret, providing crucial reinforcement, as the staircase wall was considerably thinner than the rest of the keep. If the curtain wall was destabilised by stone robbing and then started to slide down the motte, it could easily have ripped out the lower part of the stair turret.

Artillery fire, slighting, stone robbing – these are all possibilities that may account for the sad state of Longtown castle, and they are by no means mutually exclusive. Stone robbing most certainly has occurred, though whether that followed episodes of damage during the Civil War will only be determined if new information comes to light.

In the fall-out from the Civil War, the manor of Ewyas Lacy was confiscated from its Royalist owner, Sir Ralph Hopton, and sold at a knock-down price to the Parliamentarian, Major General Thomas Harrison. After the restoration of the monarchy in 1660, Harrison was hung, drawn and quartered as a regicide.

The Nevill family retained ownership of Longtown Castle until 1920 when they sold most of their interests in Ewyas Lacy. One of the properties for sale was the Sun Inn beside Longtown's market place. Included in the lot, as if as an afterthought, were the ruins of Longtown Castle.

LOT 162.

(*Coloured Brown on Plan No. 10.*)

An Excellent Holding, known as "Sun Inn,"

Situate in the VILLAGE OF LONGTOWN, and comprising:

A Good Stone-built and Slate-covered House

Together with

The Ruins of Longtown Castle

and about

3 acres, 3 roods, 5 perches

OF

Pasture and Pasture Orchard Land

Lot 162 – the sale of Longtown Castle

18

The borough of Longtown

The said town is a very long town being but one street in it
Robert Dudley's surveyors, 1566

THE LONG TOWN of Ewyas Lacy was so called because most of its houses lie along a single street, running down the ridge between the valleys of the River Monnow and the Olchon Brook, before continuing south for another mile to the smaller community of Clodock clustering around the parish church.[1]

The medieval town almost certainly began as a small settlement beside the early wooden castle at Longtown, probably enclosed within the square rampart. From there, it expanded into two separate areas to the north and south of the castle, protected by ditches and embankments. The southern embanked area was the more important of the two as it contained the marketplace and later a church, two inns and a courthouse. Small-scale excavations of the embankments have confirmed that they were medieval but did not provide precise dates for their construction. A part of the northern embankment, unaffected by later development, can be clearly seen crossing an open field from outside the Salem Baptist chapel in Llanwonog Lane.[2]

Our own excavations on Castle Green found there was no domestic occupation within the square rampart of the castle after the thirteenth century. It was retained by the de Lacys and their successors, and presumably reserved for military use. Later it became the location for Longtown's fairs where local farmers bought and sold livestock and sometimes tried their skills at bare-knuckle fighting. The Green and the land immediately around the castle are still owned by the Marquis of Abergavenny.

The embankments marking the western side of Longtown are skirted by a track known as Jew's Lane. Hereford's Jewish community expanded in 1236 when Jews were expelled from Worcester and Gloucester. It is possible that some of them settled along the edge of Longtown, but there is no documentary evidence confirming this and the name may simply be a distortion of something else. Upper and Lower Jewry at Abbey Dore were apparently derived from a corruption of the old Welsh for a yew wood.

When exactly the early settlement of Longtown was further developed as a borough is unknown. No founding charter has been unearthed and there may not have been one. Recently, LiDAR imagery has been successfully used to discover more about the medieval borough and has provided insights into its form and extent. LiDAR is a survey method that involves firing pulses of laser light vertically downwards from an aircraft and recording the time it takes for them to be reflected back from objects on the ground. Software can then process this data to create three-dimensional digital models of the landscape. By filtering out all but the last received reflections, it is possible to remove buildings, trees, and hedges in order to arrive at an accurate picture of just the land surface, known as a terrain model. By lighting this with a virtual sun, shadows can be cast to accentuate features on the ground that would normally be invisible. The LiDAR image of Longtown shows that a remarkable amount of the medieval landscape still exists in the form of usually unnoticeable earthworks.

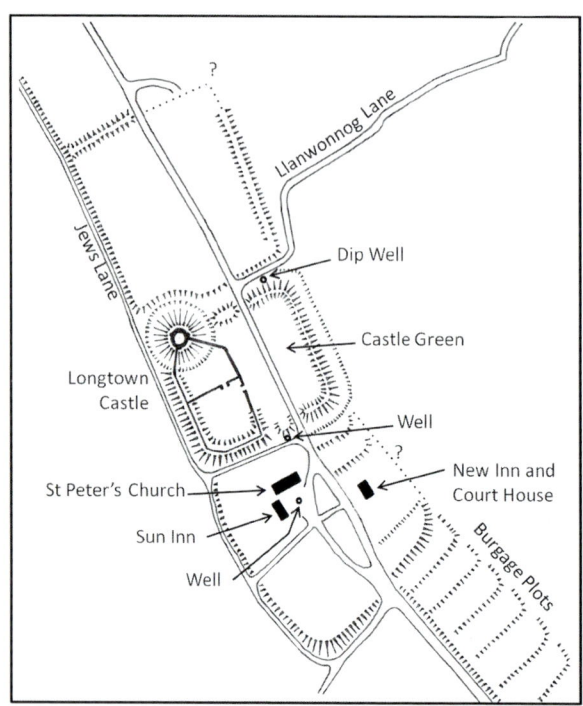

A plan of the central borough

The northern embankment from Llanwonog Lane

The six large fields or closes immediately east of the castle rampart were demesne land, not rented out to tenants but held by the de Lacys and their successors for their own use. They are identified on the 1718 plan as 'Lords Land' and were then still part of the Abergavenny lordship.

Along the east side of the road running south of the castle there are 20 or so rectangular plots, clearly seen as terraces bounded by low banks. In the area to the north

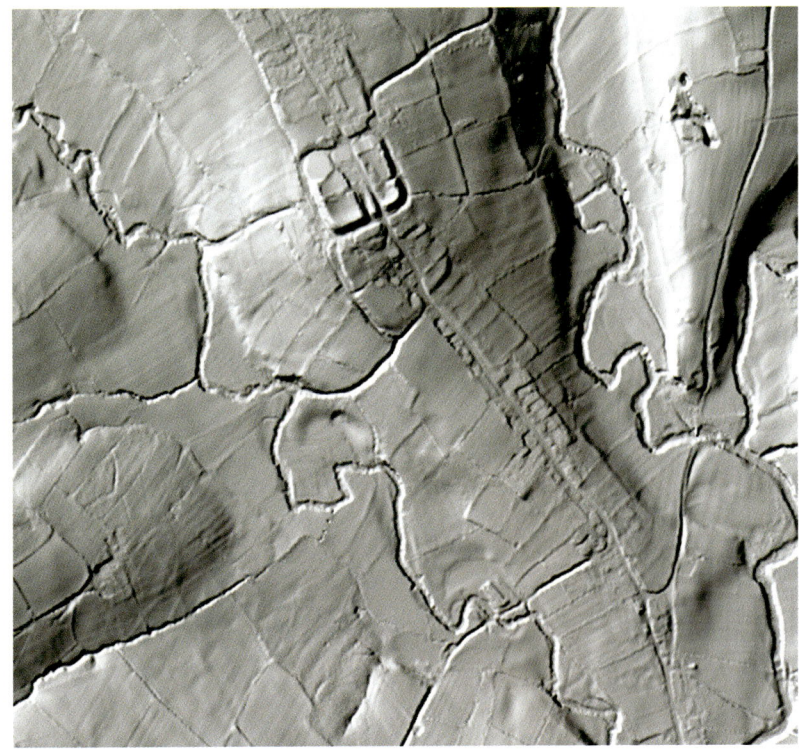

LiDAR image of Longtown

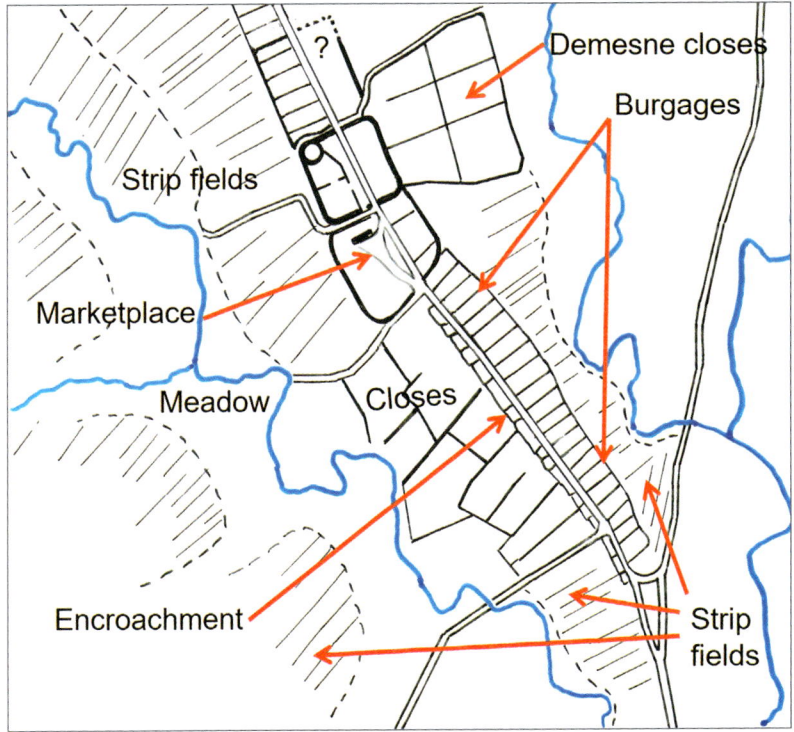

The LiDAR interpretation

of the castle, medieval activity has been largely obscured by modern development, but this too may have been divided into similar sized parcels. These were burgage plots, a standard feature of medieval town planning.

Burgage plots were rented out to burgesses or freemen to generate an income for the lord of the manor. They were more or less a standard size, large enough to build a house from where the burgess could practice a trade, as well as grow some food for his family. At Longtown the burgages are around 26 metres wide and 70 metres long, reducing to around 50 metres as they get further away from the castle. They appear to have been laid out within the boundaries of earlier strip fields. Eventually most of these burgage plots reverted to open fields. Even so, recent house-building in Longtown has respected the medieval plot boundaries, although dividing them in two. During the dry summer of 2018, some of the burgage plots and the footprint of their buildings showed up clearly as parch marks in the fields.

Parch marks showing burgage plots and their buildings

A valuation of 1310 recorded that Ewyas Lacy had 100 burgages. LiDAR shows that this number must have included properties in the outlying settlements and not just the nucleus of Longtown. Around 1234, Isabel Bigod, the widow of Walter de Lacy's son, Gilbert, endowed Craswall Priory with a fulling mill at Ewyas and a burgage with eight acres of land attached to the mill. Obviously a burgage with that amount of land and enough water to run a mill was not one of those seen on the LiDAR plot.[3]

On the opposite side of the road, the boundaries show a very different picture. Here, the houses have no land at all and back directly on to an area divided into roughly rectangular fields or closes. These houses may have originated as encroachments along the side of the road. Before being surfaced with tarmac, rural roads were usually much wider than they are now, wide enough for wagons to pass, and allowing travellers to weave around potholes. Encroachment commonly occurred where there were absentee landlords.

Beyond the burgage plots and the enclosed fields most of the surrounding land appears to have been an open field system, divided into selions or strip fields, occasionally still visible as areas of ridge and furrow, known locally as 'cop and reen'. Only the damper parts of the river valley bottoms were left unploughed and used as meadows. It is evident that in medieval times Longtown's farms were much more agrarian than they are today, and far less dependent on grazing livestock.

'Cop and reen' revealed as linear puddles after heavy rain

Although it had a weekly market and an annual fair, Longtown never really flourished as a market town, unlike the other de Lacy *caputs* of Weobley and Ludlow. By 1500 the market had ceased to function. With only one side of the road laid out in burgage plots, our initial thought was that the expected influx of craftsmen and traders must have failed to meet expectations. However, it is more likely that the real reason for Longtown not reaching its full potential lay with the division of the lordship after the death of Walter.

In 1566, Queen Elizabeth, gave the Crown's half of the lordship to her favourite and master of horse, Robert Dudley, the earl of Leicester. His surveyors reported that:

the most part of all my Lord of Burguany's [Abergavenny's] houses are kept in good reparations, the rest being now your Lordship's portion utterly in decay, and many house and burgages that have yielded rent now hath waste, not possible to be re-edified again because there is no man (if they were built again) that would take them to dwell in for that there is no manner of ground belonging to them, but the very plot where the house stood.[4]

Comparing this description with the LiDAR evidence leads to the conclusion that the division of the lordship of Ewyas Lacy between Walter's granddaughters, resulted in Longtown being divided along the road. Margaret received the east side of the road, while Matilda had the west side. Margaret and her descendants also had the castle, which gave them an incentive to develop the borough, but Matilda and her descendants declined to invest, resulting in the parlous state of the west side of the road commented on by Dudley's surveyors. It follows that the burghal development of Longtown did not take place until after the two sisters inherited the town from their mother, Isabel Bigod, in 1250, rather than when the castle was rebuilt in stone or during Walter's lordship, as suggested by other writers.

Robert Dudley himself had no interest in investing capital to improve his share of Longtown and quickly sold it for ready cash.

If the divided lordship led to problems for the people of Longtown, these can only have been exacerbated by the Great Famine and the Black Death that struck during the middle of the fourteenth century. The reported income of one of the lordships fell dramatically from £82 in 1332 to only £49 in 1369. At this time Ewyas Lacy had three watermills held in moiety or half-shares by the two lordships. One of these was at Clodock and another at Michaelchurch Escley. The location of the third, known as Castle Mill, is something of a mystery since the nearest mill to Longtown Castle, Pontynys Mill, is half a mile away. It is, however, possible that Castle Mill can be identified with Trewyn Mill, near to the first Ewyas Lacy castle at Walterstone. By 1493 both Clodock Mill and Castle Mill were 'ruinous for want of repair' and Michaelchurch Mill ceased working soon after. For the whole of the sixteenth century the Abergavenny estate bailiffs recorded that none of the three manorial mills brought in any profit 'because for many years past they have been thrown down and are totally in ruins.' This is probably explained by the fact that, during this period, the other side of the divided lordship was vested in the Crown, under the Tudor dynasty, until Elizabeth made her gift to Dudley. It seems that the mills of Longtown were too insignificant to capture the interest of the agents of the Crown and the lords of Abergavenny. It wasn't until the seventeenth century that the mills of the lordship came into private hands and started working again, now in competition with several others.[5]

The inhabitants of Longtown were served by two churches. For a time, the residents of the castle were inconvenienced by the two-mile round-trip to St Clydawg's church at Clodock. Then, in the thirteenth century, a chapel of ease dedicated to St Peter was built in the market place. Nonetheless, St Clydawg's always retained its precedence as the parish church for the borough. The fact that it kept both its primacy and its Welsh dedication suggests that the de Lacys had some consideration for the traditions of the native population.

When the de Lacys first arrived in Ewyas the church at Clodock would almost certainly have been a simple timber construction and they, or possibly the canons of Llanthony, went to considerable effort and expense to rebuild the old church in stone. The tiny, round-arched Norman windows located in the chancel and the nave indicate a twelfth-century date, although there have been several phases of enhancement, most notably the incorporation of larger windows of various dates. A defensible bell tower was added in the early fifteenth century. At some time during the sixteenth or seventeenth centuries the walls of the nave started leaning outwards, threatening the collapse of the entire church. The spread of the walls resulted in a lowering of the roof, which can be clearly seen on the east face of the tower. 'Toothings' in the chancel walls show where the walls had started to be torn apart by the movement of the nave. Fortunately, the destruction of this very special church was halted in time by strengthening the walls with massive buttresses and fitting new tie beams to the roof.[6]

The people of Longtown had the use of a number of public wells but there is no knowing when these first came into use. Saint Peter's well was located in the centre of the market place below the church. It has now been capped and covered over. Two wells were dug into the filled-in moat around the rampart. One, no longer visible, was south of the rampart on the corner of Pen-y-Dre Lane. The other, north of the rampart beside Llanwonog Lane, is known as the Dip Well (*see overleaf*) because here the water table is high enough to dip vessels in rather than use a bucket on a rope. The stonework of the Dip Well is not original, having been rebuilt as a community project in the 1970s. To the south of Longtown, Saint Clydawg's Well is to be found on the east bank of the river, 60 metres below Clodock Bridge.

For those who prefer to drink stronger stuff, until recently Longtown and Clodock enjoyed the benefit of seven hostelries – the Sun, the New Inn, the Greyhound, the Crown, the Black Lion, the Anchor and the Cornwall Arms – as some said, one for every day of the week. At the time of writing, only the Crown and the Cornwall Arms are still serving drinks.[7]

Those inhabitants of the borough who fell foul of the law would have had to answer to the de Lacys and their successors. As Walter de Lacy had recommended a gallows to Llanthony Priory it seems very unlikely that there would not have been one at Longtown. The earl of Abergavenny continued to hold his manorial courts to settle disputes and judge minor offences at Longtown Castle well into the nineteenth century, adjourning to the New Inn when the ancient house where they were customarily held became too dilapidated for comfort. After Henry VIII's reforms, the Marcher barons could no longer try capital crimes, so when, in 1790, William Jones of Longtown, poisoned his wife with arsenic, in order to take up with a young Monmouth girl of easy virtue, he was tried and executed at Hereford. His corpse was then hung in chains on a gibbet at Castle Green near to his home, as a warning to others. The rotting corpse caused a plague of flies and it was said that in Abergavenny market no one would buy butter from the Longtown farmers' wives.

Above: St Peter's Church in the 1920s with the well visible in the foreground (*photograph courtesy of Jenny Houston*)

Left: The Dip Well

19

The denouement – who built Longtown Castle?

The temptation to form premature theories upon insufficient data is the bane of our profession

Sherlock Holmes

THIS HAS BEEN a whodunnit. We have sifted through the evidence and told a new history of Ewyas Lacy that goes a long way to explaining the previously unexplained. Two crucial questions remain outstanding. Who built the stone castle at Longtown and when?

As with all good detective stories, there has to be a denouement, so now is the time to line up all the suspects, review the evidence for and against them, dispense with all of the false leads and reveal who actually built the stone castle at Longtown.

WILLIAM FITZOSBERN

The Revd Charles Robinson wrote in 1869, 'There seems little doubt that the Romans had occupied the site for military purposes and possibly left materials enough for William Fitzosbourne, the first Norman Earl of Hereford, to construct a border fortress, which passed from his hands to Walter de Lacy.'[1]

Those border castles that were built by William FitzOsbern are recorded in the Domesday Book and the Book of Llandaff, and there is nothing to suggest that he held Longtown before it passed to Walter de Lacy. There are good reasons for believing that William FitzOsbern built the keep at Chepstow and incorporated Roman stone and bricks into its structure. However, a close inspection of Longtown Castle reveals no Roman stonework or ceramic building materials, and our excavations found no evidence that these materials had been used in the buildings of the Roman fort.

WALTER DE LACY I, ROGER DE LACY OR HUGH DE LACY I

It seems almost certain that Walter de Lacy built the first castle at Longtown and that it was a typical motte and bailey with a timber tower on the motte. It would have been a hazardous enterprise if he or his sons, Roger and Hugh, had attempted to replace the timber tower with a stone keep, because of the very real danger of subsidence on a newly-built earthen motte.

PAIN FITZJOHN

Based on the carved stones over the north window of the keep at Longtown, Malcolm Thurlby has suggested that Pain FitzJohn might have ordered the building of Longtown Castle before his death in 1137, at the time when the Herefordshire School of Romanesque Sculpture was known to be active.[2]

According to received wisdom, this is too early for a round keep – and besides, Pain isn't known to have built stone castles. His castle at Caus in Shropshire wasn't rebuilt in stone until 1198, and Painscastle in Powys was only rebuilt in stone in 1231, long after his death.

The inability to protect Llanthony Priory during Pain's lordship rather suggests the absence of a strong castle at Longtown, just two miles away. And besides, a new stone castle only 14 miles from Hereford might have been expected to attract the attention of the warring parties during the following years of the Anarchy; yet, unlike the other de Lacy castles at Weobley and Ludlow, it receives no mention in any of the accounts.

MILES OF GLOUCESTER

The early nineteenth-century historian, John Duncumb, wrote that in 1146 the Castle of Ewyas fell to the Welsh, who had come against its solid stone walls with battering rams and stone throwers. It might therefore be inferred that Longtown Castle had already been rebuilt in stone, perhaps when Ewyas Lacy was under the control of Miles of Gloucester.

However, Duncumb's source, which was a sixteenth-century translation of the twelfth-century *History of Wales* by Caradoc of Llancarfon, in fact describes an action against the Castle of Gwys. This castle is correctly identified not as Longtown but as Wiston Castle in Pembrokeshire, held by the family of a Fleming, Wizo, known in Welsh as Gwys. Unfortunately, other authors have been misled by Duncumb's erroneous claim.[3]

HUGH DE LACY II

Early in the project we suspected that Hugh II might have been responsible for rebuilding Longtown in stone using the revenues from his huge estates in Ireland.

His endowments to Llanthony Priory show that his attention was not entirely focussed on Ireland and he may have taken measures to improve the security of Ewyas Lacy.

Ron Shoesmith cautiously proposed that the motte and bailey at Ponthendre was the Castle of Ewyas. On the basis of Duncumb's error, he then suggested that, after it had fallen to the Welsh in 1146, a decision was made to replace it with the New Castle on the more defensible site at Longtown, probably with Hugh II as the builder.[4]

Shoesmith was right to be cautious. We now know that Ponthendre was never built in stone and did not fall to the Welsh in 1146, so these theories about Ponthendre do not help answer the question of who built Longtown Castle in stone.

WILLIAM DE BRAOSE

Paul Remfry was also of the opinion that Hugh built a stone castle at Longtown to replace the motte and bailey at Ponthendre, which he thought was the work of Pain FitzJohn. Hugh's stone castle was then supposed to have collapsed or been demolished during the Braose rebellion of 1207 to 1210. Apparently, the present keep was then rebuilt either by William de Braose, while holding Longtown on behalf of Walter de Lacy, or later by Walter himself using material from the remaining ruins. This elaborate theory is based on (a) the absence of any mention of Longtown Castle in the accounts of the de Braose wars, and (b) the presence of the decorated stones over the north window and some dressed quoins mortared into the foot of the wall next to the breach.[5]

The validity of the first of these points must be viewed in the light of the acute paucity of any extant records concerning Longtown Castle, although it seems likely that the destruction of a new stone castle might be expected to be mentioned somewhere in the archives. On the second point, referring to reused materials, the decorated stones have been explained in Chapter 2, while the quoins are almost certainly fallen stones that were mortared into their present position during stabilisation work carried out by the Ministry of Works/ Department of the Environment in the 1970s.

There is no convincing evidence that the present stone keep was rebuilt on the ruins of an earlier one, and we are no nearer to knowing who its builder was.

WALTER DE LACY II

Derek Renn said that Longtown was probably the New Castle of the 1186–87 Pipe Roll and then inconsistently suggested that it was founded at the later date of 1190 plus or minus five years, merely on the basis of rounded ashlar pilasters found on some rectangular keeps of that age. This date range covers the last year of Hugh's lordship, the two years and eight months when Ewyas was being held by the Crown and the early years after Walter inherited. There is no possibility that a new castle was being built when Ewyas Lacy was in Crown custody or there would certainly have been a record in the Pipe Rolls.[6]

Joe Hillaby, a veteran researcher into the de Lacy family, also begins with what we now know to be the false premise that Ponthendre was the Castle of Ewyas. He makes the case that the New Castle was a timber motte and bailey built at Longtown by Hugh de Lacy II, which was in turn rebuilt in stone by his son, the second Walter de Lacy. He is of the opinion that the design for the stone replacement at Longtown was based on the great keep at Pembroke, built by William Marshal after 1200, with the three turrets added at Longtown to deal with the problem of building on a fairly new earthen motte.[7]

Leaving aside the fact that Walter de Lacy was massively in debt at the time when the castle was supposed to have been built, there are a number of fundamental flaws to this theory. It fails to explain why Hugh would have wanted to build a second motte and bailey at Longtown when the earthworks for one already existed at Ponthendre, or why he would have contemplated such an old-fashioned timber castle for his *caput* at Ewyas Lacy, when at the same time he was building the magnificently innovative stone castle at Trim in Ireland.

Walter would have been all too aware of the serious danger of building a heavy stone keep on a newly raised motte, as in 1212 the keep being built at Athlone in Ireland collapsed, killing nine men. Nevertheless, if Walter had risked building Longtown's stone keep on a recently erected motte, the three turrets would not have added any extra stability because they were not provided with deep enough foundations and are far too small to have any significant buttressing effect.[8]

As for Longtown's keep being based on the one at Pembroke, if we compare the main elements of their structures we find far more differences than similarities.

	PEMBROKE	LONGTOWN
Symmetrical plan	No	Yes
Number of storeys	Five	Three
Floor structure	Radial joists	Set back and main beam
Projecting turrets	None	Three
Arrowslits	Yes	No
Wall-walk	Two-tiered	Single
Hoarding	Yes	No
Roof	Stone dome	Timber rafters

It appears that the only real similarity between the two keeps is their basic drum-shape, which surely is not a sufficient reason for believing that Longtown was modelled on Pembroke.

Cathcart King classified castles as being either 'primitive' or 'scientific'. Primitive castles showed little change from early Norman motte and baileys. They have basic curtain walls with simple gateways and do not have arrow-slits for crossbow fire. Scientific castles adopted measures to counter the latest developments in siege-craft.

Pembroke Castle (*photograph* © *Mario Sánchez Prada CC BY-SA 2.0*)

They have curtain walls defended by enfilading towers, complex gateways and arrow-slits. In England, the transition between the two styles coincided with Henry II taking the throne at the end the Anarchy in 1154. Cathcart King specifically cites Pembroke as an example of a scientific castle. Longtown, on the other hand definitely falls within the category of primitive castles. Stylistically, it appears that Longtown probably pre-dated Pembroke and we should therefore look elsewhere for Longtown's inspiration.[9]

THE ONGOING ENQUIRY

It seems that the evidence that any of these lords of Ewyas rebuilt Longtown's castle in stone is, at best, somewhat flimsy. We were not at all convinced that there was a plausible case for any of them being responsible. So if it was none of the above, who was it? What were we missing?

Although there is a complete absence of any good historical record of when Longtown castle was built, there was other evidence available:

i. The dump of material, found during the excavation and interpreted as resulting from the truncation of the motte in order to build the stone keep, was dated to the twelfth century.
ii. The carved stonework over the north window, which we were now sure was an original feature of the castle, dates roughly from the second quarter of the twelfth century.
iii. the primitive nature of Longtown Castle suggests that it was built no later than the mid-twelfth century, although the round keep is unusual for a primitive castle and might imply a later date.

Taken together, these factors seem to point towards a mid-twelfth-century date for Longtown. There was one lord of Ewyas during the middle part of the twelfth century who is conspicuously absent from the above list – Gilbert de Lacy. Could he be the builder of the round keep at Longtown? As the owner of Ludlow Castle, he would have been well aware of the advantages of stone castles. His association with the Templars is likely to have made him conversant with recent developments in castle-building across Europe. As a Templar, he had the chapel at Ludlow Castle built in the form of a round keep, which strongly suggests that he was familiar with the form; but were round keeps being built in Britain during his time as lord of Ewyas Lacy?

The general consensus was that round keeps were not built in Britain until later in the second half of the twelfth century or thirteenth century, although the earliest well-dated round keep in England is at New Buckenham in Norfolk, constructed around 1145–50. However, in France, round keeps are known to have been built from the beginning of the twelfth century – much earlier than in Britain – and there is no obvious reason why Normans with estates in both Britain and France would adopt different building practices in the two countries.[10]

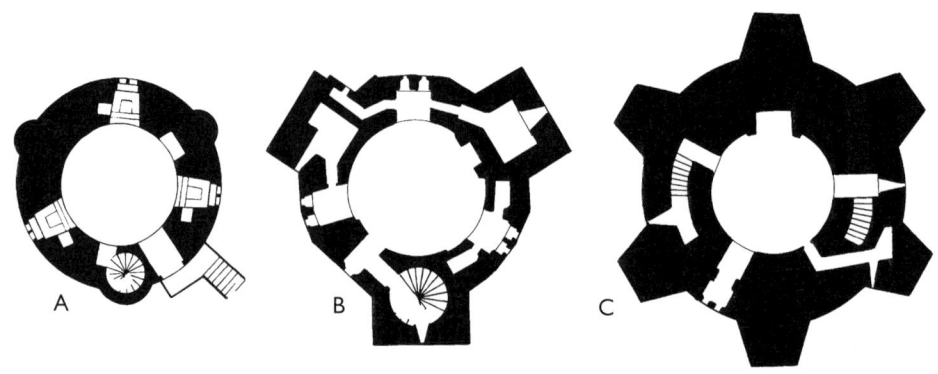

Plans of Longtown (**A**), Orford (**B**) and Conisbrough (**C**)

We searched through the gazetteers of British castles looking for any that resembled Longtown, and were left with the conclusion that Longtown's symmetrical plan of three round turrets projecting from a round keep is unique in Britain. The nearest parallels we could find were (a) Henry II's polygonal keep at Orford, built between 1165 and 1173, with three rectangular projecting turrets, and (b) Henry's half-brother, Hamelin de Warenne's round keep at Conisbrough with six trapezoidal turrets, built during the 1170s or 1180s. These two keeps were built to symmetrical designs but are very different from Longtown, being constructed on a much grander scale reflecting the resources available to the Angevin royal family.[11]

Casting our net further afield, we looked at castles in Normandy and the rest of France. Around the middle of the twelfth century, four keeps were built not far from Paris, each having a geometrical design based on arcs of circles. They are certainly impressive and practical strongholds for their time, but their complex and unique plans offer no particular defensive advantages in either structural strength or improved sightlines. It seems that their master builders simply had an appreciation of geometry and a liking for symmetry.[12]

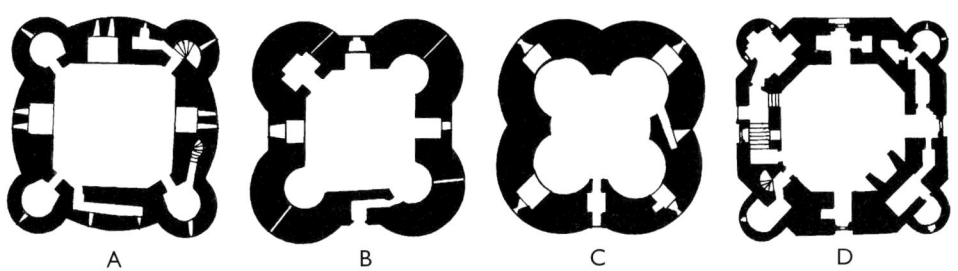

Mid twelfth-century geometrical keeps in France:
Houdan, 1120–37 (**A**); Ambleny, c.1140 (**B**); Étampes, 1130–50 (**C**); Provins, post-1150 (**D**)

The one French castle most similar to Longtown is at Houdan, Île-de-France, guarding the approach to Paris from Normandy. The drum-shaped keep has four projecting round turrets. Unlike Longtown, there are four rather than three storeys, but the different quality of the masonry of the fourth storey suggests that it may be a later addition. Like Longtown, the first floor has relieving arches of dressed stone over the windows. Houdan is thought to have been built between 1120 and 1137 by Amaury de Montfort who was Count of Évreux in Normandy. Currently, it is used as a water tower, which coincidentally was a role served by Longtown Castle until the 1970s.

Having noticed the similarity between the two keeps, we wondered whether this was entirely coincidental or if there might be a connection between them. Raised in Normandy after his father, Roger de Lacy's rebellion and exile, Gilbert may well have known Houdan. But we soon found that there were very specific connections between Gilbert de Lacy and Amaury de Montfort. Gilbert held a knight's fee from Amaury

Houdan keep (*photograph © GFreihalter CC BY-SA 3.0*)

Longtown keep

de Montfort in Évreux and he named his youngest son Amaury. Gilbert and his sons, Hugh and Amaury, witnessed charters for Amaury de Montfort's son, Simon. The Herefordshire Devereux family (from d'Évreux) had close links with the de Lacys, dating from when Walter Devereux held Lyonshall from Roger de Lacy at the time of the Domesday Book until Nicholas Devereux served as *seneschal* to Gilbert de Lacy's grandson, Walter de Lacy, the last of the dynasty.[13]

On the balance of probabilities, it appears that the builder of Longtown was Gilbert de Lacy and that Longtown's design is based on the keep at Houdan, built by his friend, Amaury de Montfort, but with only three turrets rather than four.

Gilbert may have regained control of Ewyas Lacy soon after Pain FitzJohn's death, but it is unlikely that he would have been in any position to start rebuilding the castle in stone until the more settled times after he had recovered Weobley and Ludlow in 1149. If this was the case then Longtown Castle was probably constructed in the decade after 1150. The elapsed time of around 80 years between Walter I raising the motte and Gilbert building the stone keep would have been adequate to allow for settlement, and deep foundations were not required. It may well be that the tax relief King Henry granted to Gilbert in 1157/58, was intended to help defray the building costs he was incurring. If the work was not finished by the time Gilbert left for the Holy Land in 1160, Longtown may have been completed by his sons, Robert and Hugh (the latter a noted castle-builder in Ireland).

The persistent use of the number three in the design of Longtown's keep, (three storeys, three turrets, three equal windows, three water spouts between each turret) is so unusual in castle plans that it may have been deliberate on Gilbert's part. One of the authors of this book lived for a time in the village of Rushton in Northamptonshire. It was here in the sixteenth century that the recusant Catholic landowner, Sir Thomas Tresham, built the remarkable Triangular Lodge. All the elements of its design are based on the number three and the lodge was conceived as a symbolic expression of Tresham's profound belief in the Holy Trinity. There is a possibility, but certainly no more than a possibility, that a similar motivation lay behind Gilbert de Lacy's plan for Longtown.

The Triangular Lodge, Rushton (*photograph © Daderot*)

20

Summing-up

History is a collection of lies that are generally agreed upon
Napoleon Bonaparte on St Helena, 1816

It all began with a desire to explain the mystery of why the rural parish of Longtown apparently had two castles, little more than half a mile apart. This developed into the Longtown Castles Project – a research project involving excavations at both the castle sites. The excavation objectives were defined in 19 questions. Two seasons of fieldwork produced some important and unexpected results, and remarkably all 19 questions were answered. Yet, together the answers didn't shed much light on the one original question of why Longtown had two castle sites.

We realised that we needed to widen our horizons and look at Longtown in its broader context, as the centre of the lordship of Ewyas Lacy and a significant piece of the jigsaw that was the southern Marches of Wales. It soon became apparent that much of what had previously been written about Longtown and Ewyas Lacy didn't have a strong evidential basis. The Longtown Castles Project provided an ideal opportunity to produce a comprehensive revision of the history of the March of Ewyas, and that is how this book came about.

The evidence from the archaeological investigation, complemented by a review of the documentary records and published research, has generated some noteworthy outcomes. We now *do* have a rational explanation for why Longtown has two castle sites, and the project has produced other significant information. This includes: -

i. evidence for a Roman fort at Longtown, suspected by antiquarians but until now dismissed by modern researchers;
ii. a sound case for Longtown being Harold Godwinson's camp beyond the Straddele;
iii. insights into the early Norman colonisation of the Marches and the siting of some of the first castles along the border between Ewyas and Gwent;

iv. evidence to support a revised date for the building of the stone castle at Longtown, recognising it as one of the earliest round keeps in Britain and probably the first to be built in Wales and the Marches;
v. a better understanding of the castle's structure, function and use of the earlier earthworks;
vi. new evidence for Longtown Castle's active involvement in conflict;
vii. new information on the founding and formation of the borough of Longtown.

It is to be hoped that these findings will raise interest in our local heritage and encourage a greater appreciation of it.

This was an ambitious project for a small village, with plenty of opportunity for things to go seriously wrong. Many people living in the area were unaware even that there were two castles at Longtown, and it might perhaps have been of only limited interest to them, but we could not have realised this project without involving the local community. Longtown had a population of just over 600 in the last census in 2011. We hoped that perhaps we would be able to persuade around 60 volunteers to work with us. In fact, over 130 people stepped forward to give their time and efforts to making the project a success. We were not permitted to involve young children on the excavations because of the restrictions applied to working on Scheduled Monuments, but otherwise our volunteer profile closely mirrored that of the community as a whole. The ages of those who took part ranged from 15 to 80, and there were roughly equal numbers of males and females.

Around 60% of the volunteers worked on the excavations. Others were involved in historical research, illustration, website design, writing educational material and helping organise events, as well as more mundane tasks like reinstatement of the sites after the excavations were over. Many of the volunteers were complete beginners who learned new skills from the project. More than half of them received some form of training. The majority of these were given instruction and supervision in basic excavation techniques. Others received tuition in documentary research, the use of archives and the design and maintenance of websites. A few of the volunteers were experienced archaeologists or heritage workers who brought amazing expertise and specialist experience to the project.

Although children couldn't work on the dig, we were keen to involve our two local primary schools. In 2017 the Normans were on the National Curriculum so we produced teaching aids on castles and medieval weaponry. Four groups of pupils and families from a home-learning circle were given tours of the castle and the excavations by a guide wearing a Norman helmet and carrying a sword and shield.

We wanted to make sure people knew why we were digging up the village green, so at the end of each day's excavation there was a tour of one of the sites, alternating between Ponthendre and Castle Green, for volunteers, locals and visitors, led by one of the professional archaeologists. We also gave guided tours to parties from a local secondary school, students from Manchester University working on another dig nearby, five local historical societies, Historic England, CADW and Herefordshire County Council. As well as the arranged visits, many casual visitors, both local people and tourists, stopped off at Castle Green during the excavations. Altogether we estimate that between 300 and 400 visitors came to the sites during each season of excavation.

The project received extensive media coverage. Our press releases produced articles in a number of local newspapers, also covered on their websites. There was a broadcast from the excavations on BBC local radio during both seasons. The project had a Facebook group and set up its own website (longtowncastles.com) to disseminate the results of the excavation and historical research.

After both seasons of excavation, exhibitions were staged in the village hall with photographs, artefacts, interpretations and an amazing display of works by the school children, who had been engaged in their own project producing colourful views of the castle and the surrounding countryside in the style of David Hockney! Each year during the project we also had stands at the Longtown Show and we were invited to give illustrated talks to several local societies.

The close-out of the excavations was celebrated with a pageant and medieval fair on Castle Green, complete with a hog roast. This was a family event, attended by most of the pupils from the two primary schools and their parents, many of whom came in medieval costumes. Entertainment was provided by an archer displaying use of the longbow, a stilt-walking jester and a falconer who flew his hawks while mounted on a magnificent Spanish stallion. Minstrels sang and played early musical instruments, while a motley gaggle of mountebanks added to the revelry with juggling, fire-eating, and trickery. The children needed no encouragement to take part in tugs-of-war, a swordplay workshop and a bespoke historical play. Around the Green there were traditional craft demonstrations, including spinning, basket weaving and woodturning using a pole lathe, while our local blacksmith fired up a mobile forge and produced a formidable-looking broadsword.

If possible, we wanted the project to benefit the local economy. The enabling grant from the Heritage Lottery Fund was virtually all spent in Herefordshire, paying wages and supporting local businesses. We produced two pamphlets to help boost tourism, one giving information on Longtown Castle, the other on a historic walk around Longtown. These are available at the castle and are distributed to local pubs, guesthouses and campsites. They have proved to be very popular with visitors to the area. We also published a booklet on the project, *The Mystery and History of the Castles of Longtown*. Copies were given to every pupil in our two primary schools and it is now sold at the village shop.

Some of the many volunteers, and scenes from the medieval fair on the Green ...

An ongoing result of the project has been a dialogue with English Heritage, the custodians of Longtown Castle. With the new information we had garnered, we were invited to update their website entry on the history of the castle. More importantly, working through Longtown Village Pride, we have now entered into an agreement with English Heritage, giving direct community involvement in the management and maintenance of the castle. This has resulted in more work being done by volunteers and local contractors. The enhanced relationship between the custodians and the people of Longtown has been held up by English Heritage as an example of how small heritage sites can be cared for in the future.

In all, it has been a very rewarding project. We were extremely fortunate in having the right partners in place and a pool of willing volunteers within the community. Were it not for their skills, enthusiasm and encouragement, the project would not have been such a success. Many of the participants have expressed an interest in doing further voluntary work and it is gratifying that a frequently asked question is, 'When are we going to do the next one?'

APPENDICES

A sketch of Longtown Castle in 1864, by Lady Frances Vernon-Harcourt, from *A History of the Castles of Herefordshire and Their Lords* by Revd Charles John Robinson. The keep has been perilously undermined by stone robbers

A timeline for Ewyas and the de Lacys

c.2,300 BC	Beaker graves in the Olchon Valley.
c.2,000 BC	A Bronze Age burial cairn in use in the Olchon Valley.
c.400 BC–50 AD	Iron Age forts occupied at Twyn-y Gaer, Pentwyn and Walterstone.
c.50 AD	The Romans build a fort at Longtown.
c.500	The churches of St Clydawg and St Beuno founded.
c.1048	Osbern Pentecost builds a timber castle at Ewyas Harold.
1055	Harold Godwinson's army camp at Longtown.
1067–71	William FitzOsbern refortifies Ewyas Harold Castle as part of a chain of castles around Hereford. Walter de Lacy builds castles at Walterstone, Longtown and along the border with Gwent.
1175	Walter de Lacy helps put down Roger de Breteuil's rebellion.
1085	Walter de Lacy dies while inspecting church building at Hereford.
1086	The Domesday Book records Roger de Lacy's landholdings in Ewyas and elsewhere.
1088	Roger joins the rebellion against William Rufus.
1095	Roger is implicated in another rebellion and is exiled.
1108	Roger's brother, Hugh, founds the priory at Llanthony.
1119	Pain FitzJohn has the lordship of Ewyas Lacy, along with other landholding in the Marches.
1135	The beginning of the 'Anarchy'. The canons of Llanthony retreat to Gloucester after repeated attacks from the Welsh.
1137	Pain FitzJohn is killed. Gilbert de Lacy bids to recover Ewyas, Weobley and Ludlow.
1139	Ludlow and Hereford under siege.
1147	Dore Abbey founded.

APPENDIX 1

c.1150	Having regained his patrimony, Gilbert de Lacy starts rebuilding Longtown Castle in stone.
c.1158	Gilbert becomes a Templar and departs for Palestine.
1171	Hugh de Lacy II joins Henry II's expedition to Ireland and is soon made lord of Meath.
1182	Hugh appointed governor of Ireland.
1186	Hugh assassinated. Ewyas and Weobley are held by the Crown until 1189. Hugh's son, Walter de Lacy II, comes of age in 1189.
1195/1197	Differences with Prince John in Ireland and King Richard in Normandy result in huge fines being levied on Walter.
1210	Walter and his brother Hugh expelled from Ireland and banished to Normandy.
1213–15	Walter recalled and supports King John against the barons calling for the reforms of the Magna Carta.
1216	Walter appointed sheriff of Hereford.
1233	Longtown Castle seized by the rebel forces of Richard Marshal but recovered by Henry III.
1241	The death of Walter results in the division of the lordship of Ewyas Lacy.
1316–18	Longtown Castle garrisoned against a Welsh rebellion.
1328	The castle is reported as being in ruins.
1348–49	The Black Death.
1403	Henry IV orders the castle to be defended against possible attack by Owain Glyndŵr.
1535	The abolition of the Marcher lordships. Ewyas Lacy is divided by the new Welsh border, and Longtown officially becomes a part of Herefordshire.

Were the de Lacy brothers at Hastings?

The record of who actually fought at Hastings is remarkably scant and much disputed. A list of the main combatants was compiled soon after the battle and kept at Battle Abbey, but it was removed following Henry VIII's dissolution of the monasteries and subsequently destroyed in a fire. Various supposed copies survived but they are inconsistent with each other and even the original was unreliable because the monks of the abbey were not above adding names to the roll in return for a suitable inducement. Two versions survive from the sixteenth century. Leland's list includes a *Lascy* and a *Lascels*, while Holinshead has the name *Lacy* twice.[1]

Master Wace, writing a century after Hastings, records many who were present at the battle, and describes the exploits of a troop of knights that included one of the de Lacy family:

> And Richard d'Avrencin was there, and with him were the sire de Biarz, and the sire de Solignie, and the butler d'Aubignie, and the lords de Vitrie, de Lacie, de Val de Saire, and de Tracie; and these forming one troop, fell on the English off hand, fearing neither fence nor fosse; many a man did they overthrow that day; many did they maim, and many a good horse did they kill.

Later, Wace also mentions a '*chevalier de Lacie*', so it appears that at least two members of the de Lacy family served in Duke William's cavalry at Hastings.[2]

The '*lord de Lacie*' ought to refer to Hugh, who was in his mid-forties at the time, while the '*chevalier de Lacie*' could be either Ilbert or Walter. But if Hugh had been present at Hastings it is odd that there is no record of him ever receiving any English land. Orderic Vitalis may provide an explanation for this. He wrote:

> Meanwhile, some of the Norman ladies were so inflamed by passion that they sent frequent messages to their husbands, requiring their speedy return, adding that, if it were not immediate, they would choose others. They would not venture as yet to join their lords, on account of the sea voyage, which was entirely new to them. Nor did they like to pass into England where their husbands were always in arms, and fresh expeditions were daily undertaken, attended with much effusion of blood on both sides. But the king naturally wished to retain his soldiers while the country was in so disturbed a state, and made them great offers of lands with ample revenues and great powers, promising still more when the whole kingdom should be freed from their opponents. The lawfully created barons and leading soldiers were in great perplexity, for they were sensible that, if they took their departure while their sovereign, with their brothers, friends and comrades, were surrounded by the perils of war, they would be publicly branded as base traitors and cowardly deserters. On the other hand, what were these honourable soldiers to

APPENDIX 2

do, when their licentious wives threatened to stain the marriage bed with adultery, and stamp the mark of infamy on their offspring? … and many others departed, deserting, with regret and reluctance, their king struggling amongst foreigners. They returned obsequiously to their lascivious wives in Normandy, but neither they nor their heirs were ever able to recover the honour and domains which they had already gained, and relinquished on this occasion.[3]

More recently, French antiquaries compiled a new roll of those present at Hastings, which in 1862 was inscribed on the wall of the Norman church at Dives-sur-Mer, the mustering harbour for William's invasion fleet. This roll is unreliable, as it appears that the compilers plucked many names from the Domesday Book, written 20 years after the battle. They not only included *Hugue, Ibert and Gautier de Laci*, (Hugh, Ilbert and Walter) but also *Roger* who was only about four years old in 1066.

In 1931 the French government commissioned a bronze plaque to be erected at Falaise, the birthplace of William the Conqueror, naming those who took part in the invasion. The compilers of the *Roll de Falaise* included only two de Lacys, *Ibert* and *Gautier*, presumably concluding that both Ilbert and Walter were at Hastings from the rewards in land they later received. However, they may have received these rewards for services during the later stages of the Conquest or when putting down rebellions.

So there appears to be no conclusive proof as to whether it was Hugh de Lacy and one of his sons, or both the de Lacy brothers, who fought at Hastings. However, very soon after the Conquest there is sound evidence that Ilbert and Walter were resident in England, while there is no record of their father, Hugh. On the balance of probability, it seems most likely that the two brothers came over with the invasion force, while their father remained in Normandy looking after the family estates.

Roger de Lacy's holdings in Herefordshire

Held directly by Roger de Lacy as tenant-in-chief			
HUNDRED	MANOR	PRESENT SUBTENANT	FORMER HOLDER
Cutsthorn	Ewyas Castlery	William/ Osbern	
Ewyas	Ewyas		
–	Clifford Castlery		
Greytree	Putley	William	Tosti
Thornlaw	Ocle Pychard		6 free men
	Maund	William	Alric
	River Wye		
	Hereford		
	Maund	Hugh	Wonni
	Bodenham	Herbert	Edwy
	'same hundred'		Edwy cilt
	Marden	Ingelrann	Edwy cilt
Wolphy	Woonton	Gerald	Ernwy
	Heath	Gerald	**Leofwin**
	Pudleston	Hugh	Wulfward
	Whyle?	**Alwin**	Edwy cilt
Stradelei	Bacton	Gilbert	Edwy
	Wadetune	Gilbert	Alfward
	Elnodstune	William	
	Edwardstune	Walter	
Dinedore	Bullinghope		Alnoth
	Cobhall	Gerald	Alfward
	Mawfield	Ingelrann	Edwy cilt
	Webton	Berner	Alfward
	Webton	Gerald/ Berner	Edwy

APPENDIX 3

NOTES
1. Carucates are converted to hides at 2 : 1
2. Places in italics are unidentified
3. English and Welsh subtenants are shown in **bold**

Hides	Ploughs in Lordship	Villagers' Ploughs	Value in shillings	Notes and payments in kind
2	2	1	20	Waste
5	11			15 sesters of honey + 15 pigs
2				Waste
1	2	2	20	
7	2	9	75	
2	2		25	
			120	A fishery
			20	Burgesses
1	1		15	
1.5	2	6	60	A mill at 16s + 16 sticks of eels
0.25		1	2	
1	2	2	60	
0.75		1	4	
0.75			6	
3	2	2	40	
1.5	1	0.5	10	
5	1		9	+ 3 sesters of honey
1				
3	2		10	*Pontrilas?*
			8	*Poston?*
2	1	2.5	50	One third of 2 mills 14s 8d
1	2		50	
2	2		46	**Leofwin** holds 1 virgate
0.5	1		15	
2.5		3	10	

ROGER DE LACY'S HOLDINGS IN HEREFORDSHIRE

Held directly by Roger de Lacy as tenant-in-chief			
HUNDRED	MANOR	PRESENT SUBTENANT	FORMER HOLDER
Cutsthorn	Stretton	Robert	Edwy Cilt
	Lyde	Ralph	Thorkell from Earl Harold
	Lyde	Ralph	Browning
Radlow	Weston Beggard		Ginfrid
	Yarkhill		Arkell
	Halmonds Frome		Tosti from Queen Edith
	Castle Frome		Brictmer from Earl Harold
	Munsley	Ralph	Brictmer
	Little Marcle	Odo	Thorkell from Earl Harold
	Canon Frome	Gerard	Thorkell
	Evesbatch	Odo	3 men from Earl Harold
	Monkhide	Tesselin	Osgot
	Tarrington	Ansfrid	Alric
	Leadon	St Peter's	Thorkell
	Leadon		Thorkell
	Mathon	Odo	Merwin from Earl Oda
Hazeltree	Lawton	**An Englishman**	Wulfric
	Street	William	King Edward
	Ledicot	Gilbert	Aelfled
Elsdon	Hopleys Green	Walter	Wulfric
	Lyonshall	Walter	Thorkell from Earl Harold
	Woonton		Algar
–	Eardisley	Robert	Edwy
	Letton	Tesselin	Edwy cilt
Stretford	Weobley		Edwy cilt
	Fernhill		Edwy cilt
	Kings Pyon		King Edward
	Birley	**Godmund**	Saeric
	Alton	Osbern	Alnoth
	Swanstone	**Godmund**	Saeric
	Staunton	Leofric	Ernwy from Edwy Cilt
	Mansell Gamage		Aelfled from Earl Harold
	Staunton	William	Alric
	Yazor	Robert	Ludric, thane of Earl Algar
	Yarsop	Robert	Edwy/ **Leofwin**/ Saemer
	Byford	Walter	Alfward

Hides	Ploughs in Lordship	Villagers' Ploughs	Value in shillings	Notes and payments in kind
2.5	2	3	50	A mill 32d
2	1	2.5	25	
1	2		60	
6	2	9	100	A mill 10s
2	2	7	50	A mill 100d
4	2	8	60	A mill 7s 6d + 5 sticks of eels
5	3	7	60	A mill at 10s
3.35	2	9	60	
5	1	11.5	100	A mill pays corn
4	2	7	73	A mill at 10s 10d
1	4	2	28	
1	1		5	
0.5	1		6	
0.5	1	1	20	
0.5			4	Waste
0.5	1		10	
1	1	1.5	20	
1			15	
1	1	1	10	
2				Waste. Men pay 10s 8d to settle
5	2	5	50	Men pay 100d to settle
1		1.5	5	
?	1		No tax	A fortified house in a wood
3	1	1	30	A mill pays nothing
3.5	3	9.5	100	A park
2	1	10	60	
5	2	9	80	A gift from King William to Walter
0.5	2	1	40	
0.3	2		10	
1		2	15	
2	0.5	2	5	
8	3	10	160	
4	2	1	30	
5	2	3	60	
1.5	1	0.5	15	
5	1	2	100	A mill at 20s

Held directly by Roger de Lacy as tenant-in-chief			
HUNDRED	MANOR	PRESENT SUBTENANT	FORMER HOLDER
	Wormesley	**Leofric**	Alfwy/ Wulfnoth
	Wormesley		Hadwic
Plegelgate	Stoke Lacy		Aelmer Cilt
	Collington	Hugh	Wulfward
	Sawbury	Hugh	Wynric
	Wolferlow	Hugh/ Walter	Alwin
	Bishops Frome	Hugh	Leofsi
	Tedstone		Ernsy
	Bredenbury	Herman	Leofsi
	Butterley	**Alwin**	Edwy Cilt
	Marston Stannett	**Godmund**	Saeric
	Grendon	William	Edwy/ Ordric
	Stanford	**Thurstan**	Edwy Cilt
	Chipelai	**Edric**	Leofsi
	Hanley	St Peter's	Alnoth
		Total held directly by Roger as tenant-in-chief	

Held by Roger de Lacy as tenant from others			
HUNDRED	MANOR	PRESENT SUBTENANT	FORMER HOLDER
Held by Roger from the King			
Kingstone	Cusop		
Hazeltree	Hopleys Green		King Edward
	Street		
	Lawton		
			A pigman
Bromsash	Cleeve		Earl Harold
Leominster	Leominster		Queen Edith
	– Humber		
	– Brockmanton		
	Hampton Wafre		Browning
	Hampton	Gilbert	Edwy
	Sarnesfield	**Godmund**	Saeric
	Gattertop	Walter	Alwin

Hides	Ploughs in Lordship	Villagers' Ploughs	Value in shillings	Notes and payments in kind
1.25	1.5	1.5	15	
0.5			3	
10	3	6	200	A mill at 5s
2	1	0.5	20	
0.5				Waste
6	2	3	65	1.5 hides to Roger from King William
1	1	1	15	A mill at 32d
1	2	2	20	
1	1	3	10	
3.5	1	3	30	A mill at 16d
0.5	1		5	
4				'Nothing is recorded there'
1	1		10	
1	1	1	12	
0.5	1		8	
170.15	105	178	2,604 shillings = £130	

Hides	Ploughs in Lordship	Villagers' Ploughs	Value in shillings	Notes and payments in kind
2				Earl William gave these to Walter
1				"
1				"
0.5				"
				Half a fishery and 25 measures of salt from Droitwich
				Roger de Lacy pays 6s 8d
3.5				
1.5				
0.5	1		30	
2	2	4	40	
1.5	1	3	20	
1	1	2	30	

Held by Roger de Lacy as tenant from others			
Hundred	Manor	Present Subtenant	Former Holder
Held by Roger from the King			
Leominster cont.			
Esch, Worcs	Feckenham		Earl Edwin
Archenfield	Birch	**Costelin's son**	Costelin
	Penbecdoc	**Novi**	Novi
Wormelow	Westwood	Odo	King Edward
Held by Roger from the Bishop			
	Holme Lacy		Earl Harold
Held by Roger from St Guthlac's			
	Almeley		
Held by Roger from Ralph Tosny			
	Clifford Castlery		
Held by Roger from Henry de Ferrers			
Cutsthorn	Ewyas Castlery		
Held by Roger from Osbern FitzRichard			
	Lyde		Seisyll
Held by Roger in exchange from Urso of Abetot			
Plegelgate	Wicton, Bredbury		Alwin
Held by Roger in Worcester but belonging to his manor in Hereford			
Clent	Droitwich		Aelfric
		Total held by Roger as tenant from others	
		Grand total of Roger's Herefordshire holdings	

Hides	Ploughs in Lordship	Villagers' Ploughs	Value in Shillings	Notes and payments in kind
				What Roger de Lacy holds pays 13s 4d and 25d from tribute
				Walter de Lacy gave 1 hide out of the lordship land to Hubert
4				15s + 7 sesters of honey
4				10s + 6 sesters of honey
	2	4		Part of this manor
6	2	20.5	160	
4		8	38	
2				
0.25				3 churches, a priest, 32 acres of land; they pay 2 sesters of honey
2	2	2	30	
1.25			3	
0.5				11 burgesses 1.5 salt-houses; they pay 32.5 measures
38.5	11	43.5	351 shillings = £18	
208.65	116	221.5	2,955 shillings = £148	
Equivalent to approximately 25,000 acres or nearly 40 square miles				

NOTES
1. Carucates are converted to hides at 2 : 1
2. Places in italics are unidentified
3. English and Welsh subtenants are shown in **bold**

The de Lacys in the north of England

In the early years after the Conquest the north of the country caused problems for the Normans. During the Anglo-Saxon period Northumbria had been an independent kingdom, not integrated into England until 927, and even then still retaining much of its autonomy. With its remoteness it was all too easy for Northumbria to make alliances of convenience with Scotland, which then provided a place of safe refuge when things went wrong. In 1067, insurrection forced William to bring his army north and build two castles at York. Others were built at Nottingham, Lincoln and 'everywhere in that region'.

Northumbria had four local earls in three years – two were rebellious and the other two were murdered. Tired of the lawlessness, William appointed a Norman, Robert Comines, as earl; however, in 1069 he was ambushed and killed along with 900 men in the stronghold of Durham. The rebels then marched on York. Edgar the Ætheling had earlier either been expelled or fled from William's custody to live in exile at the Scottish court. He now saw the uprising in Northumbria as an opportunity to promote his claim to the English Crown. The Norman governor of York was killed and the people quickly capitulated to the rebels. However, William was able to launch a surprise counter-attack that dispersed the rebels, leaving Edgar no option but to flee back to Scotland. William's army then took revenge on the people of York by ravaging the town. The redoubtable William FitzOsbern was left in charge but was soon called away to deal with rebellions in Shrewsbury and Exeter.[1]

That same year a fleet of 240 Danish ships arrived at York and were joined by the Northumbrians, again led by Edgar. The insurgents took the castle, killing many hundreds of Normans and taking others back to their ships. They demolished the castle, and during the fighting the borough and its minster were burned.

Whether it was done in rage or for coldly calculated expediency, King William's retribution for this latest insurrection was harsh. Today, it would be described as a campaign of state terrorism, even genocide. After buying off the Danes and driving Edgar back to Scotland again, he ordered the entire Northumbrian countryside to be laid waste. People were killed indiscriminately, their corpses left to rot. Houses, crops and agricultural equipment were all burned. In the resulting famine the survivors were reduced to eating horses, dogs and cats, and then even human flesh. Some sold themselves into slavery, just to survive. By the end of the campaign it was said that not a single village was inhabited between York and Durham. The Harrying of the North was a scorched-earth policy designed to eliminate any further opposition to Norman rule.[2]

Subsequently, radical measures were taken to strengthen what was now effectively a new frontier zone between York and the Pennines. It seems that Ilbert de Lacy was probably party to the harrying and must have earned the respect of King William because he was given charge of a huge fiefdom around Pontefract in the West Riding of Yorkshire, extending for about 500 square miles.

APPENDIX 4

It was of great military importance, straddling Ermine Street, the Roman road that led out of the east of England to Northumbria and on to Scotland. It also controlled the Aire gap, an important trade route across the Pennines. Ilbert held many other more secure and lucrative manors in Lincolnshire, Oxfordshire and Nottinghamshire, either as tenant of Bishop Odo or directly from the king. Within a few years his domain had expanded across the Pennines to include the honour of Clitheroe in Lancashire, giving Ilbert and his successors control across much of the northern border of Norman-held England.

Ilbert's patron, Odo, fell from King William's favour in 1082 when he gathered forces for an unsanctioned expedition to Italy to assist the Pope in a war with the Holy Roman Emperor (or perhaps to make himself Pope, as others suggest). After this, Ilbert held his lands as tenant-in-chief directly from William. Ilbert in turn had subtenants who paid him fees of cash or knight's service. It is estimated that from the honour of Pontefract Ilbert was able to call on the service of 60 knights. Ilbert faithfully served both William I and William Rufus. He died sometime after 1090 and was succeeded by his son, Robert de Lacy.

Robert founded the Cluniac priory of Pontefract and probably built the castle at Clitheroe. He served William Rufus but differences with Henry I around 1114 resulted in his being banished to Normandy with his son, Ilbert II. The honour of Pontefract was granted to Hugh de Laval and then, after Hugh died without an heir, his widow and titles were sold off to William Maltravers, a wealthy commoner and court official, for 1,000 marks.[3]

On hearing of the death of Henry I, a knight loyal to the de Lacys killed the upstart Maltravers. Ilbert de Lacy was restored to the honour after the succession of King Stephen and became an active builder of castles. In 1138 he was one of the leaders of the English forces fighting against the Scots in the Battle of the Standard. His brother was one of the few English knights to be killed. Then in 1141, Ilbert led his troops at the Battle of Lincoln. Several of Stephen's earls deserted him when Matilda's forces gained the upper hand, but Ilbert fought on alongside the king until he and a handful of his remaining supporters were finally captured.[4]

Whether Ilbert died as a result of the battle is unknown, as nothing more is heard of him. He was succeeded by his brother, Henry. When King Henry II came to the throne, he granted Henry de Lacy a written pardon for the support he had given to Stephen during the Anarchy. In 1165 Henry joined the king's expedition into Wales. Like his distant cousin Gilbert, Henry took the cross, and in 1177 set off for Jerusalem only to die later that year. King Henry only allowed his son Robert II to assume the lordship of Pontefract on the payment of 1,000 marks.

Robert II was the last of the direct line of the northern de Lacy dynasty. He died without heir in 1193. A distant relative, Roger the constable of Cheshire, was allowed to inherit the de Lacy lands and titles, for the eye-watering fee of 3,000 marks. Roger changed his name to de Lacy. His family were able to join the Pontefract estates to the earldom of Lincoln, making them one of the powerful families in the country in the thirteenth and fourteenth centuries.

A view of Longtown Castle in 1840 by Charles Walter Radclyffe, published in *Picturesque Antiquities &c. of the County of Hereford*. Sheep are grazing on Castle Green and a timber wagon is passing by, pulled by a team of six draught horses

BIBLIOGRAPHY

ApSimon, A.M. et al, 'King Arthur's Cave Whitchurch, Herefordshire: Reassessment of a middle and upper palaeolithic, mesolithic and beaker site', *Proceedings of the University of Bristol Spelaeological Society*, 19 (2) (1992), 183–249.

Asbridge, T., *The Greatest Knight – the remarkable life of William Marshal*, Simon & Schuster (2015).

Aston, M., *Monasteries in the Landscape*, Tempus (2000).

Atkinson, C., *Garway Hill Common, Garway Herefordshire: An Archaeological Evaluation*, HAR Number 214 (2006).

Bloxam A., *Olchon Court Cairn: Early Bronze Age Funerary Practices in England and Wales*, unpublished report (2013).

Bartlet, W.B., *King Knut and the Viking Conquest of England 1016*, Amberley Publishing (2016).

Beresford, M., *New Towns of the Middle Ages*, Alan Sutton Publishing (1988).

Bloxam A., *Olchon Court Cairn: Early Bronze Age Funerary Practices in England and Wales*, (2013).

Brace, S. et al, 'Ancient genomes indicate population replacement in Early Neolithic Britain', *Nature Ecology & Evolution*, 3 (2019), 765–71.

Brown, R.A., (1970), *English Castles*, Chancellor Press (1970).

Burnham, B.C. & Davies, J.L. (eds.) *Roman Frontiers in Wales and the Marches*, Royal Commission on the Ancient and Historical Monuments of Wales (2010).

Caesar, J., *The Gallic Wars*, Palatine Press (2015).

Campbell, E. & Lane, A., 'Llangorse: a 10th-century royal crannog in Wales', *Antiquity*, 63, (1989).

Coplestone-Crow, B., *Herefordshire Place-Names*, Logaston Press (2009).

— 'The Fief of Alfred of Marlborough in Herefordshire in 1086 and its Descent in the Norman Period', *Transactions of the Woolhope Naturalists' Field Club* (1986).

Cownie, E., *Religious Patronage in Anglo-Norman England, 1066–1135*, The Boydell Press (1998).

Crouch, D., *The Reign of King Stephen, 1135–1154*, Pearson Education (2000).

Davies, H., *Roman Roads in Britain*, Shire Publications (2008).

Davies, M. & S., *The Last King of Wales – Gruffudd ap Llywelyn c. 1013–1063*, The History Press (2012).

Davies, R.R., *The Revolt of Owain Glyn Dŵr*, Oxford University Press (1995).

Doüet-d'Arcq, L. (ed.), *Chronique d'Enguerrand de Monstrelet*, Vol. I, Mme. Ve J. Renouard. (1857).

Duchesne, A. (ed.) *Gesta Stephani, Regis Anglorum*, Sumptibus Societatis (1846).

Dugdale, W., *Monasticon Anglorum: A History of the Abbies and other Monasteries, Hospitals and Frieries … in England and Wales*, Vol 6 Part 1, James Bohn (1846).

Duncumb, J., *Collections towards the History and Antiquities of the County of Hereford, Vol. II*, Merton Priory Press (1812, 1997 Edition).

Ellis, P., 'Longtown Castle: A Report on Excavations by J. Nicholls, 1978', *Transactions of the Woolhope Naturalists' Field Club* (1997), 64–83.

Faraday, M.A. (ed.), Herefordshire Taxes in the Reign of Henry VIII, *Woolhope Naturalists' Field Club* (2005).

Florence of Worcester, Forester, T. (tr.), *The Chronicle of Florence of Worcester*, Henry Bohn, (1854).

Gantz, J. (tr. & ed.), *The Mabinogion*, Penguin Books Ltd (1976).

Gerald of Wales, Thorpe, L. (tr.), *The Journey Through Wales/The Description of Wales*, The Penguin Group (1978).

— *Conquest of Ireland*, Forester, T. (tr.), George Bell & Sons (1905).

Handyside, P., *The Old French Translation of William of Tyre*, Cardiff University (2012).

Hanson, W.S., *A Roman Frontier Fort in Scotland: Elginhaugh*, Tempus Publishing (2007).

Hardy, T.D. (ed.), *Rotuli Chartarum in turri Londinensi asservati*, Public Records Office (1837).

— *Rotuli Litteratum Patentium*, Public Records Office (1835).

Hennessy, W.M. (ed.), *Annals of Loch Ce*, Longman (1871).

Hezlett, H., *Castles and Manors of Ewyas Lacy, Herefordshire*, Gwent Archive (1829), D 1583.107.1.

Higham, R. & Barker, P., *Hen Domen, Montgomery*, University of Exeter Press (2000).

Hillaby, J., 'Hereford Gold: Irish, Welsh and English Land Part 2', *Transactions of the Woolhope Naturalists' Field Club* (1985), 193–270.

— 'Walter II de Lacy and the foundation of Craswall Priory: the historical contexts', *Transactions of the Woolhope Naturalists' Field Club* (2016), 62–83.

Hislop, M., *Castle Builders, Approaches to Castle design and Construction in the Middle Ages*, Pen & Sword Archaeology (2016).

Holden, B., *Lords of the Central Marches: English Aristocracy and Frontier Society 1087–1265*, University of Oxford Press (2008).

John of Worcester, Forester, T. (tr.), *The Chronicle of Florence of Worcester with the two continuations*, Henry Bohn (1854).

Keynes, S. & Lapidge, M. (tr.), *Alfred the Great – Asser's Life of King Alfred and other contemporary sources*, The Penguin Group (1983).

Kemp-Welch, A. (tr.), *The History of Fulk Fitz-Warine*, In parentheses Publications (2001).

King, D.J. Cathcart, *The Castle in England and Wales: an interpretive history*, Croom Helm (1988).

Leland, J., Lucy Toulmin Smith (ed.), *The Itinerary of John Leland in or about 1535–1543*, George Bell and Sons (1908).

Lewis, H. (tr.), *Brut Dingestow*, University of Wales Press (1942).

Lieberman, M., *The Medieval March of Wales – The Creation and Perception of a Frontier, 1066–1283*, Cambridge University Press (2013).

Livingston, M. & Bollard, J.K. (eds), *Owain Glyndŵr – A Casebook*, Liverpool University Press (2013).

Llewellin, F.G., *The History of Saint Clodock: British King and Martyr*, John Heywood Ltd. (1919).

Lock, G., Ralston, I. et al, *Atlas of Hillforts of Britain and Ireland*, https://hillforts.arch.ox.ac.uk

Lloyd, D., *Ludlow Castle*, Powys Castle Estate (undated).

Lloyd, J.E., 'Geoffrey of Monmouth', *The English Historical Review*, Vol. LVII, (1942).

Murphy, D. (ed.), *Annals of Clonmacnoise*, University of Dublin Press (1896).

Marshall, G., 'Report on the discovery of two Bronze Age cists in the Olchon Valley, Herefordshire', *Transactions of the Woolhope Naturalists' Field Club* (1932), 147–53.

Molinus, M., *Pura Walia*, Corby Press (1948),

Nennius, *History of the Britains, Mirabilia*, https://en.wikisource.org/wiki/History_of_the_Britons

Nennius, Evans, A.J. (tr.), *The Wonders of Britain*, University of Leeds, (2003). http://www.wondersofbritain.org

Olalde, I. et al, 'The Beaker phenomenon and the genomic transformation of northwest Europe', *Nature*, 555 (2018), 190–96.

Orderic Vitalis, Forester, T. (tr.), *The Ecclesiastical History of England and Normandy*, Henry G. Bohn (1854, 1856, 1865).

Orpen, H.G., (ed.), *The Song of Dermot and the Earl*, Clarendon Press (1892).

Paris, M., Giles, J.A. (tr.), *Historia Anglorum*, Henry G. Bohn (1852).

Phillips, N., *Earthwork Castles of Gwent and Ergyng AD 1050–1250*, PhD thesis, University of Sheffield (2005).

Powell, D. (tr.), *The History of Wales by Caradoc of Llancarvon*, W. Williams (1812).

Powlett, C.L.W., Duchess of Cleveland, *The Battle Abbey Roll*, John Murray (1889).

Probert, A., 'Twyn-y-Gaer hill-fort, Gwent: an interim assessment', in Boon, G.C. & Lewis, J.M. (eds.), *Welsh Antiquity; Essays Mainly on Prehistoric Topics Presented to H.N. Savory*, National Museum of Wales (1976), 105–19.

Rasmussen, S. et al, 'Early Divergent Strains of Yersinia pestis in Eurasia 5,000 years ago', *Cell,* 163 (2015), 571–82.

Ray, K., *The Archaeology of Herefordshire: An Exploration*, Logaston Press (2015).

Ray, K. & Bapty, I., *Offa's Dyke – Landscape and Hegemony in Eighth-Century Britain*, Oxbow Books (2016).

Rees, W.J. (tr.), *The Liber Llandavensis*, Welsh MSS Society, (1840), 444.

Remfry, P.M., *Longtown Castle 1048 to 1241*, SCS Publishing (1997).

— *The Castles of Ewyas Lacy 1048 to 1403*, SCS Publishing (1998).

Renn, D.F., 'The round keeps of the Brecon region', *Archaeologia Cambrensis* (1961).

— *Norman Castles in Britain,* John Baker Publishers Ltd (1968).

Reynolds, P.J., *Grain Storage in Underground Silos*, Butser Ancient Farm Yearbook (1986).

Richard of Hexham, Stevenson, J. (tr.), *The Church Historians of England, vol. IV part I*, Seeleys (1856).

Roberts, G., *Some Account of Llanthony Priory, Monmouthshire*, W. Pickering (1844).

Robinson, C.R., *A History of the Castles of Herefordshire and Their Lords*, Longman & Co. (1869).

Roger of Wendover, Giles J.A. (tr.), *Flowers of England*, Henry G. Bohn (1849).

Royal Commission on Historical Monuments, England, *An Inventory of the Historical Monuments in Herefordshire, Vol. 1 – South-West*, HMSO (1931); *Vol. 3 – North-West*, HMSO (1934).

Salter, M., *The Castles of Herefordshire and Worcestershire*, Folly Publications (1989).

Shoesmith, R., *Castles and Moated Sites of Herefordshire*, Logaston Press (2009).

— & Johnson, A., *Ludlow Castle: Its History and Buildings*, Logaston Press (2000).

Simeon of Durham, Stevenson, J. (tr.), *The Church Historians of England, vol. III part II*, Seeleys (1855).

Stanford, S.C., *Croft Ambrey*, Woolhope Naturalists' Field Club (1974).

— 'Credenhill Camp, Herefordshire: An Iron Age Hill-Fort Capital', *Archaeological Journal*, 127 (1970), 82–129.

— *The Archaeology of the Welsh Marches*, privately published (2nd ed. 1991).

Stone, B. (tr.), *Sir Gawain and the Green Knight*, Penguin Books (1964), 34–41.

Swanton, M. (tr. & ed.), *The Anglo-Saxon Chronicles*, Phoenix Press (2000).

Tacitus, Jackson, J. (tr.), *The Annals*, Delphi Classics (2014).

Tapper, A., '1. Early Settlements', in Thomas, J. & B. (eds.), *Garway Hill through the Ages*, Logaston Press (2007).

Thomas, J. & Ray, K., *An Interim Report on Excavation at Dorstone Hill, Herefordshire 2011–14*, University of Manchester/Herefordshire Council (2015).

Thomas, M., 'An Ancient Track in the Golden Valley', *Transactions of the Woolhope Naturalists' Field Club* (1987), 186–92.

Thorne, F. & C. (eds.), *Domesday Book 17, Herefordshire*, Phillimore (1983).

Thurlby, M., *The Herefordshire School of Romanesque Sculpture*, Logaston Press (2013).

Topping, J., Hurst, D. & Pearson, E., *Evaluation at Longtown Outdoor Education Centre*, Archaeology Service, Worcester County Council, Report 657 (1998).

Veach, C., *Lordship in Four Realms: The Lacy family, 1166–1241*, Manchester University Press (2014).

Venning, T., *Kingmakers – How power in England was won and lost on the Welsh frontier*, Amberley Publishing (2017).

Vincent, N., *Peter des Roches: an alien in English Politics, 1205–38*, Cambridge University Press (1996).

Wace, Taylor, E. (tr.), *Roman de Rou*, William Pickering (1837).

Wade-Evans, A.W., 'Beuno Sant', *Archaeologia Cambrensis*, Vol. 85, 315–41.

Wardle, T., *England's First Castle*, The History Press (2009).

Watkins, A., *Early British Trackways, Moats, Mounds, Camps, and Sites*, Simpkin, Marshall, Hamilton, Kent & Co, (1922), 1.

— 'Archaeology', *Transactions of the Woolhope Naturalists' Field Club* (1925).

— 'Archaeology', *Transactions of the Woolhope Naturalists' Field Club* (1932).

Wedell, N., *Self portrait of a village school: Longtown School log books 1879–1910*, Nina Wedell (2014).

Whitehead, D., *The Castle Green at Hereford*, Logaston Press (2007).

Wightman, W.E., *The Lacy Family in England and Normandy 1066–1194*, Oxford University Press (1966).

William of Malmesbury, Giles, J.A. (tr.), *Chronicle of the Kings of England*, Henry G. Bohn (1847).

William of Newburgh, Hamilton, H.C. (ed.), *History of English Affairs*, Sumptibus Societatis (1856).

William of Newburgh, Stevenson, J. (tr.), *The Church Historians of England, vol. IV part II*, Seeleys (1855).

Williams, A. & Martin, G.H. (eds.), *Domesday Book*, Penguin (2002), 715.

Williams, D.B. (ed.), *Rental of Ewias Lacy on behalf of Robert Dudley, Earl of Leicester*, Longleat DU/Vol. XVII.

— transcriptions of HARC G33/I/1-5.

Williams, P. (ed.), *Historic Texts from Medieval Wales*, Modern Humanities Research Association (2012).

Wilson, D. & Hurst, D., 'Medieval Archaeology in 1965', *Medieval Archaeology*, Vol 10 (1966).

ADDITIONAL PRIMARY SOURCES

Calendar of the Liberate Rolls of Henry III, HMSO (1916).

Calendar of the Patent Rolls of Henry III, 1216–72 HMSO (1901–1913).

Close Rolls of the Reign of Henry III preserved in the Public Records Office, HMSO (1905).

Henry III Fine Rolls Project, www.finerollshenry3.org.uk

NOTES AND REFERENCES
Historians get grumpy when it's not their period

Chapter 1: Ponthendre motte and bailey castle today
1. Kenyon, 11.
2. Orderic Vitalis, vol. II, 19.
3. Higham & Barker, 47; Salter, 10–51. Different interpretations give different numbers.

Chapter 2: Longtown Castle today
1. The inside diameter of the keep, ID = 7m
   The outside diameter of the keep, OD = 13m
   The plinth diameter, PD = 18m
   The footprint of the tower less the plinth is $\pi (OD^2 - ID^2)/4 = 94m^2$
   The footprint of the tower with the plinth is $\pi (PD^2 - ID^2)/4 = 216m^2$
   In his PhD thesis, Phillips incorrectly speculated that Longtown is an enmotted tower, in other words a tower with earth piled around the bottom to form the motte. However, the 1978 excavation by Nicholls, (Ellis 1997), clearly confirms that the keep was built on a pre-existing motte with only a shallow foundation of pitched rubble.
2. Ellis describes this as a post-medieval feature but, lacking dating evidence, later says it may have been medieval.
3. Hillaby (2016), 73 misconstrued the simple floor structure at Longtown and inexplicably imagined that it attempted 'to follow the elaborate design of radial beams at Pembroke.'
4. RCHME, 183; Shoesmith, 213.
5. Thurlby, 169–84.

Chapter 3: Why build a round keep?
1. Renn (1961), 1–2.
   Derek Renn, a highly respected writer on castles, bears a lot of responsibility for propagating dubious opinions about round keeps. The following is an extract from his 1961 article:

   > The rectangular keep dominated the military architecture of England and Wales for a century after the Norman Conquest, but the assaults of time and man revealed certain defects in the design. Structural stress was greatest at the angles, where the parallel jointing made attack with ram or pick easy. Once the quoins decayed, were undermined, or removed, the unsupported wall

collapsed. One remedy was the provision of stout buttresses at the angles, but this aggravated another defect. However wide the splay of defensive loopholes and crenels, there is always dead ground adjoining the angles of a tower. This zone is limited by the planes of the outer splays of adjoining loopholes, and can only be eliminated by having a loophole through the angle – and thus weakening it structurally. An angular tower had to be defended on several separate fronts. The multangular plan (and its limiting case, the circular) lessened these structural and defensive weaknesses by spreading the load more evenly, and by providing neither buttress nor sharp corner to be levered out or undermined. It was easier to mass men at a threatened point and, with less dead ground and an allround view, the defence recovered the initiative.

While superficially this appears to be a well-argued case, hardly a single sentence stands up to serious scrutiny.
2. Roger of Wendover, 338; Spencer, 94.
3. Paul Drury Partnership, 37–8.

Chapter 4: The excavations

1. Neil Phillips carried out a resistivity survey of Ponthendre for his PhD thesis in 2002. He suggested that anomalies below the bailey scarp might be the remains of buildings. However we could see nothing in either his results or our own beyond what might be caused by solid geology near to the ground surface.
2. Wedell, 24 & 62.

Chapter 5: Post-excavation analysis and interpretation

1. Watkins (1922), 1.
2. Phillips, 300–2.
3. http://www.gatehouse-gazetteer.info/English%20sites/1461.html
4. Radiocarbon dates are calibrated and given to 95.4% probability.
5. The perimeter of the rampart is 4 x 120 = 480m.
   The average height is 6m. The average width is 15m.
   With a roughly triangular profile the volume is 480 x 6 x 15/2 = 20,000 m^3.
   At a density of around 2 tonnes per m^3, the mass of material moved is around 40,000 tonnes.
6. The material removed is a truncated cone.
   The upper radius, $r = 6m$. The lower radius, $R = 10m$.
   The motte has a slope of around 35°
   So the reduction in height, $h = \tan 35° \times (R - r) = 2.8m$
   The volume of a truncated cone $= 1/3 \, \pi \, h \, (r^2 + rR + R^2) = 575m^3$

Chapter 6: Ewyas in prehistoric times

1. ApSimon et al.
2. Brace et al.
   Recent DNA analysis has shown closer affinities between Iberian and British Neolithic skeletal material than between British and northern European material. The data on pigmentation and eye colour come from the same study and are a remarkable result of our understanding of the human genome.
3. Thomas & Ray.

4. Pers. comm. Frank Olding, Blaenau Gwent County Borough Heritage Officer, 5 Nov 2018.
5. Marshall.
6. Olalde, I. et al; Rasmussen et al.
7. Bloxam.
8. Lock, Ralston et al.
9. Atkinson.
10. Reynolds.
11. Stanford, 1974.
12. Stanford, 1970; Stanford 1971.
    Ray (2015) disagrees with Stanford's interpretation of the numbers occupying Credenhill.
13. Probert.
14. Caesar, Book 4:33.
15. The Portable Antiquities Scheme database is an extraordinarily useful asset for studying different types of artifact by location.
16. Caesar, Book 5:12.

Chapter 7: The Roman occupation of the southern Marches

1. The title *Valeria Victrix* was only awarded to *legio XX* after the Boudiccan revolt in AD 61. *Legio XIV Gemina* also received the title *Martia Victrix* at this time.
   Auxiliary units comprised men from the provinces who were not usually Roman citizens. Citizenship was granted after 25 years service. The units were nominally 500 or 1000 strong, provided backup to the legions, but were not usually involved in front-line service.
   The Dobunni, whose tribal lands lay to the west of the Fosse Way, were on friendly terms with the Romans and provided a buffer zone against the hostile Silures.
2. Burnham & Davies give a good recent summary.
3. Tapper, 6.
4. Cartimandua was Queen of the Brigantes, a tribe occupying approximately what is now northern Derbyshire and Yorkshire.
5. Tacitus, *The Annals,* Book 12, 38.
   The author Raymond Williams in his 1989 book *The People of the Black Mountains* gives a fictional, but dramatic account of this attack. He took the view that the fort in question was the one at Clyro, which has also been suggested elsewhere. The Clifford forts appear to have been overlooked. These large campaign bases seem unlikely candidates for the attack, however, being hardly 'garrison-posts'. They would also have been amongst the first forts to be built in the campaign. Williams's account does, however, describe the incident from the Silurian point-of-view, which is a refreshing perspective!
6. The legion in question was commanded by G. Manlius Valens, according to Tacitus, but which legion and where the defeat occurred is not revealed.
7. Burnham and Davies, 192, provide an account of the later Usk fort and its relationship with Caerleon.
   The numbers of auxiliaries is estimated from Diploma documents of AD 103 (Ibid. 47).

8. Auxiliary units were organised into 6 categories. The smallest, the *cohors quingenaria peditata* consisted of about 480 foot-soldiers; the *cohors milliaria peditata*, 1,000 infantry. Equivalent *ala* units comprised cavalry. In addition, there were part-mounted battalions – the *cohors quingenaria equitata*, consisting of 360 foot-soldiers and 120 cavalry and the larger *cohors milliaria equitata* units of 800 infantry and 240 cavalry. Even small forts may have had significant numbers of cavalry (*see 9 below*).
9. Hanson, 2007.
10. Thomas, 1987.
    A more detailed account of the Roman road between Longtown and Bacton, together with others in the area, can be found at www.longtowncastles.com

Chapter 8: Ewyas in the Dark Ages
1. Geoffrey of Monmouth, 15; Williams, 4.
2. Lloyd, 460–8.
3. Nennius, *The Wonders of Britain*, 13.
4. Gerald of Wales, *Journey*, 96.
5. Gantz, 135–76.
6. Rees, 444.
7. Llewellin, 47.
8. Gantz, 447.
9. Wade-Evans, 315–41; Stone, 34–41.

Chapter 9: Anglo-Saxons and Vikings in the Welsh borderlands
1. Ray & Bapty, *passim*.
2. Swanton, 98–100; Campbell & Lane, 675–81.
3. William of Malmesbury, 133–4.
4. Swanton, 173–4.
   The eponymous Harold of Ewyas Harold was the son of Earl Ralph of Hereford. Although Ralph died in 1057, Harold didn't come into his inheritance at Ewyas until some time after 1086 when the Domesday Book simply refers to the castlery of Ewyas, then in the hands of Alfred of Marlborough.
5. Swanton, 176.
6. Davies, M. & S., 55–6.
7. Florence of Worcester, 156–7.
8. Swanton, 188–9.
9. Swanton, 191.
10. Gerald of Wales, 266.
    An Old Testament term, found in the books of Samuel and Kings, meaning a man or a boy who stands while urinating.
11. Swanton, 191.

Chapter 10: William FitzOsbern and the Norman Conquest
1. Wace, 103–8.
2. Swanton, 200.
3. Swanton, 200; Florence of Worcester, 171; Orderic Vitalis, vol. II, 4.
4. Orderic Vitalis, 26.

5. Ibid. 29–30.
6. Wace, 171.
7. Orderic Vitalis disagrees with Wace, saying that Roger de Montgomerie remained in Normandy during the invasion of England and was co-governor with King William's wife, Matilda. Whichever of the chronicles is correct, Roger de Montgomerie was well-fitted to be earl of Shrewsbury.
8. Turner, 6–8.
9. Orderic Vitalis, vol. II, 59; William of Malmesbury, 289–90.

Chapter 11: Walter de Lacy I and the castles of Ewyas

1. Orderic Vitalis, vol. II, 47
2. Wace, 220 & 231.
3. Wightman, 118–9; Thorne, 184a–185b.
4. Thorne, 184a.
5. Orderic Vitalis, vol. II, 26; Higham & Barber, 43.
6. Coplestone-Crow, 57.
7. Remfrey (1997) offers a completely different synopsis, with the early de Lacys having no need of castles because northern Ewyas was occupied by 'friendly Welsh'. We are expected to believe that it took the Normans 50 years or so to advance three miles north of Walterstone to incorporate Clodock and Longtown into Ewyas Lacy, during which time lesser Marcher lords had gone as far as Pembroke.
8. Rees, 512 & 550.
9. Thorne, 185c; Coplestone-Crow (1986), 376–7.
10. It has been suggested that these castles were built during the civil war of the twelfth century, later known as the Anarchy. However, small motte and bailey castles like these would have been a totally inadequate response to the sort of armies that were deployed during this period.
11. Thorne, 179b.
12. Swanton, 210–2; Florence of Worcester, 178–9, Orderic Vitalis, vol. II, 78–82.
13. Lieberman, 108.
14. Thorne, 182d & 184a,

Chapter 12: Roger de Lacy – Rebel

1. Thorne, 184a–185b.
2. Williams & Martin, 715.
3. This account of the 1088 rebellion is assembled from the various accounts given by the Anglo-Saxon Chronicles, Orderic Vitalis, Florence of Worcester, John of Worcester and William of Malmesbury.
4. According to William of Malmesbury, this same goodly Bishop Wulfstan, along with the archbishop of Canterbury, endeavoured to persuade the king to prohibit the sale of slaves into Ireland, a practice banned by his father, William I. Wulfstan was the last Anglo-Saxon prelate to remain in office and was later canonised.
5. Wightman, 132–3, 139–40, 142.
Wightman notes that the de Lacy estates of Ewyas, Weobley and Ludlow were all well-placed for further expansion into Wales but does not appear to have happened.
6. Molinus, 69. *Saes* is the Welsh word for the English.

7. William of Malmesbury, 340.
8. Orderic Vitalis, vol. III, 21.
9. Orderic Vitalis, vol. IV, 25.

Chapter 13: Hugh de Lacy I – a nobleman of noble behaviour

1. Orderic Vitalis, vol. 3, 21; Wightman, 175.
2. Florence of Worcester, 203; Thorne, 233.
3. RCHME, vol. 3, 192–203.
4. Wightman, 182, 208; Cownie, 61.
5. Gerald of Wales, *Journey*, 96–100.
6. Coplestone-Crow (1986), 394; Wightman, 183.
   Hugh's donations included the Herefordshire churches of Llanwarne and Much Birch, and the Gloucestershire churches of Painswick and Stanton, plus land at Tidenham, Madgett and Canons' Frome.
7. Dugdale, 130.
8. Eyton, 239; Wightman, 174–5.

Chapter 14: Pain, Anarchy and Gilbert de Lacy

1. Coplestone-Crow (2013), 2.
2. Rees, 561 & 576.
3. Sewell, 15–6.
4. Gerald of Wales, *Journey*, 94–5.
5. Henry of Huntingdon, 64.
6. Gerald of Wales, *Journey*, 108; John of Worcester, 252.
7. Gerald of Wales, 100.
8. Duchesne, 16; John of Worcester, 252.
9. A sixteenth century genealogy says Gilbert was Roger's nephew. However, see Wightman, 169 & 185. Duchesne, 38; Eyton, 248; Richard of Hexham, 42.
10. Henry of Huntingdon, 70.
11. Orderic Vitalis, vol. VI, 518; Duchesne, 38.
12. Henry of Huntingdon, 70; John of Worcester, 263.
13. Henry of Huntingdon, 72–3; Asbridge, 56.
14. Henry of Huntingdon, 73; John of Worcester, 267.
15. Coplestone-Crow (2013), 5; Crouch 102; Eyton, 245.
16. Eyton, 246.
17. Wightman, 208.
18. John of Worcester, 269; Duchesne, 69.
19. William of Malmesbury, 515–21; John of Worcester, 282; Henry of Huntingdon, 81.
20. Eyton, 251; Henry of Huntingdon, 75–81.
21. Crouch, *passim*.
22. Duchesne, 100–1.
23. Duchesne, 129.
24. Aston, 77; Banister, 23; Thurlby, *passim*.
25. Coplestone-Crow, (2013), 4, 18–9, 28–9; Eyton, 231; Wightman, 186.
26. Crouch, 257 & 274.

27. Eyton, 252; Wightman, 189.
   Remfry (1997) argued that Gilbert's gift of the churches of Clodock and Weobley to Llanthony is evidence that Clodock was probably not incorporated into Ewyas Lacy until the time of Pain FitzJohn. This ignores the fact that Weobley was certainly not a recent acquisition, being listed as one of Roger de Lacy's manors in the Domesday Book.
28. Kemp-Welch, 16–28.
29. Wightman, 188–9.
30. Eyton, 252; Wightman, 207.
31. Wightman, 189; Handyside, 104–5.

Chapter 15: Hugh de Lacy II – governor of Ireland

1. Veach, 289.
2. Wightman, 193.
3. Orpen, 111.
4. Lloyd, D., 4.
5. Gerald of Wales has Rodry suing for peace and submitting, but soon being again at war with the Normans (Forester, 231). Veach maintains that Rodry did not submit; Wightman, 200.
6. Gerald of Wales, *Conquest of Ireland*, Book 1, 41.
7. Veach, 38.
8. Ibid, 79.
9. William of Newburgh (Hamilton), 237–8.
   The medieval Latin is obscure. William of Newburgh (Stevenson), 526, says Hugh actually had a diadem made for himself, but Gerald of Wales (*Conquest of Ireland*, Book 2, 64) makes no mention of it.
10. *Conquest of Ireland*, Book 2, 65.

Chapter 16: Walter de Lacy II – last of the dynasty

1. Pipe Rolls, 1187–1190.
2. A fuller version of this mandate, in both Latin and English, is provided by Veach, 98.
3. Some authors, following Wightman, put the confiscations down to Walter's supposed misdemeanours in Ireland. The evidence does not support this view, as Walter remained on good terms with Prince John, his overlord in Ireland, throughout the period.
4. *Rotuli Chartarum in turri Londinensi asservati*, vol. 1, 1199–1216, 66–7.
5. Annals of Loch Ce, vol. 1, 239.
6. *Historia Anglorum*, vol. 2, 117; Roger of Wendover, 248.
   De Braose's brother, Giles, Bishop of Hereford, also took part in the Leominster raid and was forced to flee to France.
7. *Rotuli Litteratum Patentium*, 91; Remfry (1997), 17; Veach, 139–40 discusses the conspiracy with France in detail.
8. Whitehead, quoting the Exchequer Pipe Rolls, provides a figure of £129 12s as the cost of the Athlone keep; see Veach, 145 for a list of castles involved.

9. Hillaby (2016) claims that Walter rebuilt the castle in the years after 1216, but provides no primary sources to support this. Certainly considerable sums were spent on strengthening and refortification during Walter's tenure as sheriff, as the pipe rolls testify (Pipe Roll 2 Henry III, 90; Pipe Roll 3 Henry III, 165), but as Whitehead details, this was part of an ongoing castle rebuild which lasted from 1200 until 1240, when the 'new tower' was completed (Liberate Rolls, 1226–1240, 488).
10. Leland, Part V, 64–5.
11. Roberts, 76.
12. Annals of Loch Ce vol. 1, 295–7; Annals of Clonmacnoise, 232–3.
13. Close Rolls, 1227–1231, 115; Patent Rolls, Henry III vol. 3, 42.
14. Roger of Wendover, 553–96, provides a contemporary account of the Marshal rebellion, although he is clearly biased in favour of the rebel faction. Some of the details may also be inaccurate or exaggerated, e.g. the whereabouts of the king on certain dates do not correspond to those of the Close Rolls.
15. Ibid, 566 & 569; Fine Rolls, C60/32, 311; Vincent, 389.
16. Patent Rolls Henry III, vol 3, 25; Close Rolls 1231–1234, 257, 264–5; Liberate Rolls of Henry III, vol. 1, 1226–1240, 235; Fine Rolls 39 Henry III C60/52 1255, 333; Fine Rolls 42 Henry III C60/55 1258, 531.
17. Close Rolls 1231–1234, 352. Roger of Wendover, 573.
18. Liberate Rolls of Henry III vol. 1 1226–1240, 235.
19. Roger of Wendover, 574.
20. Close Rolls 1231–1234, 547; Roger of Wendover has the letter to the Irish barons being sent from des Roches and Rivalles, instead of the king. There is some evidence that Marshal did extend his activities into other barons' territories, Veach, 218.
21. Close Rolls 1231–1234, 553; Roger of Wendover, 586.
22. Ibid, 592.
23. Close Rolls 1231–1234, 414, 399; a number of authors, including Holden and Veach, take the view that the Marshal rebellion in the Welsh Marches ended in early September 1233, ignoring or missing the later stages, including the battle of Grosmont. Our fuller account attempts to rectify this.
24. Close Rolls, 1227–1231, 80, 565.
25. Annals of Clonmacnoise, 236–7.

Chapter 17: After the de Lacys

1. Ewyas Lacy Study Group Research Paper: The Lordship of Ewyas Lacy from Norman times to the present day, ewyaslacy.org.uk
2. Calendar of Patent Rolls of Edward II, 9 April 1322.
3. Calendar of Patent Rolls of Edward II, 25 May 1359.
4. Calendar of Close Rolls, Henry IV II, 111; Livingston & Bollard, 174–5; Davies, R.R., 235.
5. Doüet-d'Arcq, 81–3.
6. Faraday, 144.
7. Bannister, 88–92, 132–3; Llewellin, 182.
8. Watkins (1932), 186–7.
9. Bannister, 91.

Chapter 18: The borough of Longtown

1. Coplestone-Crow (1989), 57.
   Coplestone-Crow says that Longtown was called *Nova Villa* or New Town in 1232. However, this might be a reference to the nearby village of Newton.
2. Wilson & Hurst, 199; Topping, Hurst & Pearson, 5.
3. Beresford, 451 cites C134/14/19; Duncomb, 282.
4. Williams, D.B., *Rental*, 40.
5. For borough income Hezlett, *passim*.
   For mills HARC G33/I/1–5; Gwent Record Office D1583.107.2.
6. RCHME, vol. 1, 179–80.
   The surveyors for the Commission missed the movement of the walls and mistakenly believed that the toothings were intended for an unfinished building project.
7. According to Dudley's surveyors there were no inns in Longtown at the time. Presumably they meant lodging houses, rather than drinking dens.

Chapter 19: The denouement – who built Longtown Castle?

1. Robinson, 97.
2. Thurlby, 175.
3. Duncumb, 275–7, Powell, 166–7.
   An alternative source, *Annales Cambriae*, refers to '*castellum Wiz*'. In his account, Duncumb also claimed that Longtown was a pre-Conquest Norman castle and confusingly managed to conflate the two castles of Ewyas Lacy and Ewyas Harold.
4. Shoesmith, 209.
5. Remfry (1997), 17 & 34.
6. Renn (1961), 3.
7. Hillaby (2016), 69–74.
8. Hillaby (1985), 223–6.
9. King, passim.
10. Brown, 77–8.
11. Renn (1968), 157 & 271.
12. Hislop, 110–2.
13. Veach, 26.

Appendix 2: Were the de Lacy brothers at Hastings?

1. Powlett, vol. II.
2. Wace, 219–22 & 231.
3. Ordericus Vitalis, vol. II, 20–1.

Appendix 4: The de Lacys in the north of England

1. Orderic Vitalis, vol. II, 22.
2. Swanton, 202–4; Orderic Vitalis, vol. II, 28; Simeon of Durham, 550–551.
3. Wightman, chaps. 1 & 2.
4. Richard of Hexham, 35; Henry of Huntingdon, 72; Orderic Vitalis, vol. IV, 217–8.

INDEX

Abergavenny *viii*, 76, 78, 83–6, 156, **157**, 163, 177, 181–2, 189, 192, 196, 198
  Alice of 154
  earl of 197
  marquis of 191
Aberystwyth 24, 182–3
Abbey Dore *x*, 84–5, 149, 191
  Dore Abbey 182, 186, 216
Aconbury Priory 168, 180
Ælfgar, Earl 102–4
Ælfnoth, sheriff of Hereford 104
Æthelflæd, Lady of the Mercians 97–8
Æthelred the Unready, King 98–100, **99**, 103, 111
Æthelstan, King 98
Alfred, King (Alfred the Great) *xiv*, 97, 99, 110
Amesbury Archer, the 63, **63**
Amphora 39, **43**, **48**, 49
Anarchy, the 139–52, 200, 203, 216, 229
Angevins 141, 144, 147–9, 205
Anglo-Saxons *xi*, 7, 50, 95–9, **95**, 102, 104, 109, 121, 124–5, 127, 228
  Burh *xi*, 7, 104
  Chronicles *xiv*, *xvi*, 101, 110, 115
Archenfield 88, 93, 96–7, 101, 116, 118, 124, 143, 226
Arthur, King *ix*, 89–91, 94
  Arthur's Cave 59, 88, 90
  Arthur's Stone 61, **61**, 88–9, **89**
  Arthur's Chair 88, 90, **90**
Athleague *see* Ireland
Athlone *see* Ireland

Bacton *x*, 84, 86, 124, 220
Bamburgh Castle 131
de Barentin, Drogo 180
Bayeux Tapestry *xv*, 6, 104, **105**, 107, **107**, 110, **110**, **129**
Beaker culture 63–7, **64**, **67**, 216
Beaumaris Castle 24, 182
Berkeley 112–3, 128
Beuno, Saint 94, 216
Bigod, Isabel (m. Gilbert de Lacy, John Fitz Geoffrey) 175, 181, 194, 196
Black Mountains *ix–xi*, 78
Blestium *see* Roman, town
de Bohun, Henry, Earl of Hereford 168
Boudicca 79
Braose 146, 150
  de Braose family 163–5
    Giles, bishop of Hereford 164, 168
    Maud, wife of William the 4th Lord 163, 165
    Margaret/ Marjory, wife of Walter II de Lacy 163, 168
    Reginald, son of William the 4th Lord 168-9
    William (the 'Ogre of Abergavenny'), 4th Lord of Bramber 150, 156, 163–5, 168, 201
    William, son of William the 4th Lord 165
Brecon *viii*, 123, 163, 184
  Beacons 90, **90**
  Town 80, 131, 141, 156, 168
Breifne *see* Ireland

de Breteuil, Roger 125–6, 130, 216
Brigantes 78
British Camp 70
Bronllys Castle 26, **26**
Bronze Age 62–8, **65**, **68**, 105, 216
Brycheiniog, kingdom of 88, 96–7, 120–1, 124, 131, 139, 147
de Burgh
   Hubert, justiciar of England 173, 175, 180
   Richard, justiciar of Ireland 174–5, 180
   William, Lord of Connaught 162–3, 174

Caesar, Julius 73–4
Caernarfon Castle 24, 182
Caerphilly Castle **19**, 22, **23**, 80, 188
Caerwent (*Venta Silurum*) 113
Caldicot Castle 13, 26, **26**
Canute *see Cnut*
Caradog ap Gruffydd 105–6
Caratacus *ix*, 75–8
Cardiff 76, 79, 136
Cardigan Castle 141, **142**
Carrickfergus Castle 165
Cartimandua of the Brigantes 78
Castle Green *see Longtown*
Catevellauni 75
Chepstow Castle *viii*, 20–2, 112–3, **114**, 116, 123, 125, 145, 154, 199
Chester 76, 111, 126, 172–3, 179
de Clare, Baldwin 141
de Clare, Richard (Strongbow) 141, 153–4, 156–7, 159, 164
Clifford Castle *x*, 76–8, 84–5, 112, 116, 119, 123, 125, 131, 178, 220, 226
de Clifford, Walter 177
Clodock *x*, *xi*, *xv*, 84, 88, 91–3, **92**, 121, 191, 197
   Church 93, **93**, 124, 151, 188, 196–7
   mill 29, 92, 196
Clonmacnoise *see Ireland*
Clydawg, King and Saint *xv*, 91–2, 124, 196–7, 216
Civil War, English (1642-51) 41, 188–90
coinage *see minting*
Cnut, King 99–100, **99**

Colchester 72, 75, 110, 113
Conisbrough Castle **204**, 205
Connaught *see Ireland*
Council of Wales 184
de Courcy, John 162, 164
crannog 97, **98**, 172
Craswall Priory *x*, 61, 167, 170, 186, 194
Credenhill 70–1, 77, 84
Croft Ambrey 70
Crusades 133–4, 148, 152, 162
   Edessa 134, 148
Curthose *see Robert Curthose*
Cusop *x*, 119, 123, 224

Danes 7, 97–9, 125, 127, 228
Dark Ages 87–8, 95
David, King of Scotland 145, 148
Devereux family 24, 207
de Dinan, Joce *xvi*, 144, 146, 148, 151
Dives-sur-Mer, Calvados *see France*
Dobunni 73, 76
Domesday Book *xiv*, 113, 116–9, **117**, 123–4, 128, 199, 207, 216, 219
donjon 6, 7
Dorstone 60–61, 71, 85, 89, 124
Doward, Great/ Little 59, 70, 88
Drogheda *see Ireland*
Dublin *see Ireland*
Dundrum Castle *see Ireland*
Durrow *see Ireland*

Eadric 'Streona', ealdorman 99, 111
Eadric the Wild 111–2, 119
Eaton Camp 70
Edessa *see Crusades*
Edgar the Ætheling 109, 228
Edmund Ironside 99, 109
Edward I, King 24, 181
Edward II, King 181–2
Edward IV, King 181, 184
Edward the Elder, King 97–8
Edward the Confessor, King 99–108, **100**, 112–3, 116, 124, 222, 224
Edith, Queen (Godwin) 100
Emma, Queen 99–100, 116

248 THE MARCH OF EWYAS

Eustace, count of Burgundy 101
Évreux *see* France
Ewyas *viii–ix*, 71, 88, 120, 122–4, **185**
    Harold *x*, 6, 47, **65**, 101–2, 112, 116–23, 125, 141, 148–9, 182, 186, 188–9, 216
    Lacy *xiii–xiv*, 24, 103, 117–20, 123, 127, 132, 136, 138, 141, 148, 150, 153, 161, 164, 175, 181–2, 184–6, **185**, 189–91, 194, 196, 199–202, 204, 208–9, 216–7
    Vale of *x*, 71, 119, 122, 124, 184, **185**
Exeter 75, 110–11, 141, 228

de Ferrers, Henry 119, 226
FitzGeoffrey, John 175
FitzGerald, Maurice 155–6
FitzHarold, Robert, lord of Ewyas Harold 141
FitzHenry, Meilar 164
FitzJohn, Pain *xvi*, 139–46, 200–01, 208, 216
FitzJohn, Sybil *see de Lacy, Sybil*
FitzMiles, Roger, of Gloucester 149–50
FitzOsbern, William *xvi*, 107–16, 119, 121, 123–4, 126, 131, 199, 216, 228
FitzScrob, Osbern, son of Richard 112, 129
FitzScrob, Richard 102, 112–3, 129
FitzWarine, Fulk 151
flint 25, 31, **31**, **43**, 53–4, **59**, 60, 62–3, **62**, 66
Flanders 100, 102, 109, 111, 114
Flemings *xvi*, 108, 111, 141, 200
Florence of Worcester *xiv*, 130, 133
Forest of Dean 113, 147–8, 178
France 7, 20–21, 49, 97, 108–9, 134, 148, 164, 166–7, 169, 172, 175, 183, 204–5
    Dives-sur-Mer 108–9, 219
    Évreux 109, 166, 205, 207
    Houdan Castle 205, **206**
    king of 114, 152, 162, 165
    Lassy *xiii*, 109, 115
    Normandy *xiii*, 6, 97, 100–2, 107–109, 114–5, 125, 128–34, 136, 140–41, 144, 146, 148–9, 155–6, 161, 163–4, 166, 205, 217, 219, 229

Geoffrey, count of Anjou 141, **141**, 148
Gerald of Wales (Giraldus Cambrensis) *xiv*, 58, 90, 105, 133, 136, 139, 143, 149, 155–6, 160, **160**
Gerbod the Fleming 111
Gloucester *viii*, 75–6, 79, 97, 100–3, 112–3, 126, 128, 136, 139, 141, 143, 146–7, 169, 177–8, 186, 191, 216
Glywysing (Glamorgan) 88, 93
Glyndŵr, Owain 182–4, 186, 217
Godwin, Earl 99–102
Godwin, Edith *see Edith, Queen*
Godwinson, Harold, Earl, later King 102–7, **105**, **107**, 111, 113, 116, 120, 209, 216
Godwinson, Sweyn 100–2
Godwinson, Tostig 102, 104, 109
Golden Valley *ix*, 60, 85, 103–4, 112, 119, 124, 188
Goodrich Castle 21–2, 188–9
Grandmont Abbey 167
    Grandmontine monks 167, 170
Grosmont Castle *x*, 143, 164, 177, **178**, 182, **183**
Gruffydd ap Llewelyn 100, 102
Gruffydd ap Rhydderch 100–5, 124
Gwent 62, 79, 88, 93–4, 96, 105, 113, 120, 122–3, 131, 139, 143, 156, 209, 216
Gwern Castle 122–3
Gwys (Wizo) the Fleming 200

Harald Hardrada 104, 109
Harlech Castle 24, 182–3
Harold Harefoot 99
Harold's Stones, Trellech 105, **106**
Harthacanute 99–100
Hastings 6, 109–11, **110**, 115–6, 123, 128, 218–9
Hatterall Ridge *x*, 36, 184
Hay Castle *viii*, *x*, 123, 168, 177–9
Hay-on-Wye *viii–ix*, 78, 104, 177
Henry I, King 128, 132, 136, 139–41, 143–4, 229
Henry II, King 148–60, **176**, 203, 205, 208, 217, 229

Henry III, King 169, *169*, 170, 172–80, *176*, 217
Henry IV, King 182–3, 217
Henry V, King 183
Henry VIII, King 184, 186, 197, 218
Henry of Huntingdon *xiv*
Hereford *viii*, 70, 84, 95–8, *99*, *100*, 100, 103–4, 111–3, 123, 125–6, 128, 141, 144–5, 147, *147*, *149*, *169*, 170, 173–4, 177–8, 180, 186, 188–9, 191, 198, 200, 220, 226
  Castle 111–2, 119, 144, 147, 168, *169*, 216
  Cathedral 17, 103, 147, 149, 153
  churches 126, 136, 147, 152, 216
  Museum 64–5
Herefordshire School of Romanesque Sculpture 17, *17*, 149, *150*, 200
hillforts 68–74, 77–8
hoarding, hourds 18–9, *19*, 23, *23*, 202
Holme Lacy 153, 226
Honddu, River *see* Rivers
Houdan Castle *see* France

Ireland *xiii*, *xvi*, 20–21, 24, 58, 62, 69, 89, 91, 97, 102, 153–68, 170–7, 179–81, 200, 202, 208, 217
  Antrim, County 62
  Athboy 155
  Athleague 172
  Athlone 155, 156, 162–3, 166, 174, 202
  Breifne 163, 171–2
  Clonmacnoise 155, 158, 180
  Connaught 155, 158, 162–4, 172, 174–5
  Drogheda 155–7, *158*, 163, 167–8, 173
  Dublin 154–7, 160, 163, 168, 172–4
  Dundrum Castle 155, 157
  Durrow 155–6, 160
  Leinster 153, 155–8, 163–5, 174, 179
  Limerick 163–5, 170
  Lough Oughter 172
  Lough Ree 172
  Meath 58, 155–8, 160, 162–3, 165–7, 171–4, 181, 217
  Munster 162
  Shannon, River 155, 158, 172

Ireland cont.
  Trim 20, *24*, 155, 157, *159*, 166, *166*, 167, 174, 180–81, 202
  Ulster 163–6, 173–4
  Wexford 163, 165, 173
Iron Age *xi*, 6, 21, 49, 62, 68–74, *69*, 77, 87–8, 124, 216

Jerusalem 102, 134, 136, 152, 162, 229
Jews 134, 165, 170, 180–81, 191
John of Monmouth 178
John, Prince, later King 22, 159, 162–8, *167*, *176*, 217
Julius Caesar *see* Caesar, Julius

King Arthur's Cave *see* Arthur, King
de Kinnersley, Hugh 180
knight's service 114–6, 128, 153, 205, 229

de Lacy family *xi*, *xiii–xvi*, 20, 47, 184, 191–2, 195, 197
  Amaury, son of Gilbert I 207
  Gilbert I, son of Roger 144, 146, 148, 150–2, 204–5, 207–8, 216–7
  Gilbert II, son of Walter II 170, 175, 181, 194
  Henry, son of Robert 229
  Hugh I, son of Walter I *xiii*, 24, 115, 128, 132–3, 136–9, 146, 200, 216
  Hugh II, son of Gilbert I *57*, 58, 153–61, *160*, 200–2, 207, 217
  Hugh III, earl of Ulster, son of Hugh II 163–6, 172–4, 179, 217
  Ilbert I of Pontefract 115–6, 144–5, 218–9, 228–9
  Ilbert II, son of Robert 229
  Isabel, wife of Gilbert II *see* Bigod, Isabel
  Margaret, daughter of Gilbert II (Margery, m. John de Verdun) 175, 181, 196
  Matilda, daughter of Gilbert II (Maud, m. Geoffrey de Geneville) 175, 181, 196
  Robert, son of Ilbert I 229
  Robert I, son of Gilbert I 152–3
  Robert II, son of Henry 229
  Robert, son of Ilbert 229

de Lacy family cont.
   Roger, son of Walter I 116–9, 124, 127–32, 144, 200, 205, 207, 216, 219–27
   Sybil (m. Pain FitzJohn, Joce de Dinan) 139, 144, 146
   Walter I *xiii*, 24, 115–26, 128, 130, 200–01, 216, 218–9
   Walter II, son of Hugh II 161–75, **167**, 177, 179–81, 194, 196–7, 199, 201–2, 207, 217
   Walter III, grandson of Walter II 175, 180
   William 'Gorm', half-brother of Walter II 168, 171-2, 174
Lassy *see France*
Law of Wales Act, 1535 184
Leofgar, bishop of Hereford 104
Leinster *see Ireland*
Leominster 102, 165, 224–7
   abbess of 100
   Priory 17
LiDAR 192–4, 196
Limerick *see Ireland*
Lincoln, Battle of 147, 169, 229
Llancillo 24, 119, 122–3, 138, 161
Llandaff 139
   bishop of 92–3, 97
   Book of 123, 199
   Cathedral 17, 93
Llangorse Lake 97, **98**, 139, **140**
Llangua 122–3
Llanthony 141, 150, 184
   Priory *x*, 124, 133, 136–8, **137**, **138**, 141, 143, 151, 170, 175, 184–6, 197, 200, 216
   Secunda 141–3, **142**, 186, 216
Llanveynoe *x*, 88, 94, **94**
Llanwonog 93
Llywelyn ap Iorwerth 167, 170, 172, 175, 177
Longtown *ii*, *vii*, *x–xi*, 3–56, 59, 61–2, 72, 76–85, **81**, **82**, 103–4, 120–21, 209–11, 216–7
   borough 191–8
   Castle *ii*, *xii*, *xiii*, **1**, 2, 8–20, **8**, **10–20**, 24, 26, **32**, 45–7, 51, **55**, **56**, 72, 76, 103, 120–2, 124, 126, 161, 170, 175, 177, 181–2, 186–90, **187**, 199–208, 211, 214, **215**, 216, **230**

Longtown cont.
   Castle Green (the Green) 28, 31–6, **33**, **36**, 38–44, **38–43**, 48–55, **52**, **55**, **56**, 62, 104, **212–3**
   Castles Project *vii*, *xiv*, 209
   School *xi*, 34–5, 210–11
Lough Oughter *see Ireland*
Louis, Prince of France 152, 168–70
de Lucy, William 180
Ludlow *viii*, 20, 24, 58, 128, 132–3, 139, 150–51, 153, 167, 173, 184, 195
   Castle 126, 128, 144–6, **145**, 151–2, **152**, 154, **154**, 157, 163, 166–7, 174, 180–81, 184, 200, 204, 208, 216
Lyonshall 24, 126, 207, 222

Magnis see Roman, town
de Mantes, Ralph (the Timid) 103
March, earl of 181–2
Marches *viii*, *xiv*, 13, 21, 26, 68, 75–86, 95–6, 116, 176, 128, 130–3, 139, 143–5, 149–50, 152, 154, 156–7, 163–5, 168, 170, 175, 178–9, 181, 184–6, 209–10, 216–7
de Marisco, Geoffrey 165, 171, 174
Marshal family 113, 173
   Richard, 3rd earl of Pembroke, brother of William II 175–80, **179**, 217
   William, 1st earl of Pembroke 145, 164–5, **164**, 169, 173, 202
   William, 2nd earl of Pembroke 173–5
Matilda, Empress 140–41, **141**, 144–5, 147–8, 150, 229
Meath *see Ireland*
Mercia 95–9, 102, 111
Merlin 89–90
Mesolithic **59**, 60
Michaelchurch Escley *x*, 196
Midsummer Hill 70
Miles of Gloucester *xvi*, 139, 143, 146–7
Milville, Hugh 180
minting and coinage 73, 79, 87, 98, **99**, **100**, 149, **149**, **169**
Monmouth *viii*, *xi*, 76, 78, 83, 85, 178–9, 198
   Castle 112–3, 123, 178

Monnow
   River *see Rivers*
   Valley 19, 59, 78
de Montfort, Amaury, count of Évreux 205-7
de Montfort, Simon 172, 207
de Montgomerie, Roger 111
Mortimer family 146, 153, 181-2
   Sir Edmund 182-3
   Edmund, 5th earl of March 182
   Hugh 149, 151
   Ralph 129, 131
   Roger, 1st earl of March 181
   Roger, 2nd earl of March 182
motte and bailey castle 3-9, *3*, *4*, *5*, 12-3, 15, 22, 24, 26-31, 37-8, 45-7, *46*, 49, 51, 53, 102, 119-24, *158*, 161, 168, 189, 200-2, 204, 208
Mouse Castle *x*, 104, 123-4
Mowbray, Robert, earl of Northumberland 128, 131-2
Munster *see Ireland*
Mynydd Ferddin (Moneyfarthing Hill) 89, 188

Neolithic 60-61, *61*, 89, *94*
de Neufmarché, Bernard 129, 131, 139
Nevill family *vii*, 181, 190
New Buckenham 25, 204
New Forest 134, *135*
Normandy *see France*

O'Connor
   Aed, King of Connaught 174
   Rodry, High King of Ireland 155-6, 158, 162, 172
O'Rourke, Teirnan 155-6, 171
Odo, bishop of Bayeux 109-10, *110*, 115-6, 125, 128-31, *129*, 133, 222, 226, 229
Offa, King of Mercia 95-6, 183
Offa's Dyke 96, 101
Olchon
   Brook *x*, 3, 19, 82, 119, 121, 191
   Court cairn 66, *67*, 216
   Valley 63-4, 66, 94, 216

Orderic Vitalis *xiv*, 3, 7, 107, 115, 121, 127, 218
Ordovices 73, 75-80
Orford Castle 205

Pembroke
   Castle 26, 156, 202-3, **203**
   earl of 145, 154, 173, 175
Pentecost, Osbern 101-2, 112, 216
Pentwyn 71, *72*, 216
Pen-y-Clawdd Castle 122-3
Pevensey 109, 130
Pipe Rolls *xiii*, 48, 161, 201
Plantagenet 149, 181
Ponthendre *vii*, *xi*, 3-6, 29-31, 62, 117
   Castle/ motte *xi*, *xiii-xiv*, *3*, 4, 6, 27-9, *29*, *30*, 37, 45-8, *46*, 51, 53, 119-22, 161, 201-2
   excavation 29-31, *29*, *31*, 37-8, *37*, 53, 62, *62*, 211
   Pont Hendre, Pont Henry *xv*
Portskewett 105
Pura Walia 181

Ranulf, earl of Chester 172
Revolt of the Earls 125
Rhydderch ap Caradog 123-4
Rhys ap Gruffydd 139-40
Richard I, King 161-3, *162*, 174, *176*, 180, 217
Richard's Castle 102, 112, 119, 146
de Rivallis, Peter 175, 177-9
Rivers
   Honddu 119, 136, *137*
   Monnow *viii*, *ix-x*, 71, 77-8, 82, 84-5, 91-2, *92*, 113, 119, 123, 191
   Severn *viii*, 78-9, 91, 96-7, 105, 111-3, 125, 139, 183
   Shannon *see Ireland*
   Usk *viii*, 77, 101
   Wye *viii*, 76-8, 90, 96, 98, 105, 111-2, 127, 220
Robert Curthose, duke of Normandy 128, 130, 132-4, 136
Robert, earl of Gloucester 144, 147

Robert the Bruce 182
des Roches, Peter, bishop of Winchester
    175, 179
Rochester Castle 22, 130
Roger of Wendover *xiv*, 22, 177, 179
Roman *xi*, 36, 39–40, 71, 75–87
  emperors
    Claudius 79
    Flavian 80
    Nero 79–80
  forts 76–85, 88
    Abergavenny 76–8, 80, 83–6
    Ariconium 77, 85
    Blackbush 80, 84–6
    Brecon Gaer 80
    Caerleon 80
    Caerphilly 80
    Canon Frome 76
    Cardiff 76, 79–80
    Carmarthen 80, 86
    Castlefield 76–8, 85
    Chepstow 199
    Chester 76, 80, 111
    Clifford 76–8, 84–5
    Clyro 76–8, 84–5
    Colchester 110
    Credenhill 71, 77–8, 84
    Elginhaugh, Scotland **81**
    Gloucester (Glevum) 76, 79–80
    Hindwell Farm 76, 80
    Jay Lane 76
    Kingsholm 75
    Little Doward Hill 88
    Longtown 39, 49–51, 53–5, **55**, **56**, 76–85, **81**, **82**, 104, 120–21, 199, 209, 216
    Monmouth 76–8, 80, 83, 85
    Pen-y-Gaer 76, 79–80, 85
    Stretford Bridge 76
    Stretton 85
    Usk 76–7, 79–80, 85
    Whitchurch 76, 80
    Wroxeter 76–7, 79–80, 86
  governors
    Aulus Plautius 75

Roman cont.
    Aulus Didius Gallus 79
    Gaius Julius Agricola 80–81
    Ostorius Scapula 75–9
    Quintus Veranius 79
    Seutonius Paullinus 79
    Sextus Julius Frontinus 80
  pottery *xi*, 39, 41, 43, 48, 50, 78
  roads 75, 77, 79, 83–5, **83**, **84**, **86**, 96, 111–3, 229
  towns
    Ariconium 77, 85
    Blestium *xi*, 78, 85
    Magnis 77, 84–6
    Venta Silurum 113
Rose of Monmouth 157, 160
Rowlestone 17, 119, 122–3, 138, **150**
Rhuddlan 104
    Robert of 126, 129

Samian Ware 49
Sandwich, Battle of 170, **170**
Scotland 21, **81**, 97–9, 102, 145, 165, 228–9
Scots 141, 145, 182, 229
Scottish army *see Civil War*
Severn Valley ware 48, **48**
Shannon, River *see Ireland*
Shrewsbury *viii*, 139, 173, 178
    Castle 111, 145, 168
    earl of 126, 129, 131–2
  siege 7, 12, 20, 22–3, 47, 111, 130, 133, 141, 144–8, 175, 177, 183, 188, 202, 216
Silures 75–6, 78–9
Skenfrith Castle 13, **26**, 26, 143, 164
Skirrid mountain 71, **122**
Snodhill *x*, 104, 124, 129
Stamford Bridge, Battle of 109
Stephen, King 140–50, **144**, **149**, 229
Stone Age 59–62
Stonehenge 60, 63, 89
Straddele 103–4, 209
Strongbow *see de Clare, Richard*
Sweyn Forkbeard 99

INDEX 253

Tacitus 75, 76, 78–9
de Talbot, Geoffrey 144, 147
Templars 152–3, **152**, 204, 217
Treaty of Windsor 156, 158
Tre-fedw 122, **122**
Tremorithic 84
Tretower Castle 26, **26**, 166
Trim Castle *see Ireland*
Twyn-y-Gaer 71, **72**

Usk
  Castle 177–8, 182
  fort 76, 79–80, 177
  Valley 78–80

Vikings 97–104, 111,
Vortigern 88, 90

Walterstone 119, 122–3, 182
  Castle *x*, 28, 47, 51, 119–22, **120**, 126, 161, 196, 216
  Church 119, 138
  fort/ camp 71–2, 216
Walter of Therouanne 6
Watkins, Alfred 46, 188
Weobley *viii*, 126–8, 132–3, 136, 139, 144–5, 150–1, 153, 195, 216–7, 222
  Castle 24, 58, 126, 144, 150, **151**, 161, 181, 200, 208
  Church 151
White Castle, Llantilio 20, 143, **143**, 164
Wigmore Castle 48, 112, 119, 129, 149
William I, duke of Normandy, king of England *xv, xvi*, 107–16, 123, 125, **129**, 133, 218, 223–5, 228–9
William II, Rufus, king of England 128–34, **135**, 216, 229
William of Malmesbury *xiv*, 132
Winchester 110, 147–8
  bishop of 148, 169, 175, 179
Wiston Castle (Castle of Gwys) 200
Worcester *viii*, 50, 104, 129–30, 150, 170, 183, 191, 226
  bishop of 101, 125
  Castle 126, 150

Wormelow Tump 88, 90, 118, 226
Wulfstan, bishop of Worcester 130
Wye
  River *see Rivers*
  Valley 41, **43**, 59, 113, 123–4

Also from LOGASTON PRESS (www.logastonpress.co.uk)

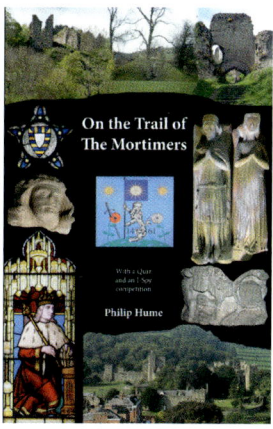

On the Trail of the Mortimers
Philip Hume
144 pages, 234 × 156 mm
75 colour photographs, as well as maps and family trees
ISBN: 978-1-910839-04-1
Paperback with flaps, £7.50

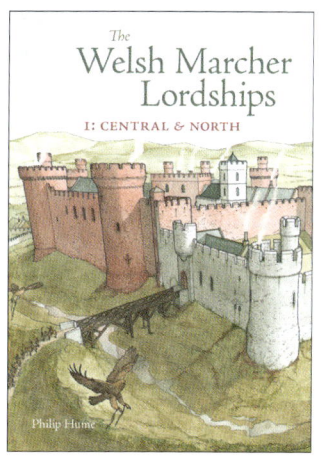

The Welsh Marcher Lordships
1: Central & North
Philip Hume
288 pages, 242 × 171 mm
200 colour and b&w illustrations
ISBN: 978-1-910839-45-4
Paperback with flaps, £15.99

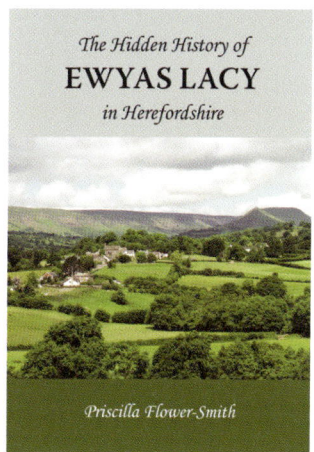

The Hidden History of Ewyas Lacy
Priscilla Flower-Smith
224 pages, 242 × 171 mm
37 colour and 28 b&w photographs and maps
ISBN: 978-1-906663-81-0
Paperback, £12.95 NOW £6.00

The 1718 plan of Longtown Castle (*photograph © The British Library Board, Add. 60746 f11*)